THE WAR
and its Shadow

The Cañada Blanch / Sussex Academic Studies on Contemporary Spain

General Editor: Professor Paul Preston, London School of Economics

Richard Barker, *Skeletons in the Closet, Skeletons in the Ground: Repression, Victimization and Humiliation in a Small Andalusian Town – The Human Consequences of the Spanish Civil War.*

Germà Bel, *Infrastructure and the Political Economy of Nation Building in Spain, 1720–2010.*

Gerald Blaney Jr., *"The Three-Cornered Hat and the Tri-Colored Flag": The Civil Guard and the Second Spanish Republic, 1931–1936.*

Michael Eaude, *Triumph at Midnight in the Century: A Critical Biography of Arturo Barea.*

Francisco Espinosa-Maestre, *Shoot the Messenger?: Spanish Democracy and the Crimes of Francoism – From the Pact of Silence to the Trial of Baltasar Garzón*

Soledad Fox, *Constancia de la Mora in War and Exile: International Voice for the Spanish Republic.*

Helen Graham, *The War and its Shadow: Spain's Civil War in Europe's Long Twentieth Century.*

Angela Jackson, *'For us it was Heaven': The Passion, Grief and Fortitude of Patience Darton – From the Spanish Civil War to Mao's China.*

Gabriel Jackson, *Juan Negrín: Physiologist, Socialist, and Spanish Republican War Leader.*

Sid Lowe, *Catholicism, War and the Foundation of Francoism: The Juventud de Acción Popular in Spain, 1931–1939.*

Olivia Muñoz-Rojas, *Ashes and Granite: Destruction and Reconstruction in the Spanish Civil War and Its Aftermath.*

Linda Palfreeman, *¡SALUD!: British Volunteers in the Republican Medical Service during the Spanish Civil War, 1936–1939.*

Cristina Palomares, *The Quest for Survival after Franco: Moderate Francoism and the Slow Journey to the Polls, 1964–1977.*

David Wingeate Pike, *France Divided: The French and the Civil War in Spain.*

Hugh Purcell with Phyll Smith, *The Last English Revolutionary: Tom Wintringham, 1898–1949.*

Isabelle Rohr, *The Spanish Right and the Jews, 1898–1945: Antisemitism and Opportunism.*

Gareth Stockey, *Gibraltar: "A Dagger in the Spine of Spain?"*

Ramon Tremosa-i-Balcells, *Catalonia – An Emerging Economy: The Most Cost-Effective Ports in the Mediterranean Sea.*

Dacia Viejo-Rose, *Reconstructing Spain: Cultural Heritage and Memory after Civil War.*

Richard Wigg, *Churchill and Spain: The Survival of the Franco Regime, 1940–1945.*

To the memory of
Fernando Ruiz Vergara, 1942–2011
and
David Vilaseca, 1964–2010

THE WAR
and its Shadow

Spain's Civil War in Europe's Long Twentieth Century

HELEN GRAHAM

sussex
ACADEMIC
PRESS
Brighton • Portland • Toronto

2 4 6 8 10 9 7 5 3 1

First published in 2012 in Great Britain by
SUSSEX ACADEMIC PRESS
PO Box 139
Eastbourne BN24 9BP

and in the United States of America by
SUSSEX ACADEMIC PRESS
920 NE 58th Ave   Suite 300
Portland, Oregon 97213-3786

and in Canada by
SUSSEX ACADEMIC PRESS (CANADA)
8000 Bathurst Street, Unit 1, PO Box 30010, Vaughan, Ontario L4J 0C6

Published in collaboration with the
Cañada Blanch Centre for Contemporary Spanish Studies.

British Library Cataloguing in Publication Data
A CIP catalogue record for this book is available from the British Library.

Library of Congress Cataloging-in-Publication Data
Graham, Helen, 1959–
The war and its shadow : Spain's civil war in Europe's long twentieth
  century / Helen Graham.
pages cm.
Includes bibliographical references and index.
ISBN 978-1-84519-510-6 (h/b : alk. paper) —
ISBN 978-1-84519-511-3 (p/b : alk. paper)
  1. Spain—History—Civil War, 1936–1939—Influence. I. Title.
DP269.8.I5G73 2012
946.081′1—dc23

2011051609

Typeset & designed by Sussex Academic Press, Brighton & Eastbourne.
Printed by TJ International, Padstow, Cornwall.

Contents

The Cañada Blanch Centre for Contemporary Spanish Studies

In the 1960s, the most important initiative in the cultural and academic relations between Spain and the United Kingdom was launched by a Valencian fruit importer in London. The creation by Vicente Cañada Blanch of the Anglo-Spanish Cultural Foundation has subsequently benefited large numbers of Spanish and British scholars at various levels. Thanks to the generosity of Vicente Cañada Blanch, thousands of Spanish schoolchildren have been educated at the secondary school in West London that bears his name. At the same time, many British and Spanish university students have benefited from the exchange scholarships which fostered cultural and scientific exchanges between the two countries. Some of the most important historical, artistic and literary work on Spanish topics to be produced in Great Britain was initially made possible by Cañada Blanch scholarships.

Vicente Cañada Blanch was, by inclination, a conservative. When his Foundation was created, the Franco regime was still in the plenitude of its power. Nevertheless, the keynote of the Foundation's activities was always a complete open-mindedness on political issues. This was reflected in the diversity of research projects supported by the Foundation, many of which, in Francoist Spain, would have been regarded as subversive. When the Dictator died, Don Vicente was in his seventy-fifth year. In the two decades following the death of the Dictator, although apparently indestructible, Don Vicente was obliged to husband his energies. Increasingly, the work of the Foundation was carried forward by Miguel Dols whose tireless and imaginative work in London was matched in Spain by that of José María Coll Comín. They were united in the Foundation's spirit of open-minded commitment to fostering research of high quality in pursuit of better Anglo-Spanish cultural relations. Throughout the 1990s, thanks to them, the role of the Foundation grew considerably.

In 1994, in collaboration with the London School of Economics, the Foundation established the Príncipe de Asturias Chair of Contemporary Spanish History and the Cañada Blanch Centre for Contemporary Spanish Studies. It is the particular task of the Cañada Blanch Centre for Contemporary Spanish Studies to promote the understanding of twentieth-century Spain through research and teaching of contemporary Spanish history, politics, economy, sociology and culture. The Centre possesses a valuable library and archival centre for specialists in contemporary Spain. This work is carried on through the publications of the doctoral and post-doctoral researchers at the Centre itself and through the many seminars and lectures held at the London School of Economics. While the seminars are the province of the researchers, the lecture cycles have been the forum in which Spanish politicians have been able to address audiences in the United Kingdom.

Since 1998, the Cañada Blanch Centre has published a substantial number of books in collaboration with several different publishers on the subject of contemporary Spanish history and politics. A fruitful partnership with Sussex Academic Press began in 2004 with the publication of Christina Palomares's fascinating work on the origins of the Partido Popular in Spain, *The Quest for Survival after Franco: Moderate Francoism and the Slow Journey to the Polls, 1964–1977*. This was followed in 2007 by Soledad Fox's deeply moving biography of one of the most intriguing women of 1930s Spain, *Constancia de la Mora in War and Exile: International Voice for the Spanish Republic* and Isabel Rohr's path-breaking study of antisemitism in Spain, *The Spanish Right and the Jews, 1898–1945: Antisemitism and Opportunism*. 2008 saw the publication of a revised edition of Richard Wigg's penetrating study of Anglo-Spanish relations during the Second World War, *Churchill and Spain: The Survival of the Franco Regime, 1940–1945* together with *Triumph at Midnight of the Century: A Critical Biography of Arturo Barea*, Michael Eaude's fascinating revaluation of the great Spanish author of *The Forging of a Rebel*.

Our collaboration in 2009 was inaugurated by Gareth Stockey's incisive account of another crucial element in Anglo-Spanish relations, *Gibraltar. A Dagger in the Spine of Spain*. We were especially proud that it was continued by the most distinguished American historian of the Spanish Civil War, Gabriel Jackson. His pioneering work *The Spanish Republic and the Civil War*, first published 1965 and still in print, quickly became a classic. The Sussex Academic Press/Cañada Blanch series was greatly privileged to be associated with Professor Jackson's biography of the great Republican war leader, Juan Negrín.

2011 took the series to new heights. Two remarkable and comple-mentary works, Olivia Muñoz Rojas, *Ashes and Granite: Destruction and Reconstruction in the Spanish Civil War and its Aftermath* and Dacia Viejo-Rose, *Reconstructing Spain: Cultural Heritage and Memory after Civil War*, opened up an entirely new dimension of the study of the early Franco regime and its internal conflicts. They were followed by Richard Purkiss's analysis of the Valencian anarchist movement during the revolutionary period from 1918 to 1923, the military dictatorship of General Primo de Rivera and the Second Republic. It is a fascinating work which sheds entirely new light both on the breakdown of political coexistence during the Republic and on the origins of the violence that was to explode after the military coup of July 1936. The year ended with the publication of *France Divided: The French and the Civil War in Spain* by David Wingeate Pike. It made available in a thoroughly updated edition, and in English for the first time, one of the classics of the historiography of the Spanish Civil War.

An extremely rich programme for 2012 opened with Germà Bel's remarkable *Infrastructure and the Political Economy of Nation Building in Spain*. This startlingly original work exposed the damage done to the Spanish economy by the country's asymmetrical and dysfunctional transport and communications model. It was followed by a trio of books concerned with the International Brigades and the Republican medical services in the Spanish Civil War. Already published are Angela Jackson's rich and moving account of an extraordinary life – that of the left-wing nurse Patience Darton, and the comprehensive account of the Republican medical services by Linda Palfreeman. These books will be followed later in the year by a life of Tom Wintringham by Hugh Purcell and Phyll Smith.

It is difficult to exaggerate the importance of the present volume. Helen Graham is probably the most profound historian writing about the Spanish Civil War in the English language today. *The War and its Shadow* manages, in an entirely original way, to focus our perceptions of the after-life of the Spanish Civil War, not just during the long dictatorship which was the institutionalization of Franco's victory but in Spain's present-day democracy. Especially striking is the way in which she relates it to the mass violence taking place across Europe in the inter-war period. Despite being at the heart of that dark continent where dreadful things were happening everywhere, Spain and its civil war are often omitted from reflections about the meanings of that violence. In that regard, as in so many other ways, this book crams a cornucopia of remarkable insights into a very short space.

PAUL PRESTON
Series Editor
London School of Economics

List of Illustrations

The author and publisher gratefully acknowledge the following for providing photographs and/or giving permission to reproduce copyright material:

Cover Photographs
One of a series of photographs taken by Robert Capa of International Brigaders and Spanish Republican soldiers in March 1939, *en route* between two zones of Le Barcarès internment camp, one of several camps erected on France's south-eastern beaches, over the border from Spain. (The Mexican Suitcase, Magnum/International Center of Photography, New York).

The back cover photograph records an event in Madrid in September 2010 organized by civic memory associations and the Plataforma contra la Impunidad del Franquismo (Platform against the impunity of the Franco dictatorship) when a 14 × 3 metre photograph of a mass grave, one of several excavated in 2007 in El monte de La Andaya, Burgos (northern Spain), was displayed every Thursday in the capital's central square, the Puerta del Sol, directly on the spot said to measure Spain's 'dead' centre (kilómetro zero) in order to focus attention on the plight of tens of thousands of families still searching for the remains of their disappeared – those extrajudicially killed by Francoist paramilitary forces. (Puerta del Sol photograph by Óscar Rodríguez, Asociación para la Recuperación de la Memoria Histórica (ARMH). Andaya photograph by Claudio Albisu).

In-text Photographs
INTRODUCTION: Burgos, 2004, Francesc Torres; Srebrenica, 2010, Robert Jinks; Sarajevo (1993–2003), Miquel Ruiz Avilés.

CHAPTER 2: Spanish legionaries with severed heads of Moroccan prisoners, anonymous photograph from J. Roger-Mathieu (ed.), *Mémoires d'Abd-el-Krim* (n.p. [Paris] 1927). Reproduced courtesy of the Biblioteca Nacional, Madrid.
Seers from Ezkioga in the Basque Country. Photograph by Joaquín Sicart. Reproduced courtesy of William A. Christian Jr.
Young women with heads shaved, Montilla (Córdoba), Spain. Collection of

the late Ignacio Gallego. Reproduced courtesy of Francisco Moreno Gómez.

Murdered civilians, Talavera del Tajo (Toledo). Fondo Serrano, Hemeroteca Municipal de Sevilla.

Sagrado Corazón, Cerro de los Ángeles, Madrid. EFE, Madrid.

Disinterment, Salesian Convent, Barcelona, July 1936. Ministerio de Cultura (Spain), Archivo General de la Administración, Alcalá de Henares.

CHAPTER 3: All photographs of Amparo Barayón and family members reproduced courtesy of Ramón Sender Barayón.

CHAPTER 4: Manuel Moros, Republican cavalry, Collioure, France. Courtesy of Jean Peneff, Estate of Manuel Moros.

Bill Aalto, from K. E. Heikkinen and William Lahtinen (eds), *Meidän Poikamme Espanjassa* (n.p. [New York]: Finnish Workers' Federation, USA Inc., 1939). Tamiment Library and Robert F. Wagner Labor Archives, New York University.

Gustavo Durán on the Aragón front. Courtesy of Cheli and Jane Durán.

Ernst Toller with Walter Hasenclever. Ullstein Bild, Berlin.

CHAPTER 5: Republican soldiers on the Catalan front, Robert Capa, Mexican Suitcase collection, International Center of Photography, New York/ Magnum Photos.

Republican boy refugees, Collioure, France. Jean Peneff, Estate of Manuel Moros.

CHAPTER 6: Prison column of captured Republican soldiers. Fondo Serrano, Hemeroteca Municipal de Sevilla.

Prison Gallery, Barcelona. Carlos Pérez de Rozas, Arxiu Històric de la Ciutat de Barcelona/Arxiu Fotogràfic.

Camp de la Bota (Barcelona). Arxiu Històric de Poblenou.

Laundry day, Camp de la Bota. Arxiu Històric de Poblenou.

Maes–Barayón family photograph. Courtesy of Ramón Sender Barayón.

Acknowledgements

This book has benefited immensely from the wisdom, intellectual support and practical help of colleagues and friends in the UK, Spain and North America. I would like to thank:

John Aalto Jr, Montse Armengou, Richard Baxell, Hilary Canavan, Cathie Carmichael, Peter Carroll, Ángela Cenarro, Jane and Cheli Durán, Francisco Espinosa Maestre, Mercedes Esteban-Maes Kemp, Sebastiaan Faber, Giuliana di Febo, James Fernández, María Jesus González-Hernández, Penny Green, Joel Isaac, Lala Isla, Angela Jackson, Becky Jinks, Jo Labanyi, Andrew Lee, Magdalena Maes Barayón, Jorge Marco, Mayte Martín, Josie McLellan, Judith Meddick, Carole Naggar, Linda Palfreeman, Bernard Perlin, Lisa Power, Alex Quiroga, Michael Richards, Isabelle Rohr, Francisco Romero, Rúben Serém, Scott Soo, Sandra Souto, Maria Thomas, Bill Thornycroft, Francesc Torres, Piero Tosi, Vanessa Vieux, Marta Vilaseca, Ángel Viñas.

I would also like to thank the following for help with textual and photographic research and the provision of images:

Peter Anderson, John Aalto Jr and family, Manuela Alonso, staff of the Arxiu Històric de Poblenou, Barcelona, Tom Bannan, Sara Bhagchandani, EFE (Madrid), Jonathan Bell (Magnum); William A. Christian Jr., Elena Delgado, Florence Dumahut (Maternité Suisse d'Elne), Helen Ennis, John Foot, Emilio Grandío, Elena Hormigo León (Hemeroteca/Fototeca Municipal de Sevilla), Robert Jinks, Martin Jönsson, Nathan Kernan, Robert Lubar, Gail Malmgreen (Tamiment Library, NYU), Philomena Mariani (ICP, New York), Matti Mattson†, Francisco Moreno Gómez, Dieter Nelles, John Palmer (ARMH, Zamora), Jean Peneff, nephew of Manuel Moros, for the Moros Estate, Victoria Ramos (Archivo Histórico, Partido Comunista, Madrid), Óscar Rodríguez (ARMH), Miquel Ruiz Avilés, Javier Santacruz, Peter G. Schmitt (Tamiment Library, NYU), Ramón Sender-Barayón, Juan Salas (NYU), Emilio Silva (ARMH, Madrid), Sue Susman, Rémi Skoutelsky, Maria Thomas, Francesc Torres, Grégory Tuban, Sylvia Thompson, Ricard Vinyes, Nik Wachsmann, Mikko Ylikangas (Helsinki), Cynthia Young and Claartje Van Dijk (International Center of Photography, New York).

I owe a debt to my Europeanist colleagues in RHUL History – Daniel

Beer, Rudolf Muhs and Dan Stone, for their collaboration over a number of years in the development of our jointly-taught MA course on the European civil wars. My thanks are also due to two immensely supportive Heads of Department, Justin Champion and Sarah Ansari, and also to Marie-Christine Ockenden, our Postgraduate Administrator, for offering me her calm support – especially through the final stages of the book in the summer and autumn of 2011.

I am also deeply grateful to the staunch team of friends and colleagues who read draft versions of the book and offered me shrewd and invaluable advice – my thanks here to Becky Jinks, Rudolf Muhs, Alex Quiroga, Dan Stone and Maria Thomas.

Anthony Grahame, Editorial Director at Sussex Academic Press, and his staff, offered kind and efficient guidance at every stage of the publishing process.

Paul Preston has been a constant source of advice and encouragement throughout, his careful reading of the text and general assistance extending well beyond his duties as the series editor. All remaining errors in the text are, of course, my own.

This book is dedicated to the memory of two people: the Andalusian film director and artist, Fernando Ruiz Vergara, who suffered directly in his own life the structural violence of Spain's transition. His documentary film, *Rocío*, is discussed in chapter 7. I also dedicate the book to the memory of my friend, the Hispanist scholar David Vilaseca, who was killed in a cycle accident in central London in February 2010. His work was far removed from my own, and about theory we often disagreed – precisely in these ways I learned a lot from him. I miss our conversation and his quiet presence.

Introduction

Photographs { . . . } enact a reckoning with history that takes the measure of the residual effects of the past in the present, as well as in the future.[1]

The civil war in Spain stands at a crossroads in Europe's "dark twentieth century": that is, in the story of how, not so long ago, the mass killing of civilians became the brutal medium through which European societies came to terms with structure-shattering forms of change.

The Spanish conflict was all about this. But although its exterminatory dimension was *sui generis* – triggered by a domestic military coup – the escalation of the war, and of its bleak heart of extrajudicial killing, is inconceivable without the intervention of Nazi and Fascist state arsenals, which both equipped the Spanish military rebels in their "cleansing" offensives against civilians, while also directly bombing open cities and refugee columns of "enemies". As chapter 1 indicates, Spain is thus doubly emblematic of a larger European story, in prefiguring the many other latent civil wars across the continent – dense and fraught confrontations over social identities and values, which from September 1939 onwards were, in sequence, triggered and intensified as full-scale confrontations by Nazi occupation/annexation.

In Europe north, south, east and west – from the Baltic to the Balkans (Greece, Serbia, Croatia), in Ukraine and France, these conflicts ran their own violent course beneath the carapace of the Third Reich's wars of imperial conquest. This Introduction lays out a conceptual frame for these conflicts, while the rest of the book opens up the human stories of those who confronted, endured and (sometimes) survived the cataclysm in Spain.

The thousand-year Reich was defeated militarily in only six, but not so the belief in the superiority of "homogeneous nations" it had lethally intensified, nor the realization that war remains the most effective means of creating them. This "knowledge", deployed both by states and other actors – which was already incubating within the war-born Francoist project in Spain – has ever since victoriously stalked wars and genocides (the line between the two constantly blurs) inside Europe and beyond. The specific

Burgos mass grave, 2004

"The task to be accomplished is not the conservation of the past, but the redemption of the hopes of the past": the photograph shows the excavation by volunteers in July 2004 of a mass grave near Villamayor de los Montes (Burgos, northern Spain) of 46 male civilians who on 24 September 1936 were extrajudicially murdered by other local people, almost certainly civilian vigilantes connected to organizations of the political right. Their actions were endorsed by the new military authorities who, having made the coup of 17–18 July 1936, successfully took control in most of northern Spain.[*] (Photograph: Francesc Torres, 2004).

economic and cultural circumstances may vary.[2] But common to all is the relationship between crisis and the resulting social fear which generates a cultural script that can justify aggression.

In Spain in July 1936 all the civilian supporters of the coup had in common an immense fear of what the future might hold for their sense of themselves and their most cherished environments. These potent fears were inextricably linked to other very tangible conflicts over the redistribution of economic and political power, but it is the melding of the two factors of fear and power which explains why the coup-makers were successful in projecting back to their supporters an image of their own fears as a myth about the intentions of "the enemy"; of how "the plan was to kill you all", thus justifying the strongly felt need for a pre-emptive form of "defensive" and "cleansing" violent attack (see chapter 1).

* Francesc Torres, *Dark is the room where we sleep* (New York and Barcelona: Actar, 2007), pp. 64–5 for photograph and witness testimony and pp. 14–25 for Torres' own acute introductory essay. The caption quote is from Max Horkheimer and Theodor Adorno, *Dialectics of Enlightenment* (London: Verso Editions: 1979), p. xv.

Not only does the attack create its own dynamic, uncontrollable in the end even by those "victors" who most benefit from it, but it is also, almost immediately, out of date as a response to the perceived danger. The processes of change continue mutating, while the "victors" clutch at their victims. One is inevitably reminded of the elaborately constructed siege defences which appear in Sebald's seminal novel of European memory, *Austerlitz* – hugely costly and evidence of subtle human ingenuity, but obsolete even before completion.[3]

Notwithstanding the very real differences of empirical history, a strikingly similar mechanism to that deployed by Spain's military rebels in 1936 worked equally well in the 1980s and early 1990s during the Yugoslav wars when a new Serbian national memory and identity was forged through precisely the same sort of mythological mobilization. Croatian nationalists fomented and deployed exactly the same kind of mythological ethnic mobilization for political ends, of course, and their responsibility in the wars that followed was also great. But it is the particularity of *a fearful imaginary projected into war*, as I outline it here, which makes the Serb case analogous with Francoism. Generated by economic fears and political uncertainty, Serban national memory solidified as a perception of existential threat which was then projected as the "murderous intentions of the enemy".[4] There are, inevitably, many substantive differences between the Francoist case of the late 1930s and 40s and the Serbian case of the 1980s and 90s.[5] The point of thinking comparatively is not to *equate* these two forms of nationalism, but rather to indicate a resonant parallel that could allow us to think more deeply about the mechanisms which generated the violence in each case: once an aggressor unleashes war – whether military rebels in 1936 Spain or Serbian nationalists in Yugoslavia/Bosnia – then it engulfs everything to make its own new meanings, and in any war whose stakes are supremely about the dreamed-of post-war society and civil order, then atrocity against civilians is everywhere; every "side" acquires its perpetrators, is implicated in the violence.

Aggrieved Serbs cite the raids undertaken by Muslim forces around Srebrenica as a justification for the mass killing of Muslim civilians there in July 1995. But for a historian, unlike for a nationalist, the fact of Muslim war crimes cannot obviate the meaning that is embedded in the chronology of events. Bosnian Serbs, like Franco's military rebels before them, unleashed a war which was publicly justified as a means of "resisting" a fearful fate which was first attributed to, and then inflicted upon the "enemy", thereby reducing the opponent to the same level; forcing them to engage, making them ugly, while simultaneously positing the originating

Srebrenica, 2010

Bosnia and the rest of Yugoslavia emerged from the Second World War, like many regions of Europe, as if from an apocalypse, the landscape so riddled with mass-graves that "the very earth seemed to breathe".[**]

The photograph shows the former battery factory-cum-UN barracks in the "safe haven" of Srebrenica, which fell to the Bosnian Serb army on 11 July 1995. From this place thousands of Bosnian Muslim adult male refugees were taken and killed by the conquering forces. Some were murdered in the "heat" of conquest, in the vicinity of the factory, even within the sight of Dutch UNPROFOR personnel; many more were killed during the subsequent days of "cold" operational terror in farm buildings and schools of the surrounding area. Yet more were hunted down by hundreds of Bosnian Serb soldiers-become-perpetrators in the surrounding woods as the refugees sought to reach safe territory. Of the 7,000 to 8,000 killed and buried in mass graves, thousands are still unaccounted for, and their remains lie scattered in the earth of the surrounding landscape.[†] (Photograph: Robert Jinks, 2010).

aggression as a "lasting solution", which, in both the Francoist and Serbian cases, meant the bid to create a homogeneous national community within the territory it controlled.

It remains true of course that the ethnic dimension of the mass killing

[**] Milovan Djilas, *Wartime* (London: Secker and Warburg, 1980), p. 447.

[†] Figures are those of the International Criminal Tribunal for the former Yugoslavia (ICTY), http://www.icty.org/x/file/Outreach/view_from_hague/jit_srebrenica_en.pdf, p. 1. By 11 July 2011, the sixteenth anniversary of the fall of Srebrenica, the remains of 4,522 people have been identified and interred. (It is policy not to inter unidentified bones.) See the Srebrenica museum site at Potočari: http://www.potocarimc.ba/ and also http://srebrenica-genocide.blogspot.com/ (all accessed 11 July 2011).

that occurred during the Yugoslav civil war of the Second World War period – whose memory was repressed under Tito's rule, indeed was repressed as a foundational axiom of that rule – offered the Serbian nationalist elite much collateral for incubating and intensifying popular anxieties, unresolved grief, and a sense of victimhood, as grist for their work of mythological mobilization in the 1980s.[6] There was nothing of comparable scale in the arsenal of Spanish ultra-nationalists in the 1930s. But there was, nevertheless, more than enough. The iron grip of Spain's long-lived monarchical system (re-imposed in 1875 and in power until 1931) had been predicated on repressing directly or indirectly any political or social reform that might have fostered a process of gradual opening to a genuine constitutional democracy. This had as its singular – though not at all paradoxical – consequence an intense and mounting social fear among elite groups and those retainer constituencies who depended on the status quo. These fears crystallized in the rise of black propaganda, conspiracy theories and also actual "conspiracies" invented by the police in order to justify exemplary repression. All of this was probably most intense in the rural deep south, where huge landed estates and socially feudal relations of power held captive a mass of starving landless day labourers. But these fears extended also to the north and to the comfortable classes of the bigger cities, where the memory was strong of popular rebellions against military conscription (1909) and later explicitly against economic hardship and political exclusion – the cycle of rural risings and street warfare/violence known as the "bolshevik three years" which followed the end of the Great War. These fears may have been temporarily lulled by dictatorship in the 1920s, all the more especially as that dictatorship was floated on a European economic boom which for a time softened the edges of Spain's underlying structural impasse. But the fears remained just under the surface, and would soon become the substance for the sociological mobilization of a new mass conservatism in 1930s Spain, as they were filtered and recast by the discourses of the Catholic, military and agrarian right under pressure of the accelerating cultural change symbolized by the coming of the democratic Second Republic in 1931. Indeed such was the power of this recasting of social fears that it effectively "prepared" socially conservative constituencies for the depradations that the Franco regime would later inflict. The sheer rapidity of the post-coup mobilization of civilian forces behind the military rebels in July 1936 is only comprehensible if one takes into account these already high levels of social and psychological "conscription" beforehand.[7]

This psychological conscription of social fear by political actors is what has driven civilian-upon-civilian massacre in the many subsequent conflicts that have "run" with Hitler's – and Franco's – lethal belief that killing is the most effective means of establishing a "rational political community" (see chapters 2, 3 and 6). It is a realization of this which underpins our growing sense of the enormity of what the Republican war effort once held back, in resisting the advance thrust of Nazi adventurism, with all the many wars of ethnic, cultural and political "purification" that it would unleash. The human and social costs for Spaniards of this purificatory project, in both the short and long term, are explored in the individual study in chapter 3, just as they also run through the second half of the book, in its analysis of the structural violence of the Franco regime and its enduring effects into present times; while chapter 4 explores on a broader canvas some of the most resonant forms of political, social and cultural resistance to that purificatory project, both as they coalesced in Spain in 1936–39, and also in the memory and legacy these have left behind in Europe and beyond, a theme that also re-emerges in the final chapter. Throughout the book I tell this bigger history through the human stories of people who felt its full force in their personal lives.

Precisely because Francoism was born of a war made viable by Nazi and Fascist intervention, with a political project conceived therein as a fundamentalist nationalism, extreme in its virulent extirpation of difference, then the major terms of analytical reference deployed here are those of the Nazi new order which Franco fervently wished to be part of. The comparisons made between Francoism and Stalinism are fewer, though no less pertinent for that, particularly in regard of a similar deployment of ideas of "work" and "sacrifice" in the conceptualization of forced labour and the prison universe (see chapter 6). In the Soviet Union, the other major example of brutal state-making during the European inter-war period, the ostensible ideological goal was to abolish nationalism. Yet the mass killing and extreme violence perpetrated by the Stalinist system retained a strong ethnic charge, targeting whole groups of "enemy peoples" during the 1930s and the Second World War. And while it was not the aim of Stalin's regime to create a homogeneous nation state, the system (as Stalin personally) demonstrated a fearful obsession with ethnic difference.[8]

While the chapters of this book always have the fundamentalist core of nationalism in their analytical sights, none engages explicitly with the polemics about the definition of genocide, which often shed more heat than light and, certainly, could add little to what this book seeks to explain. It is, however, worth noting that, as with the fraught definitional debates around genocide, so too those surrounding related forms of mass extrajudicial killings as war crimes and/or crimes against humanity often suffer from a similar decontextualization, a mesmerising focus on the acts of lethal violence themselves which fail singularly to place in their proper historical context either the motives or the forms of violence.[9] This is in part a reflection of how scholars themselves have co-opted legal categories, but in all cases this obliviousness to historical context (which as well as the "close-up" contemplation of the act also comprises the reduction of complex events to hackneyed myths, clichés and racist stereotypes) also conveniently others the phenomenon, thus providing alibis for "normal" societies today, and permitting the pigeonholing of the violence as "aberrant" – thus once again ignoring what is by now clearly the "elephant in the room": that it is in such normal societies, including ones self-defined and perceived as "modern" and "civilized" where, under stress, and once specific configurations of crisis combine, ordinary individuals, ordinary human beings murder their neighbours.[10]

In virtually all cases too there operates a crucial intermediate phase when intense social fears are mythologized, transformed, usually by some form of political mediator (Church hierarchy, military elite or ultra-nationalist party) which may or may not itself believe in these social fears, or which believes in them to some degree, while also having other goals. This "mythological transformer" would appear to be the crucial trigger legitimizing mass participation in murder – perhaps because there is a human, or at least a broadly trans-cultural need to rationalize violence, even if that "rationale" is a mythological one – otherwise one cannot compose a *post-hoc* account of the violence that allows for some kind of social reconstruction and which, crucially, allows the perpetrators to live with themselves.[11] By the same token, an international narrative – journalistic or otherwise – which deals in de-historicized categories (Spain as an exotic, "southern", and violent culture; ancient tribal hatreds in the Balkans) or which then seizes upon the consequences of civil wars as if they were causes (Republican integral "instability", or ethnic "irreducibility" in Bosnia) also provides a crucial alibi for a certain exhausted notion of modernity itself, thus staving off the moment of recognition of its illusion of control, which would otherwise be inescapable. Knowledge of this "exhaustion" saturates the events at Srebrenica where refugees were murdered in the presence and sights of UN personnel.

After Franco's military victory in Spain, too, the international powers ignored the regime's institutionalization of killing after 1 April 1939 in the full knowledge of its perpetration.[12] (After 1945 the western Allies would be similarly complaisant, when they approved ethnic cleansing dressed up as "population transfer" or "expulsion" in central and East Europe – a process that also involved large numbers of violent deaths, all in the name of producing ethnic homogeneity.[13]) The second half of the book examines the context in which the institutionalized killing transpired in Spain and its consequences for the history and memory of long-durée Francoism, both inside Spain and beyond. The dictatorship predicated itself as an extension of the civil war as it sought to construct a monolithic national community by violently extirpating Republican political and cultural identities – a predication further intensified by the regime's persistent rhetorical denial of this violence (the "uncivil peace"). The multiple strands of war-born Francoism's "afterlife of violence", both structural and psychic, still haunt Spain, long after the end of the dictatorship. This is evident in intolerant discourse and in the endurance of clientelist political modes renovated by the Franco regime and perpetuated across the democratic transition. It is also evident in a certain disdain and arrogance which inhabit the constitutional state and which take sustenance from what we might call Francoism's still "live" field of memory. Nor have its once lethal myths yet ceased to shape European and western perceptions of Spain's recent history: that Franco was an old-fashioned nationalist; that military intervention was a necessary and patriotic response to political subversion, instability and inveterate internal division in a country culturally unsuited to constitutional democracy. Indeed, rather than these myths being neutralized or defused, they may now be increasing their purchase in the wake of late-twentieth- and twenty-first-century new ultranationalist ascendancy in central and east Europe.

At Srebrenica and elsewhere in Bosnia, the work of recuperating and identifying the victims of nationalism continues. That this offers support for family members is incontestable and amply justifies the endeavour,[14] not least because it has been hard-won, like its equivalent in Spain. But there are more ambivalent outcomes too in that the recuperation of the remains also shores up the moral credibility of an increasingly threadbare form of political and cultural "reason", whose representatives were the very signatories of an internationally brokered peace in Bosnia in 1995 which endorsed the world view of the perpetrators (or at least prevented the anti-Serb alliance from finishing the job). In 1995 as in 1945 the normativity and desirability of ethnic homogeneity was accepted, thereby endorsing the same lethal myths of nationalism.

I omit here the "ethnic" qualifier because what emerges clearly from the study of Spain is that the murderous potential belongs to nationalism itself, without adjectival qualification.[15] From today's vantage point it is quite clear that "ethnicity" has always been simply the most deadly of the myths in the arsenal of the "national idea". Except there has never been anything "simple" about it, as we see today in the continuing, even increasing, capacity of its "mythological transformer" to empower the political ambitions and mass projects of an newly ascendant populist-nationalist right across Europe.

Sarajevo (1993–2003)

"A photograph could be the subtle light that unassumingly helps us to change things."[††]
The panels in the photograph contain images originally taken in September and October
1993 by the photojournalist Miquel Ruiz Avilés, including of the war-destroyed façade of
the offices of the newspaper *Oslobođenje* in Sarajevo (right-hand side). These images were
subsequently part of a travelling exhibition designed by Photographers Without Borders
(http://photographerswithoutborders.net) to raise funds for relief work in the besieged
Bosnian capital. Coinciding with the invasion of Iraq in 2003, exhibition visitors were
invited to record their thoughts by writing on the panels. In Girona, Catalonia, one of the
exhibition's destinations, someone chose to write on the *Oslobođenje* panel "Ací s'acaba
la nit, comença el dia" (Here the night ends and the day begins.) Also visible to the left of
the *Oslobođenje* panel (and again on the left-hand side of the photograph) is the National
Library building in Sarajevo which was destroyed by the shelling of the besieging Serb forces
on the night of 25 August 1992 with the loss of 90 per cent of its books. (Photographs:
Miquel Ruiz Avilés, 1993–2003).

†† W. Eugene Smith – a remark made by the veteran American photographer after he had
documented the effects of mercury poisoning in the fishing village of Minamata (Japan) in
an episode which symbolized the clash between human/ecological needs and powerful corpo-
rate interest. W. Eugene Smith and Aileen M. Smith, *Minamata* (London: Chatto and
Windus, 1975).

I

A War For Our Times
The Spanish civil war in twenty-first century perspective

The war with its flashes of gunfire has opened our eyes. The idea of political
alternation has been replaced for ever by that of extermination and expulsion,
which is the only valid response against an enemy which is wreaking more
destruction in Spain than any ever caused by a foreign invasion.[1]

We ourselves are the War. (Freikorps diary)[2]

In Spain today the civil war, triggered nearly seventy years ago, is still "the
past that has not passed away" and a Spanish judge, Baltasar Garzón, internationally renowned for his championing of human rights, is currently
debarred for reasons connected to his bid to investigate the crimes of the
Franco dictatorship born of that war.[3] In the UK, Garzón is better known
for his bid to have another military dictator, Augusto Pinochet, extradited
from Britain to answer for the forced disappearance and murder of some
three thousand Chileans under his regime (1973–90). Franco was responsible for ten times that number of "disappeared", as well as tens of thousands
more extra- and quasi-judicial killings. Yet outside Spain there is still relatively little public awareness of this dimension of the war. The focus has
remained instead on high politics and diplomacy: on the rapid military
intervention by expansionist Nazi Germany and Fascist Italy, bent on
displacing Anglo-French hegemony in Europe – which turned Spain into
the antechamber of continental, and ultimately, world war.[4]

But it is the long shadow of the world war which is now bringing back
centre frame the most disquieting aspects of what happened in Spain. The
tectonic shift in Europe since 1989 has permitted an unprecedented
empirical excavation of the continental convulsion of 1939–45 (more
accurately, 1938–47), and is now beginning to reveal to a broader public
the stark truth already known by specialist historians – that this was a war
waged predominantly upon civilians;[5] moreover millions of them were
killed not by invaders and strangers, but by their own compatriots,

including their own neighbours.[6] A war of intimate enemies and local massacre, then, which occurred across Europe and whose intensity derived from their being culture wars as much, if not more, than of wars of politics: or, rather, they became possible as mass political conflicts by dint of their profound cultural roots. By "culture" what is meant here is the core narrative of how society is organized and how it is reciprocally explained by its inhabitants with reference to a set of collective values deemed appropriate to underpin it.

These protean conflicts were the microcosmic manifestations in daily life of "impersonal" processes of social transformation deriving ultimately from industrialization and urbanization. By the end of the nineteenth century their impact was becoming more evident, directly or indirectly, in the east, centre and south of the European continent too, an impact much accelerated by the effects of mass wartime mobilization – in the factories probably more than at the military front itself – during the Great War of 1914–18. This was a war which, before the event, had been envisaged by many, including among Europe's traditional landed and imperial elites, as a "clamp" that would hold at bay, or even neutralize, the unintended social consequences of the industrial change which was already acting as a dissolvent on older forms of social and political order. But the "event" itself was rather different to how they had imagined. The acceleration of home front labour mobilization and mass military mobilization to meet the needs of modern industrialized warfare changed the balance of power forever across the continent. Indeed from nearly a century's distance now, we can see how much of the economic mobilization and social shift which *preceded* the conflict was already actively influencing what would be the war's medium-term social and political outcomes. But, in the immediate term, the Great War produced a sort of stalemate or hung result – fatally wounding the continent's old order of empire, elite rule, social hierarchy and deference, yet not finishing these off entirely.

In the 1920s and 30s there thus erupted a maelstrom of becoming. People were on the move physically, the demographic shift intensified by military mobilization and war work. And their ideas, their very sense of their own lives, were often on the move with them. Who should now speak through politics?[7] Which counted for more – the new political rights conceded by emerging or developing constitutional systems, or duties and notions of service deriving from an older, and rigidly hierarchical, social order? What privileges – political, economic and cultural – could wealth still command over those whose only "capital" was their newly acquired membership/citizenship of a state or nation? How might secular ideas of community coexist with religious culture and values? Especially since these latter had not, by and large, been free-floating, but rather integral to bolstering and maintaining traditional (and therefore usually hierarchical) relations in the villages or small towns in which most inhabitants of continental Europe – central, east and south – still lived.

The conflicts of the European inter-war period were most saliently and predominantly ones that emerged from the meanings made by this still overwhelmingly rural majority, in which should be included the many inhabitants of provincial and market towns, in their encounter with encroaching social change – even if for many this remained a dull-rumoured one. Pre-existing economic tensions, especially where mass landlessness was present, became much more conflictive in the new atmosphere where the knowledge of mass war dead primed the emerging language of political rights. But even where no issue of landlessness obtained, the same questions loomed: how would new forms of politics, the fruit of new circumstances, address and reconfigure interests within the rural world itself? Those of the landed, with those of the ubiquitous, complex array of others of modest and middling means – whether landowning peasantry, tenant farmers, estate stewards and retainers, provincial officials, police and the broader commercial and service classes of the locality. A community of economic interest, even in the face of an uncertain future, was far from self-evident here, until a perception of it became solidified through a gradually emerging common set of social fears and anxieties – strongly felt, yet for quite some time also diffuse – appertaining to future *social* change and the threatened loss of reference points, familiar rules, the known local environment.[8] It was these that would come to underpin the "gentry pact" as a recognizable new political alliance across the states and territories of inter-war Europe between the old and landed elites and other rural/village and small-town constituencies and "imperial" service classes anchored in the pre-1914 order.

Their fears were brought into focus and crystallized as an image of the city, becoming fixed upon it as a threat and above all as a source of destabilization. Obviously this was not about urban centres *per se*, which had long existed. Nor was their configuration as alien and other about physical separation or lack of exchange, as there was a regular, indeed increasing human traffic between city and country, including of migrant workers, and intermediate forms of identity and indeed space were already coming into being. It was, in fact, precisely this sense of social flux, of the shifting meanings that could inhabit urban space, which explains the emergence of new fearful popular imaginaries identifying the city with the new, sometimes egalitarian, but always destabilizing political desires taking shape within it. This is encapsulated in the social disgust, almost existential nausea, with which officers and cadets of the imperial armies (Wilhelmine or Hapsburg) described in diaries and correspondence the scenes of popular fervour and, to their eyes, the sheer aberration and mayhem of popular presence on the streets which greeted their return to the cities from the front.[9] They evoked these scenes – in Berlin, Budapest and many other towns and cities of central Europe – as an outright confrontation, embittered by the military defeat also accelerating it, between their own honourable and order-loving values and the onset of social apocalypse embodied in the masses on the streets.

> On a grey November morning, I was allowed to leave [the barracks] for the first time . . . When I came closer to the main streets of the city, I heard wild shouting. Soon I saw a larger crowd of people, among them several soldiers in combat uniform . . . Some were wearing red armbands. Roughly twelve or fifteen of them were beating up two young officers . . . A few civilians shouted and women were screaming "beat them to death, the damned officers!" . . . I quickly approached the scene . . . [but] I didn't get very far . . . I was already surrounded by a group of soldiers and felt the first blows . . . They took my stars and my medals for bravery as well, and the "Große Silberne" [a high military decoration] with the Kaiser's face was thrust into the dirty street. Suddenly they left us alone . . . I spat out the blood and collected the pieces of my sabre and my decorations for bravery in the field. "Damned rabble", I thought, "there will be a day of reckoning for you."[10]

Similar scenes are repeatedly described, filtered through an already fear-saturated cultural script of the French revolution – and in which women out of control are notably present. This anxiety was of course precipitated by a more immediate perceived threat, the Bolshevik revolution, which as well as a new political menace, was hugely galvanizing because it crystallized everything the old order and its "gentry" supporters *already* feared socially.

Indeed one could say that most of what happens thereafter in Europe's dark mid-twentieth century appertains directly or indirectly to this highly charged "coming to terms with the city" – unevenly, reluctantly and tacitly, a coming to terms with the heterogeneities and unorthodoxy, the sheer messiness and fracture of modern urban space and the "trouble" these signal to elites and all those other constituencies with some psychological investment in the values of the gentry pact. For the old rural world under threat was not just an economic order but also a set of social and cultural values perceived as clear and "unambiguous": tradition, religion, "simple" peasant/yeoman virtues, a politically demobilized society; women in their place, in the family home. And more even than social and cultural, these

things were felt as the necessary and essential constellation for psychological well-being too.[11]

Thus it was that the gentry pact came to be constituted as an audience
for radical new incarnations of conservative nationalism, which from
1917–18 spoke directly to their needs and fears. Economic uncertainty,
battles over resources and the crises produced by structural change,
combined with war-induced dislocation, all ratcheted up the fear and intensified the operation of the "mythological transformer", defining as the
"problem" all those who did not fit. Provincial townsmen and the upper
echelons of larger villages joined citizen "national guards" of various kinds
– whether for immediate action, as in Hungary (the white terror), or, as in
1920s Spain, became members of bodies like the *Somatén* as a statement of
intent.[12] But everywhere such organizations defined "the national" from the
outset in highly exclusive terms. Patriotism itself came rapidly to be understood as that which ensured social stasis on a traditionalist basis and in
perpetuity. The organizations were both the manifestation of fears of change
and – whether in action or embryo – a paramilitary instrument for resisting
it by force by policing not only public order but also the social order.
Concomitantly thus, the 1920s saw the effective expulsion and exclusion
across Europe of many perceived not to "fit": urban progressives, autodidact
workers with attitude, labourers who were not prepared any longer to tug
their forelock/observe due deference and the old ways. Although a minority
within European populations as a whole, they were a significant one,
numbering many thousands of people who left: from Finland (1918), from
Hungary; Poland; Yugoslavia; Greece in the 1920s – part political exiles,
part economic migrants.

Ethnicity could be a trigger in some contexts – in central Europe where
this radical, ultra nationalist defence of social stasis overlapped with a
popular culture of antisemitism – so for example in 1920s Poland there was
a movement to mobilize ethnic Poles of the middling sort as a yeomanry
guard to boycott Jewish commercial enterprises. But in numerous countries
of continental Europe after the Great War a recognizably similar social and
political cleansing occurred without any ethnic component – and the latter
category which appears so clearly dominant in the light of subsequent
events, clouds somewhat too, even in central Europe, in that the categories
of Jewish people excluded often at that time mirrored the profile of non-
ethnic social and political cleansing elsewhere. The "restless refugee boys"
described in the discussion of the social history of the International Brigades
in chapter 4, were both Jewish and not, but the reasons they left the places
of their birth in the years after the Great War were very similar, whether
they went from Finland or from Hungary, as in the case of the refugee from

Budapest who became Robert Capa. In photographing the brigaders, he bore witness to their experience in Spain and afterwards, so "swept by roads and travelling" (see also the photo-essay in chapter 5 and the cover image of this book).[13] Capa's photographs provoke an immediate reaction through their intense charge of human connection. His was an immense, preternatural talent underpinned by empathy deriving not least from an awareness that he was photographing a fate that might so easily have been his own. In all this, antisemitism was by the 1920s rather more than background noise, of course; but the drive to purify and homogenize envisaged, created and targeted a greater range of human "threats" and "dangers" – those perceived as bearing social change, a protean category which was not embodied by a single ethnic group.

Of those who felt compelled to leave, some took the established, time-worn path to North America, although the USA no longer offered the relatively easy access of earlier times. Many others departed to other European countries, France especially, where wartime losses combined with a falling birth rate provoked a substantial labour shortage. But in France too exactly the same mythological transformer was soon at work, and as the international political tensions of the 1930s mounted in the face of clear Nazi expansionist intent, so too in *la France profonde,* among the rural and small town majority there began to appear an intransigent, quasi ethnic form of nationalism which identified as the "problem" those groups of migrant urban labour in their midst, now swelled further by later arrivals, including batches of political refugees – all of whom, as antifascists and foreigners, were perceived as nefariously engaged in driving France into war with Germany. By the second half of 1938, and after the final collapse of Léon Blum's last ditch (Popular Front) cabinet in April, the Daladier government decreed a series of restrictions on foreign labourers and refugees which both played in populist terms to existing fears, while also stoking a rising xenophobia and antisemitism in France which was only in part economically motivated, and which was indeed sometimes directly at odds with the macro-requirements of the French economy and defence.[14] Accordingly naturalized citizens, especially if Jewish, were increasingly hedged about with *de facto* restrictions, while migrants or the naturalized returning from service in Spain as volunteer fighters with the Republic, against the Nazi- and Fascist-backed rebels, found themselves interned in camps, frequently indefinitely, by a peacetime and Republican French government.

A [. . .] percentage of the continent's population had become quite accustomed to the thought that they were outcasts. They could be divided into two main categories: people doomed by biological accident of their race and people doomed for their metaphysical creed or rational conviction regarding the best way to organise human welfare. The latter category included the progressive elite of the intelligentsia, the middle classes and the working classes in Central, Southern and Eastern Europe.[15]

Thus wrote Arthur Koestler from his own internment in Le Vernet concentration camp near Toulouse which was "rehabilitated" by the Daladier government to intern International Brigaders who had crossed into France with the defeated Spanish Republican army after the fall of Catalonia in February 1939. Unlike the beach internment camps, such as Argelès, St Cyprien and Le Barcarès, which were hastily set up to contain the Spanish refugees, Le Vernet, like Gurs and a small number of the other camps across the south-west, was expressly conceived as a punishment or disciplinary camp. So while those refugees in the beach camps suffered appalling conditions, especially at the start, through the sheer lack of basic facilities and even shelter, in Le Vernet the inmates were subjected to an explicit prison regime – which of course says much about how the French government viewed the brigaders. Later on Le Vernet was expanded to house other "undesirable" or enemy aliens, a category to which the Hungarian-born journalist and writer Koestler was deemed to belong. Unlike the more fortunate and better connected Koestler, who spent four months in the camp, most of those incarcerated had no hope of release. Just as their counterparts in Germany had suffered "a Munich for the camps",[16] so the inmates of Le Vernet too had their fate determined by the xenophobia which now fed appeasement. Out of a camp population of over five thousand, only a small minority (approximately fifty) would be released prior to the military collapse of France. Some two thousand prisoners passed eventually from French to Nazi (Gestapo) control,[17] but not before the appalling conditions in the camp, where hunger and disease were rife, had caused a rebellion of sheer desperation in April 1941. Brutally quelled by the local police, the result was also a virtual death sentence for those who were as a consequence deported to Germany or to the infamous North African work camps – these latter a space of European deportation and incarceration still largely unexplored by historians.[18] Today all that is left of Le Vernet camp is the prison cemetery. Restored in the 1990s, it austerely commemorates the refugees and political exiles of some fifty four nationalities who endured its conditions – the largest single component of which were Spanish Republicans.

In Liberal-Centigrade, Vernet was the zero-point of infamy; measured in Dachau-Fahrenheit it was still 32 degrees above zero. In Vernet beating-up was a daily occurrence; in Dachau it was prolonged until death ensued.

In Vernet people were killed for lack of medical attention; in Dachau they were killed on purpose. In Vernet half of the prisoners had to sleep without blankets in 20 degrees of frost; in Dachau they were put in irons and exposed to the frost.[19]

But in the very possibility of comparison, Koestler reminds us that here in France in the network of internment and "punishment camps" for brigaders and refugees that covered the landscape of Roussillon in "peace time", the European concentration camp universe was already in existence. Le Vernet and its ilk were not as consistently dangerous as Dachau or the other "early" German camps where the law was already a dead letter. But Le Vernet or Gurs, Bourg-Madame or Bram and the many other camps, were still places in which inmates, whether they suffered and died, or suffered and survived, had already become bare life: they were excluded from all "nations" and thus devoid of both the symbolic value and rights such membership afforded.[20] In these camps too could be found the cruelties typical of the later concentrationary labour universe, with its arbitrary punishments, petty tyranny and pointless tasks.[21] This was the fear-induced creation – at once surreal but only too real – of a supposed "solution" to the "problem" the officers of former empires had seen on the streets of Berlin, Linz and other central European cities in 1918 – a pathology now extending across the continent and that saw itself as the re-inscription of control.

It was into this world of social fears that Hitler's war of territorial expansion was unleashed. It thus equipped myriad European civil wars that were already primed. In villages and towns across the continent, "irregular wars" of many kinds erupted, waged in the name of different possible futures, upon the uncertain terrain opened up in the wake of the Great War. These European civil wars, west, east, north and south, took on a "cleansing" intransigence – just like the Nazis' own – unsurprisingly if bleakly, as many of those driving them had long envisaged the "solution" to convulsive change as being found in the forging of "homogeneous" communities, whether ethnic, political or religious.[22] Out of these internecine clashes the socially new would emerge, although what that might mean would not be in any way properly "clear" until after the end of the much vaster – and truly "world" – war of 1939–1945 which across continental Europe constituted a brutal coming to terms with the magnitude of the supervening social change, mediated through forms of off-battlefield violence so intense and barbaric that they remain, arguably, still "unimaginable" within main-stream Western consciousness, even today.[23]

✳   ✳   ✳

So much of this was prefigured with primal intensity in Spain, a country which, already by the end of the 1920s, no longer corresponded to the image of dormancy and demobilization generally held by outsiders and indeed by segments of Spain's own elites too. The Great War, which Spain did not enter, but which entered it, generated accelerated industrial growth and population shift, which intensified the social and cultural rifts already evident in Spain, the accretion of several decades of uneven development. The boom years of the 1920s solidified these different worlds. Spain was no longer only the land of contrast beloved of foreign essayists and travellers of various hues – the urban sophistication and/or militant labour cultures of Barcelona, against the socially feudal starkness ("primitive beauty") of the agrarian deep south. Now there were medium-sized coastal cities powered by trade and small scale industry, in which the burgeoning professional, entrepreneurial and commercial middling strata had republicanized themselves in a bid to break through to achieve a political voice in a system that was still antiquated and exclusive.

Jaggedly at odds with them were the rural fastnesses and inward looking, socially locked-down provincial market towns of the central heartlands and northern interior, from which, not uncoincidentally, were drawn many of the believers and pilgrims for the post-1919 upsurge of religious apparitions in the face of domestic and international flux.[24] (In the wake of revolutionary turmoil in Europe, the Spanish king had in May 1919 unilaterally dedicated the country to the Sacred Heart of Jesus, unveiling the imposing statue on Madrid's *Cerro de Los Ángeles* – the geographical centre of Spain.[25] In the years following 1919, town councils also erected their own Sacred Hearts, on which was inscribed "I will reign in Spain". These were acts and words whose symbolic resonance echoed like a battle cry upon urban workers and liberal and cosmopolitan constituencies.)

What would "arm" the situation in the 1930s, however, was not Republican reforms in themselves – which after all were as much as symptom of these underlying developments as a cause – but the confluence of a broader social base for change (the aforementioned north-east sea board middling constituencies combined with organized labour in town and city) with a new regime that offered a legal and policy framework to realize that change, and a language of political rights and inclusion to justify it. Against them would be mobilized patrician conservatives, but most crucially, as earlier in (a somewhat less unevenly developed) central Europe, also the ranks of Spain's inland rural society. This gentry pact would, in turn, legitimize the violent action of sectors of the Spanish military, both peninsular and colonial, whose own material discontents were filtered by a driving belief in the need for social defence against a world of enemies,[26] this further sharpened by the dominant and by now strongly ideologized memory of military and imperial defeat in 1898.

Thus on 17–18 July 1936, a group of army officers rebelled against the reforming Republic in the name of a civilian coalition of forces who favoured an older, "anti-urban" social and political hierarchy which would, supposedly, guarantee their "ideal" of a static society. Saved from almost certain failure by Nazi and Fascist military intervention, and by a British inaction amounting to complicity, these army rebels, in which a colonial military elite including Franco took the lead, unleashed a conflict in which civilians became the targets of mass killing. Even in areas where there was no armed resistance to the coup, the new military authorities authorized and presided over an extermination, mainly perpetrated by civilian death squads and vigilantes, of those sectors associated with Republican change – not only those who were politically active, or who had directly benefited from the Second Republic's land, labour and welfare reforms but also those who symbolized cultural change and thus posed a threat to old ways of being and thinking: progressive teachers, self-educated workers, "new" women.[27] Even in the areas of Spain where the military coup failed, in one crucial respect it "succeeded" fully – in that there too it unleashed extrajudicial and communal killing which, combined with the killing sanctioned by the military in the rebel zone, would make radical new meanings that changed Spain's political landscape forever.

The killing in Republican territory, which for a time the government was powerless to oppose because the military rebellion had collapsed the instruments of public order, was perpetrated against civilian sectors considered to be the natural supporters of the coup. Nearly 50,000 people were killed.[28] Many of the perpetrators believed that through these "cleansing" murders they would finally break the asphyxiating social hold of old monarchist Spain which had lived on into the Republic, so a new world could be made – hence the particular targeting of landowners, but above all of priests. Notwithstanding the vehemence of anticlericalism that was peculiar to the Spanish case, the culture wars which underlay Spain's military coup were clearly part of the broader wars of social change across Europe – with a recognizable series of flashpoints: the accelerated emergence of mass suffrage as a consequence of the Great War, demands for social welfare reform, and the redistribution of land and economic power in the countryside. Nevertheless, the unprecedented level of communal violence against priests triggered by the military coup, in which some 7,000 male religious personnel were killed, would prove devastating to the international reputation of the Republic.

Its causes, however, reach much further back than the Republic (b. 1931) into the long-lived Restoration monarchy (1875–1931) where tens of thousands of ordinary people felt the daily, pervasive presence of the Catholic Church as stifling and inimical to both their "spirit" and welfare, while its symbols reminded them daily of their political and social exclusion from the Restoration order. In many respects these people – whether or not they consciously sought to espouse secularized culture values and practices – were the direct equivalents of those who elsewhere in the villages and small towns of south and central Europe had rejected the rigidities of social hierarchy and forelock tugging. The fact that in Spain this rejection went on being manifest via anticlericalism is an indication not so much (or certainly not always) of a less politically developed awareness, as an indication of the vast and sustained power of the Catholic Church itself which still endured in the 1930s.[29] Its ecclesiastical hierarchy, a model of culturally intolerant pronouncement, operated much as in absolutist times, and had, throughout the preceding and long-lived monarchy, been content to see the Church used as a disciplinary instrument to sustain an authoritarian system in which both king and political class continued to behave as if the Great War had not occurred in Europe. It is thus the political and social context of "arrested development", rather than any religious peculiarity of Spaniards, which explains why the pivotal battle for modernity in 1930s Spain ended by being waged over the bodies of the clergy. That the result was pathological is of course also true – but, in the last analysis, that too was a consequence of the political and social modes – and abuses – that had built up under the Restoration monarchy itself.

It would be six months into the war before the Republican authorities were able to rebuild public order and put an end to this killing in their zone. By then, however, it had already reinforced a social support base for Franco among those whose families and loved ones became the victims. Nevertheless, this "Republican" violence always remained more ephemeral and less effective than the death squad vigilantism simultaneously occurring in rebel-held territory, precisely because there the killing was backed and authorized by an integrated military power, the new Franco regime in the making.

After Franco achieved military victory in spring 1939 – much aided by the British government's sustained commitment to "Non-Intervention" – the genocidal dimension which had incubated in war-forged Francoism became fully apparent. Of the baseline figure of 150,000 killings – extra-judicial and judicial, based on summary military justice – for which it was responsible in the territory under direct military control between 1936 and the late 1940s, at least 20,000 were committed after the Republican military surrender in late March 1939.[30] The scale of the post-victory killing is particularly noteworthy in view of the large scale Republican exodus via Catalonia in February 1939. In a bid to create a "homogeneous" nation based on traditionalist values and social deference, both understood to be embedded in a certain "disciplinary" form of Catholicism, the regime engaged in the murder and mass imprisonment of the Republican population, as the subsequent chapters of this book will discuss.

Francoism constitutes the most significant and enduring "Western" example of how European polities, societies and "nations" of the mid twentieth century came to be reconstructed through violence – through the large-scale execution and mass imprisonment of compatriots.[31] If we ask how this happened, and, crucially, how it was legitimized, then to answer the question we need to place Spain in the context of a Europe-wide "politics of retribution"[32] which encapsulates how brutal new states were created, through the manufacture of categories of the anti-nation, of non persons without civil rights – in short, through the creation of the "other", whether Jews, "Untermenschen", enemies of the people, or, in the case of Francoism, the catch-all epithet of "red". All the rebels' wartime political opponents were described as "red". But the term was also applied indiscriminately to entire social constituencies – predominantly to urban and rural workers, but also to Republican-identified intellectuals and liberal professional sectors and to women who did not conform to the rigid gender norms deemed appropriate by Francoism. In sum, in post-war Spain "red" came to mean whoever the rebel victors chose so to label as a means of removing either their lives or their civil rights.

To achieve this in a way which maximized its own control, the Franco regime exhorted "ordinary Spaniards" nationwide to denounce their compatriots' "crimes" to military tribunals. Tens of thousands did so – out of a combination of political conviction, grief and loss, social prejudice, opportunism and fear – motives often mixed within a single denouncer. Thus did the Franco regime, born of a military coup that itself triggered the killing, pose as the bringer of justice. But this was "justice turned on its head", given the notorious lack of fit between the acts of wartime violence themselves and those denounced and tried for them – unsurprising, given no corroboration was required nor any real investigative process undertaken. But matching crimes to culprits was not the real point of the exercise: tens of thousands were tried merely for their political or social alignment with the Republic. This was the Franco regime's "fatal" moment: through its choice of legitimating strategy it mobilized a social base of perpetrators, building on their fears and losses sustained during the war, while, at the same time, it criminalized the Republican population, perpetrating an abuse of human rights on a vast scale. Worse still, the regime then kept alive these binary categories for nearly forty years, through its apartheid policies and an endlessly reiterated discourse of "martyrs and barbarians". This is what marks Francoism apart in Europe, as the singular progeny of a seemingly never-ending war, both civil war and Cold War. The violence of its origi-nating strategy is, moreover, still "live" inside the polity and society of twenty-first century Spain, some three and a half decades after the demise of the dictator and his regime.

2

The Memory of Murder
Mass killing and the making of Francoism

Violence may originate in a set of "rationally" identifiable causes, but once it is unleashed, its effects are unpredictable and all-pervasive. They saturate everything.[1]

The Spanish civil war of 1936–39 began with a military coup. There was a long history of military intervention in Spain's political life, but the coup of 17–18 July 1936 constituted something new. Like a negative philosopher's stone, it transformed the meaning of military intervention, just as surely as it radically altered the nature of all the forms of political activity which had been occurring – in the streets and in parliament – since the coming of the Second Republic in April 1931. In effect, Spaniards were disputing the future shape of their own polity and society, in part buffeted by currents reaching them from elsewhere in Europe – the Russian revolution, and more broadly, the mass political democracy set in train by the effects of the Great War. But the dispute was already an internal one, produced by decades of social, economic and cultural change which crystallized across the 1920s in the cities of Spain, but also reached numerous provincial towns under the impact of a Europe and world-wide economic boom. The radio-listening, professional republican-association-joining urban middling classes of the 1920s, combined with an army of internal labour migrants from countryside to city (including those who built the capital's metro), had already introduced a more substantial challenge to older forms of social and political order than was to be found anywhere else in southern Europe. The Republic, with its clear vocation to speak for the city, was itself a product of this development as much as generator. And it was Spain's difference in this respect which would explain the density of popular resistance to the military coup of July 1936, as well as the clear political geography of its initial success and failure. Indeed the extent of that failure in urban, populous Spain might have been decisive in cashiering

the coup, had not Fascist Italy and Nazi Germany offered crucial military
support to the rebels, right at the start, thus allowing them to escalate their
attack.

The key to the Republic's enduring popular support lay not only in its
most tangible reforms – in the areas of land, labour and welfare – crucial
though these were for the redistribution of social and economic power. It
also lay in a qualitative change, in the change of social atmosphere that it
wrought – especially via some of the secularization measures it introduced,
most particularly the ones that saw the secularization of the streets and other
public spaces;[2] including through the provision of alternative ceremonial –
civil marriage and burial – and, above all, of education and particularly co-
education. All these things were developed by the Republican authorities,
but they were not imposed in a vacuum – which is to say, they found a ready
audience, as too did the Republic's nurturing of a relative urban
eclecticism/cosmopolitanism and its attendant freedoms, including those
related to gender and sexuality. While the Second Republic was not
Weimar, it was far less minoritarian in terms of the audience it could
command than similar progressive and/or republican projects elsewhere in
southern Europe. Crucially in Spain, the cultural change that was occurring
was not only a city event – for the Republic was altering the balance of
power beyond, in deep, rural Spain. Among the conservative smallholding
peasantry of the inland north and many provincial townsfolk, again especially (although not exclusively) in the inland northern half of Spain, there
was an ingrained hostility to Republican cultural values. But elsewhere on
the strongly federalist eastern/south-eastern sea board and in the southern
half of Spain where mass landlessness obtained, the Republic's message of
change elicited a profound response. Above all, the Republic's language of
political rights did this. It was the first regime in Spain that assumed ordinary people had rights of any kind. And this language of rights the Republic
spoke – and more importantly, allowed to be spoken – permitted those
people in small town and village Spain who dared, to think differently. This,
perhaps more than anything else, was what drove patrician Spain to sheer
apoplexy. It was against this perceived threat to older ways of being and
thinking that a fear-ridden patrician and also a populist crusade conservatism "rose" behind the coup of 17–18 July 1936.[3]

It is important to bear all of this in mind because it was the relative depth
and complexity of social and cultural change which had penetrated beyond
Spain's cities into the provincial towns and even the villages; the range of
modern cultural "collateral" already present by 1936, which explains the
violence of the Francoist counter-response. Of course the armed conflict of
1936–39 would raise the stakes enormously, in terms of *making new mean-*

ings to justify extreme, state-led violence – something which will be discussed later in this chapter. But first it is important to be clear about the relative complexity of Spain's alternative social and cultural solidarities, its collateral for "modernity", already by 1936, as the co-origin that explains the force of the Francoist blast, and which at least in part played a role in creating the prison universe of later – because so much had to be definitively destroyed. Even though Spain had neither the same level nor the density of civil society which obtained in Germany, it was the extent of Spain's intermediate (if very uneven) development in smaller cities and bigger towns; the fact that it had a great deal within it that was not simply "rural backwardness" or "provincial closed-mindedness" which brings it closer to the German example. We are thus better able to understand what happened after July 1936 if we think in terms of Germany in 1933 as a more adequate comparator than Italy in 1922 – as non-Hispanists tend still to think, and perhaps some Hispanists too.

The military coup was always intended to be violent. The military rebels issued secret orders dating back to April 1936 that indicated maximum force was to be used: this was violence as the end of the argument over constitutional reform.[4] But the coup also tapped into something else, something quite literally "fearful" within society at large. In its immediate aftermath, before any international factors could come into play, extreme forms of internecine violence were occurring virtually throughout Spain. The force with which the opposing elements clashed owed more than a little to the cultural influence of the highly authoritarian and manichean brand of Catholicism still predominating in Spain, and which affected even many of those who had consciously rejected religious belief and the authority of the Church. But the detonator of events was a military coup and it was inside Spain's officer corps that there had emerged a rigid and intolerant political culture by the early decades of the twentieth century.

The final loss of empire in 1898 had deprived Spain's substantial officer corps, inherited from the continuous wars of the nineteenth century, of its chief external *raison d'être*. In so doing, imperial defeat turned the military into a powerful internal political lobby determined to find a new role while guarding against any loss of income or prestige in the interim. To take the sting out of defeat, there grew up within the officer corps a powerful myth that civilian politicians had been to blame for the loss of empire and thus had little moral claim on governing the country. This belief was already deeply ingrained by the time the fifteen-year-old Francisco Franco entered the military academy in 1907. A generation of officer cadets came to see themselves as the defenders of Spain's unity and hierarchy and of its cultural and political homogeneity, as consubstantial with the country's historic greatness. Indeed many in the military elite took this one step further, interpreting their defence of this idea of "Spain" as a new *imperial* duty. What was lethal about this new interpretation of imperial defence was that it came to be directed against those other Spaniards who symbolized the social and economic changes occurring in the towns and cities. Indeed it was among the officers who made their careers in the colonial Army of Africa, including Franco himself, that there would emerge the most fatally reductive views of what was "wrong" with metropolitan Spanish society and politics. As a result, many of the *Africanistas* came to define Spain's subaltern classes as colonial subjects, in need of the same sort of violent subjugation which the *Africanista* campaigns had already visited upon the indigenous inhabitants of Spanish Morocco.[5]

To be sure the officer corps – both colonial and peninsular – also had more material concerns which brought them into conflict with the Republic. For land and social welfare reforms cost money and the government was seeking to subsidize these by cutting the military establishment and thus its enormous salary bill. Even the prospect of this earned the government the enmity of the conservative and ultra-nationalist majority amongst the corps who read it as an intolerable attack against the institution which best enshrined patriotic value and virtue. For junior officers

Spanish legionaries with severed heads of Moroccan prisoners.

Spanish legionaries displaying the severed heads of Moroccan prisoners as "trophies" – an anonymous photograph taken in the early 1920s and which appeared in J. Roger-Mathieu (ed.), *Mémoires d'Abd-el-Krim* (n.p. [Paris] 1927). The image was subsequently deployed by the Francoist authorities during the civil war to depict "red" atrocities. (Photo reproduced courtesy of the Biblioteca Nacional, Madrid).

there was, additionally, the looming danger of personal career blight. For the colonial corps (*Africanistas*) too, the proposed budgetary cuts coincided with their being targeted by a government enquiry into "responsibilities" for military defeats supervening in Morocco in the 1920s.[6] Strategically ill-advised, this enquiry was the equivalent of placing dynamite under the Republic and then lighting the "fuse" of a powerful pre-existing ideological narrative that largely determined how the corps would interpret Republican policy towards them.

Although a good number of these army officers were the sons of Spain's landed elites, or otherwise statistically overdrawn from the old ruling order of central-southern Spain (Basques and Catalans, from the country's strongest industrial regions, being historically under-represented within the officer corps), what was emerging in the 1930s to confront the reforming Republic and its social base, was rather more than a military–civilian coalition of patrician conservatives. (Indeed the Spanish officer corps could itself be an effective route for certain sorts of upward mobility – Franco was an example of this.) But more crucially, what was emerging from 1931 were new mass, popular forms of conservatism mobilized around the vexed question of Catholicism – that is, from sectors opposed to secularizing reform. The Republic, as Spain's first democracy had itself created the framework of political opportunity for such mobilization, although it was the Church's pre-existing infrastructure of lay Catholic associations that made possible the crucial organizational connections which allowed the emergence of this new politics. Thus it was, paradoxically, that the Catholic Church in Spain, whose hierarchy was so profoundly hostile to the notion of liberal democracy and cultural pluralism, which gave the newly mobilizing mass Catholic right its great advantage over the progressive left in the new sphere of democratic politics, that is to say the very infrastructural means to launch a national movement of opposition to constitutional and cultural change. This would eventually give birth to the CEDA, a coalition of centre-right Catholic entities that would contest and win the November 1933 elections in Spain in a bid to halt social and cultural reform as well as the redistribution of economic power.

But while the Catholic Church orchestrated this mobilization in the 1930s, it did not invent it. For, sociologically, it was a movement mostly of ordinary, lay people who, well before the civil war itself, came to see themselves as engaged on a "crusade" to defend an endangered way of life, the risk to which came to be epitomized by aspects of social change accelerating under the Republic.[7] Co-education was an especially contentious point, but seen as inflammatory too was the availability of civil marriage and burial and the spread of a relative urban eclecticism and related freedoms. Thus precisely those aspects which for some groups signified the great oxygenating opportunities of the new political times were internalized by social conservatives as threatening, and in deeply personal ways. What caused most offence to practising Catholics was the interference by the progressive municipal authorities of 1931–33 with forms of local devotion that framed social identities and daily life: for example, their interference with ceremonies organized around local saints or cults of the Virgin Mary and the restrictions placed on religious processions more generally, including, in some places, on private funerals too, where the authorities interpreted funeral processions as public displays of Catholicism.[8] This interference with a world of private devotion and communal piety conjured deep emotions as it was perceived as an attack on people's core allegiance to a way of life and often to a specific place (the immediate locality or *patria chica*), which indicates how many felt their religious faith and spirituality to be inextricably bound up with a cherished social environment.

All of this stoked the storm and fed the political cause of the ultra-

Seers from Ezkioga in the Basque Country

Adult seers from Ezkioga, a village in the Basque Country, which became famous as a site of Marian apparitions that began in June 1931, some two months after the arrival of the (secularizing) Second Republic. (This photograph was taken in the early months of 1932 by the professional photographer, Joaquín Sicart. It is reproduced here courtesy of William A. Christian Jr.).

montane right.[9] As too did the erosion of deference/traditional hierarchies that was sometimes internalized as a personal affront by small town and rural social conservatives who, even though they were themselves of only modest social extraction, retained a psychological investment in the order it guaranteed. The announcement too that the publicly funded stipend to ordinary parish priests was to be phased out also alienated both clergy and laity who might not otherwise have been so ill-disposed towards the Republic, although this was a more difficult policy issue – many priests – as well as bishops and archbishops – were from the start waging ideological war against the Republic from the pulpit; and, unlike the municipal ordinances which annoyed the pious, recouping the church subsidies was pivotal in the Republic's release of funds for other reforms, especially for (public) primary education. For many, these educational opportunities, which had never before been in their purview, signified – probably more than anything else – the Republic's status as a secular redeemer.[10]

Nor were these divergent cultural readings by Spaniards always confined to separate geographical spaces. While to some extent the south was relatively more spatially segregated, in the centre and north social conservatives and social progressives/free-thinkers very often inhabited the same space[11] – including in some cases the very same family houses. In the resonant, if perhaps optimistic, words of a historian who has written about the social impulsion of religious apparitions in 1930s Spain, these were "a kind of dialogue between divinities and the anticlerical left", not only those in the cities and on the southern landed estates, but also "anarchists and socialists in the Basque coastal cities, socialist farmworkers in Navarre, republican railway officials and schoolteachers in rural areas".[12] But the railway workers and schoolteachers of pious towns such as Valladolid and Salamanca would figure *en masse* among the first victims of the extra-judicial killing unleashed by the coup.[13] Conversely, the idea of a crusade against social modernity was to be found not only in the market towns of north-central Castile, or in the remote rural north (most obviously among the theocratic and pugnacious Carlists of Navarre) but also in larger urban centres and the big cities, where Catholic youth became activists in the new mass organizations of the right. In the aftermath of the coup many of them too would, in the vacuum of a collapsed state power, become the victims of extrajudicial killing at the hands of Republican sectors who saw in them the fomenters and supporters of the military rebellion.

For its part, patrician conservatism, which included much of the Spanish officer corps, was by the early months of 1936 increasingly linked up to the self-proclaimed fascist right, as was by then occurring too elsewhere in Europe. José Antonio Primo de Rivera, the leader of Spain's fascist party, the Falange, reciprocated, quoting Oswald Spengler's *The Decline of the West* on the idea of a squad of soldiers "saving civilization". In the end, it was the failure of these popular *and* patrician conservative forces to block reform by legal means, when they lost the elections of February 1936, that determined the military coup of July. It was hatched in Spain's remaining North African enclaves by officers steeped in ideas of Catholic and imperial reconquest. But their ideas were already strongly inflected too by social Darwinist imperatives in which the metropolis had become the object to be purified and redeemed from the "alien" values of urban and cosmopolitan culture. When the Africanista army landed in late July in mainland Spain, this then was the project: the "reconquest" of the metropolis. And indeed the supervening civil war would be fought by Franco and many of his fellow Army of Africa officers as if it were a colonial war.[14] The fact that a colonial military project had fused with the new mass/populist conservatism of the crusade to produce a "mythological transformer" about to be visited murderously on the entire population of mainland Spain, is itself indicative of something very new. The fact of a military coup in July 1936 was far from being "business as usual" in a rurally demobilized southern European country – as still so often appears in the historical narrative. It meant a new form of hybrid political project fusing the colonial ideas of the *Africanista* elite with the mass warrior Catholicism of large parts of the CEDA and especially of its youth movement, the JAP, whose violent nationalist imagery (geared to a "reconquest" against "anti-Spain") was, by 1936, indistinguishable from the fear and loathing driving the Falange. Indeed their desire for decisive, violent action would see members of the JAP join the Falange in droves in the late spring and summer of 1936.[15]

The coup, by instrumentalizing the social fears which underlay the idea of "crusade", allowed hatreds and desires – terrified and terrifying popular political imaginaries – that would otherwise have remained inchoate and fragmented to take on a concrete political form and become a reality. In the days and weeks after the July coup, public declarations were made by local civilian elites in the rebel zone – whether bosses of the fascist Falange or people associated with the mass Catholic party, CEDA, or monarchist landowners or businessmen or clerics. These were made independently of each other and of the military authorities. But they were remarkably similar. Their message was that Spain needed to be purged or purified. Sometimes they even spoke of the need for a blood sacrifice.[16] These kinds of sentiments unleashed a savage repression that happened from the outset everywhere in rebel Spain, including in many areas (in the centre-north of Spain and north-west) where the military rebels were in control from the start, where there was no armed resistance, no political resistance to speak

Young women with heads shaved, Montilla (Córdoba), Spain

Young women with shaved heads in Montilla, Córdoba, photographed in early August 1936 (see Arcángel Bedmar González, *Los puños y las pistolas. La represión en Montilla (1936–1944)*, 2nd edition [Montilla: Ayuntamiento de Montilla, 2009], p. 62). Each has been left with an 'adorning' lock or tuft of hair which serves to intensify the humiliation underpinning this form of gender-specific punishment, regularly inflicted in the rebel zone from the days of the military coup onwards. The facial expressions and body language of the women (including the varied ways in which they make the fascist salute) indicate the differing ways in which this humiliation wrought its effects. (Photograph: collection of the late Ignacio Gallego, reproduced courtesy of Francisco Moreno Gómez).

of either, no "front", no advancing or retreating troops – in short, where there was no "war" according to a conventional definition of the term. What there was, however, was a culture war that the perpetrators carried in their heads. The coup had sanctioned its unleashing and thus opened the way to mass murder.

People of all ages and conditions fell victim to this "cleansing". What they had in common was that they were perceived as representing the changes brought by the Republic. The military rebels and their civilian supporters were thus redefining "the enemy" as entire sectors of society that were perceived as "out of control" because they were beyond the control of traditional forms of discipline and "order". This did not just mean the politically active – such as members of parliament elected by the centre-left, mayors and trade unionists or those who had benefited from the Republic's economic reforms (for example landless labourers or lease-holding farmers who had achieved new tenancy rights under the Republic) – although such people were killed in their thousands. It also meant "cleansing" people who symbolized cultural change and thus posed a threat to old ways of being and thinking: progressive teachers, intellectuals, unionized and/or autodidact workers, "new" women.

Rebel violence was targeted against the socially, culturally and sexually different. It saw the killing in Zamora of Amparo Barayón, wife of the Republican novelist Ramón Sender, whose independent spirit was considered a "sin" against traditional gender norms. Her story, and that of the Barayón family, is told in chapter 3. This "cleansing" violence, or *limpieza*, claimed its most famous victim in the poet Federico García Lorca, killed both for his political beliefs and his sexuality. But many thousands of less well-known Spaniards were murdered for similar reasons, like Pilar Espinosa from Candeleda in Avila, taken away by a Falangist death squad because she read the socialist party newspaper and was known to "have ideas" (*tener ideas*), thinking for oneself being considered doubly reprehensible in women.[17]

Those who did much of the killing in rebel Spain during the first months were vigilantes. What occurred was a massacre of civilians by other civilians. This mostly took the form of death squads abducting people from their homes or else taking them out of prison. In a majority of cases the assassins had close links to rightist political organizations that had backed the coup – in particular the Falange, but also the CEDA. But the military authorities made no attempt to rein in this terror. In fact the killers were usually acting with the connivance of these authorities. Otherwise the death squads who came for Amparo Barayón and thousands of her compatriots would never have been able to take their victims out of gaol at will. In other words this was a "dirty war" and it "disappeared" some 30,000 people during the war of 1936–39. Meanwhile, at the same time in the deep south of Spain, the Army of Africa was directly involved in other sorts of extra-judicial killing. As it made its way up towards Madrid, in an action explicitly described as a "reconquest", it effected a mass *limpieza*, laying waste to civilian sectors opposed to the coup – in particular the rural landless – thereby also reversing by force of arms the Republic's agrarian reform. Rural labourers were killed where they stood, the "joke" being they had got their "land reform" at last – in the form of their burial plot.[18] In some places entire villages were virtually wiped out. Both African mercenaries (the *regulares*) and Spanish legionaries went on the rampage, killing anyone on the streets and also sometimes going from house to house to drag people out.

In every town taken by the Army there were public summary executions of men and women who had resisted: tens, hundreds and sometimes thousands of people depending on the size of the places.[19] But civilians too were

Murdered civilians, Talavera del Tajo (Toledo)

Murdered civilians in the street in Talavera del Tajo (now Talavera de la Reina), province of Toledo. They were local inhabitants, plus a number of itinerant Galician reapers/agricultural labourers, killed by Army of Africa troops and Spanish legionaries on 3 September 1936 in the hours after the town was taken by rebel forces under the command of Lieutenant Colonel Yagüe. The picture was taken by Juan José Serrano, one of the photographers and journalists who accompanied the Army of Africa on its march up through the south towards Madrid – Serrano was their preferred photographer. A contemporary eyewitness account of what happened in the street in Talavera del Tajo, that of Miguel Navazo Taboada, then a young boy, is cited in F. Espinosa Maestre, *La columna de la muerte*, pp. 435-7. Like the photograph of Spanish legionaries of the 1920s with the severed heads of Moroccan prisoners, so too the Talavera image of *Africanista* killing was reproduced by the military rebels as proof of Republican atrocities. As was later reported by one of their own propaganda chiefs, Antonio Bahamonde, the rebels not infrequently mutilated both battlefield fatalities and the corpses of executed men and women, photographing them for use, similarly, as black propaganda against the Republic. Bahamonde's memoir, and an example of the practice, is cited in P. Preston, *The Spanish Holocaust*, p. 333. (Photograph: Fondo Serrano, Hemeroteca Municipal de Sevilla).

involved in this southern repression – for example, the landowners who rode along with the African columns to take revenge on the socially rebellious; or all those locals involved in perpetrating the more systematic repression once the Army of Africa had moved on to the next town or village.[20]

Both rebel troops and their civilian supporters also used rape as a weapon of war.[21] In the South the advancing columns of *regulares* and legionaries

were given to understand by their commanders that "red" women were war
booty, part of their trophy for the taking.[22] But there were plenty of other
military perpetrators, and many civilian ones too among the rebels'
supporting coalition, whether operating after the regulares or indeed in
areas of rebel territory where the Army of Africa had no presence at all. In
short, systematic rape of the female "enemy" was perpetrated everywhere
across Spain in the aftermath of the rebel takeover – whether or not that had
involved military action.[23] The loathing manifest in the act of rape was the
most extreme symptom of the rebels' misogyny, deriving from their fear of
losing control.[24] Hence the desire first to humiliate and then to eradicate
those women who had demonstrated any kind of autonomy, but especially
those who had actively participated in the military defence of the Republic
(the *milicianas*).[25] "Red" women were obsessively reduced to their sexuality
by rebel commentators and perpetrators, whether military or civilian, who
thus projected their own fears onto those they had constructed as the
Republican enemy.[26] Nor was this only the work of the most extreme
sectors, although Legionaries, Falangists, and requetés (the Carlist militia)
were heavily involved in sexual violence. The climate propitiated by the
coup meant that, for example, "ordinary" conscripts too could feel impunity
in abusing the female members of households on whom they were billeted
in recently occupied territory, safe in the knowledge, reinforced by power,
that Republican women were corrupt and depraved and thus not worthy of
respect. In such cases, and in many others involving civilian perpetrators,
priests too often defended the "honour" of their male parishioners, especially if they had significant social status locally, and instead denounced
their female victims as "reds" and thus unworthy of being believed.[27] The
exception that proved this rule occurred in the trial of a number of perpetrators in the small town of Calanda (Teruel province, Aragón), in January
1941 for the rape and murder of numerous Republicans who had returned
to the town after Franco's military victory. The incitement to kill had been
that of the local head of the Falange and the secretary of the town council,
but the events were so extreme they were denounced to the military authorities by the civil governor of Teruel. In consequence, some of the
perpetrators were sentenced to eight years in gaol, although none served
more than half the sentence.[28] The whole episode is strongly reminiscent
of the way in which both the Italian Fascist and Nazi regimes first deployed
intense violence, and then, once it had run its course and achieved its aim,
posed as the tamer of the very violence they had unleashed in order to ensure
support for their regimes from "people of order" (*gente de orden*) among the
middling and affluent classes. This core mechanism was perhaps even more
prominent during the wars of Yugoslav succession in the 1990s where mili-

tary and civilian perpetrators deployed extreme violence (including rape) which was then "controlled". But the subterranean memory of the violence remained to do its work, just as it did in Spain, where it linked and implicated both the military and their civilian supporters.

It is this complicity in the rebel zone – between the military authorities and those "ordinary Spaniards" who sought a cleansing violence – that is of particular importance here. For where that relationship went and how it was articulated by the ruling military authorities is the story of how "Francoism" was built – bottom up as a repressive, carceral society – as well as top down as a political regime. "The memory of murder" has a number of implications, but first and foremost it refers to this pivotal complicity.[29]

This complicity was strengthened by the wave of extra-judicial murders that occurred in Republican territory in the aftermath of the military coup and during the months before government control – collapsed by the coup itself – could be restored. The people targeted for killing were often those seen as active or passive supporters of the coup – which included nearly 7,000 priests and other male religious personnel.[30] An unprecedented wave of anticlerical violence, exacerbated by the Church hierarchy's vehement and explicit support for the military coup, also reinforced pro-Franco constituencies in their idea of a crusade. But whether the targets of violence in Republican territory were clerical or otherwise, the explosion was primed by anger and fear (amounting to the same thing) at what was seen as the rebels' attempt to put the clock back to old regime order by force, having failed by legislative means. It is clear from the fact that force was everywhere directed at the sources and bearers of the "old power" – whether material (by destroying property records and land registries[31]) or human (the assassination or brutalization of priests, civil guards, estate bailiffs and shop keepers associated with speculative pricing and other exploitative practices[32]). There was a clear link between post-coup popular violence and very material conflicts of the pre-war period: for example over the blocking of land or labour reform legislation in certain localities or over worker dismissals after the general strikes of 1934 or over conflicts (again, over the implementation of social and labour reforms) in the aftermath of the February 1936 Popular Front elections. In the early months of the conflict bottom-up violence in Republican territory would also be triggered by the news of mass shootings and other atrocities in rebel territory brought by terrified refugees, as well as by the direct experience of enemy air attack which saw assaults on imprisoned conservatives in a number of places.[33]

The stresses placed on the Republic's general population were much greater, not least because included in its zone were the cities and large urban centres subject to aerial bombardment and military siege. By and large that also meant people with fewer social and economic resources, since many of the wealthiest constituencies organized to leave rapidly for France, while others remained away, having been absent from Spain on summer holidays when the coup occurred.[34] Nevertheless, leaving aside both the violence triggered by aerial bombardment and also some components of the criminal and sociopathic inevitably unleashed at moments of political collapse,[35] most of the violence in Republican territory, just like that in the rebel zone, followed a discernible and intelligible course. The Republican perpetrators tended to come from constituencies which bore a long memory of social and political exclusion.[36] (There is an echo here too of a phenomenon of which historians have long been aware – that many of those who surged into the party and union militias formed to confront the military rising and rebel garrisons in Spain's cities were young men of no previous political affiliation.) The Republic had represented a hope of change, but the reforming impetus slowed up in1933, thwarted, as they saw it, by legislative and other obstruction resulting from the endurance of the old elites and the old power. The coup was the last straw, evidence of the obstinate grip of the old and its determination to exclude even their most basic needs for its purview. It was the symbolic centrality of the Catholic Church as an institution to this social exclusion that explains the notorious anticlerical dimension of the terror. For while Spain had a long history of anticlerical behaviour and iconoclasm, the wave of priest killing that occurred once the military coup had collapsed public order, was entirely unprecedented.

While this anticlerical violence was the single most important factor in undermining the Republic's reputation/credibility internationally, its origins went back much further than the Second Republic. The key to the violence lay in the role of the institutional Church and of certain forms of authoritarian Catholicism as the linchpin of social control under the Restoration monarchy (1875–1931) which meant that hundreds of thousands of Spaniards, mainly, although not exclusively, located in urban areas, experienced the Church's cultural monopoly, and through this often the very idea of religion, as something personally oppressive, cutting right to their emotional core, as a form of daily violence done to them, a claustrophobic saturation of the space through which they passed to work and live.

To understand this one must first reckon with the abyss that existed between the formal constitutionalism of the Restoration monarchy – epitomized perhaps in its press freedoms – with the lived reality of the poor, especially poor urban dwellers – whose lives and free movement were curbed repeatedly by curfew and martial law, the latter very frequently declared at some level or other by successive Restoration governments.[37] Rights of association existed only in theory and the police could and did pursue the unionized in the streets, in their workplaces and in their homes. Urban workers were subject to a growing repertoire of harsh and arbitrary measures such as detention without trial, internal deportation, extra judicial murder (the *ley de fugas* – prisoners "shot while escaping") and even arrest on grounds of "moral guilt".[38] Although these were predominantly matters of politics and public order, in the Restoration's authoritarian culture the melding of the political and the religious was absolute: religious personnel staffed prisons and reformatories; conversely, security forces were a regular feature in the public religious processional that traversed the space of Spain's cities; it was the civil governors, state appointees, who issued edicts against the "blasphemy" that was an integral part of urban popular culture, turning it into an arrestable offence.[39] In times of turbulence and street protest, the leading lights of Catholic lay associations were among those called upon to act as police informers. And harrowing for the urban poor was the Church's crucial public role in legitimating capital punishment – which would be abolished for civilians by the Second Republic. In earlier years, the sight of the desperate and the destitute being marched on foot through the streets of poor city neighbourhoods provoked, as one memoirist recalled, "an unhealthy atmosphere, like a mixture of sadness and panic".[40] What he described in those words was a form of sustained psychological abuse, and one in which the whole edifice of Restoration public culture made the Church deeply complicit.[41]

It was this spatial dimension of the Church's cultural hegemony which came to the fore in the 1930s. The reaction to clerical symbolism – and in the end to clerical flesh and blood – was, at root, a reaction to this universe of political and social subjugation, in which those subjugated had seen no clear line between the power exercised by political and by religious authority. Other more traditional dimensions of popular anticlericalism remained – the stories of lazy, corrupt, immoral priests were legion, reinforced both by continuing economic inequalities, and the role of Church in articulating mass political opposition to Republican reform: "what was the Church? Only a chain store dealing in funerals, baptisms, marriages, hospitals, education, money-lending, banks, cafés" as one Barcelona worker expressed it in July 1936.[42] But the real challenge for a twenty-first-century audience is to understand the emotional landscape, the popular imaginary that lay behind the remarkable juxtaposition of "sadness and panic". The memory of a not dissimilar emotion would mark the Catalan artist Joan Miró who recalled his repugnance when, as a conscript in August 1917, his unit was deployed against the general strike in Barcelona and he was faced with the possibility of having to fire on workers. The memory remained with him, shaping his work implicitly, and sometimes explicitly, for life.[43]

For other lives more ordinary, however, there was no outlet – just a steady accumulation of pressure and brutalization, of "everyday", structural violence. This too would be a major "protagonist" in the anticlerical killing in the summer of 1936. The perpetrators were ugly, but they had been made so by a dominant political culture that long predated the Republic, and which, in the few years of its incumbency, the new regime could barely scratch the surface of. Currents of elite/intellectual anticlerical thought may well have exacerbated these powerful popular feelings of injustice and exclusion after 1931, but they do not account for how they had been generated in the first place.

The Second Republic's major "contribution" to all of this was to have raised legislative hopes of changing Spain's public environment, of making the air more breathable, only to see these hopes dashed again, first by a two-pronged action of radical Catholic mass mobilization and filibuster in parliament, and then finally by the act of the coup itself. What came after, in the vacuum of government power, was an attempt to change things in such a way that there could never be a return to the *status quo ante* and to ensure its irrevocability through the use of violence. Unless one understands this then it is impossible to explain the way in which priests were targeted above all other rebel-identified sectors, across the cities, towns and villages of Spain where the military rising was defeated (with the exception of the parts of the Basque Country remaining to the Republic, where social relations were qualitatively rather different). This targeting bespeaks a specific purpose. Francoism subsequently wrote it up in a fearful and reductive way as a conspiracy.[44] But the singular resolve displayed by large numbers of people to murder religious personnel indicates a driving desire to eradicate the influence of the Church. It was as clear and brutal a rejection as one could imagine of the challenge/gauntlet "I will reign in Spain" thrown down in 1919 by the monarch when, in the aftermath of social and political revolution across Europe, he consecrated Spain to the Sacred Heart of Jesus.

This rejection was registered most dramatically and deliberately in stone when, in the aftermath of the military coup, Republican militia from Madrid and the surrounding area collaborated over a ten-day period in the systematic destruction of the huge statue of the Sacred Heart which had been erected on the *Cerro de Los Ángeles* (the Hill of Angels) just outside the capital to commemorate the 1919 consecration. They used gimlets and drills and vast quantities of dynamite to destroy it, but not before there were repeated theatrical displays of the Sacred Heart's "execution" by militia firing squad.[45]

Events concluded with the renaming of the site as *Cerro Rojo* (Red Hill). The strongly ritualistic component evident in such iconoclasm, or in the

Sagrado Corazón, Cerro de los Ángeles, Madrid

A firing squad of Republican militiamen symbolically "execute" the statue of the Sacred Heart of Jesus (*Sagrado Corazón*) at *Cerro de Los Ángeles* (Madrid), 7–8 August 1936. Although the destruction of the statue – as an act of iconoclasm – definitely occurred, there has always been uncertainty over the status of this particular photograph and whether it was in fact a montage created by the rebel authorities as black propaganda (i.e. by superimposing the figures of the militia upon an existing image of the dynamited statue). Certainly the photograph was used in this way, both inside the rebel zone and also disseminated abroad for the same purpose. Technical appraisal suggests that it would have been quite difficult to simulate such a photograph credibly well. But that appraisal is based on the newspaper image reproduced here. No historian has yet had access to any version of the photograph itself (although one is said to be located in an ecclesiastical archive in Getafe, the town adjacent to Cerro de los Ángeles). Any analysis of the image as it appears in the press is necessarily provisional. Whatever the truth, it does not of course alter the political and social significance of wartime anticlerical violence in Republican territory. Although, if the image were to be proven a Francoist montage, then that would substantially change our reading of the historical significance of this particular photograph. (Photograph: EFE, Madrid).

disinterring of the remains of monks and nuns or in the humiliation and torture of priests and other male religious personnel before they were killed, all speaks clearly of the power which the desecrators and perpetrators still believed was exerted by religion and the Church.

A signal element in this confrontation was also about gendered power – for anticlerical violence, and certainly the lethal violence against persons, was largely male on male in which urban working class militia both challenged/rejected the institutional authority of the Church and, at the same time, reasserted control over "their own" women (the confessional booth being seen as a site of seduction and/or sexual predation as well as a source of alien political authority).[46] Hence too the not uncommon sexual humiliation of priests as a prelude to their murder, though far more common was their general humiliation. Contradictorily, too, priests were taunted for not being "proper" men, for having been emasculated by their vocation (since this required a lifetime of celibacy, at least formally) and there were also cases of priests being castrated prior to being killed.

Conversely, the recorded cases of the sexual intimidation or killing of female religious were very few – which is likely to reflect a rarity of occurrence rather than merely a lack of reporting.[47] Rather than visit violence on nuns, militiamen were more likely to "liberate" them into the world – sometimes with the exhortation to the younger ones that they should become mothers. Such an act of "liberation" reinforced the militias' sense of their own power, just as it also revealed their still patriarchal understanding of what "freedom" constituted for women. Nevertheless the politics of patriarchy in evidence here played out quite differently to those

Disinterment, Salesian Convent, Barcelona, July 1936

The disinterment of religious personnel (here at the Salesian Convent in Barcelona in July 1936) constituted part of a wave of iconoclasm and anticlerical violence triggered by the July military coup. (Photograph: Ministerio de Cultura, Archivo General de la Administración, Alcalá de Henares, Spain).

operating in the rebel zone. The male workers of the Republican militia still sought to control women – as was manifest in the battles joined post 18 July 1936 over women's role in the new revolutionary public space, and especially within trade unions and the new collectivist workplace structures that mushroomed where workers defeated the coup. But, for all those new battles over revolutionary power, working-class men were simultaneously engaged in a thoroughgoing assault on the established structures of social and political power that had previously subjugated subaltern groups irrespective of gender. Within the militias' reading, then, religious women, just like women workers, were subaltern groups who needed freeing not punishing (being confined to a convent was almost always construed as the result of oppression/coercion). Nuns were defined primordially as women, and thus victims, rather than, like male religious personnel, as the agents/ perpetuators of a tyrannical and subjugating Catholic culture. A piece of conservative definitional logic (women are always women above any other identity they possess) that nevertheless saved many lives. This logic usually precluded any equivalent in Republican territory of the sustained sexual punishment of women – whereas, in rebel territory, the onslaught against "red" women was integrally linked to the reimposition of traditionalist forms of social order on subaltern Spaniards regardless of gender. Given this logic, it is also unsurprising, therefore, that the instances of sexual attacks on "white" (i.e. politically conservative) women were rare in the Republican zone, as pro-rebel commentators indicated at the time.[48] All in all, it was in the nature of the political action playing out there that there was no comparable phenomenon to the consistent, mass physical abuse of women as was occurring in territory controlled by the military.

The acts of violence/extrajudicial murder in Republican territory – whether targeted at clerical personnel or other secular/lay victims – were intended to exorcize fear and destroy the structures of power which had generated it. Violence here was then something being projected back by those who had long suffered it, in some ways as the language taught to them by the dominant culture. It was believed by those perpetrating it to offer a means of achieving *tabula rasa*: the instantaneous dissolution of political tyranny and, just as importantly, a form of reparation for accumulated social hurts.[49] In the context of this psychological landscape and history, then the words of Spain's famous anarchist leader, Buenaventura Durruti, in July 1936, are entirely explicable: "we are not in the least afraid of ruins. We are going to inherit the earth."[50]

Popular violence in Republican territory was then a singular outbreak of emotion and anger – frequently intense and sometimes very ugly. On numerous occasions it became caught up with other dynamics of violence also unleashed by the coup, whether these were about the settling of pre-war political scores (most notably some within the labour unions),[51] or private score-settling or driven by agents-provocateurs, or criminally motivated (looting, theft and extortion), including by some associated with political movements, especially the anarcho-syndicalists. But irrespective of these other dimensions, the popular violence was discernibly political and about the construction of something new. For the experience of the (pre-war) Republic meant there was a consciousness of political possibility – however dulled or distorted. In this regard then anticlerical killing, as with the killing of other groups who symbolized old Spain, was an instrument, consciously used by at least some of the perpetrators because it was perceived to be a way of breaking forever with the past, of ensuring that there could be no return to the social/political order of before the coup. While some killing of hated priests or estate bailiffs or others was spontaneous and "instinctive", there were also formats which bespoke greater conscious political intent. For example the many cases where annihilatory violence came as a consequence of the arrival of anarchist militia forces or other armed squads in villages and small towns, (for example those that fanned out from the cities of Barcelona and Valencia across Catalonia, Aragón and the Valencia region). Crucial here would be locals collaborating with the incoming forces, signalling who were the local rightists and supporters of the coup. The evidence too is that, as with the involvement of young workers not previously politically active, so too this small town action crossed over to include middling sectors, many of whom were participating in politics for the first time.[52] Here war was mediating social change directly. In some ways this is comparable with the process, if not the goals, of the extrajudicial killing that was occurring in rebel Spain. The attitudes exhibited by the reconstituting Republican regime/state towards these forms of communal and political extrajudicial violence were, however, not comparable with the rebel zone.

The Republican authorities could not initially prevent extra-judicial killing in their territory because the military coup itself had completely collapsed the police and army as the instruments of public order while it had also generated a huge surge of fear and anger. But the regime subsequently rebuilt public order – not least to put an end to murder. For whatever the Republic's numerous shortcomings, there is no doubt that its political culture and state-building activities, indeed its very *raison d'être* and legitimacy, were all based upon extending the rule of law. But the challenges facing the Republic here were huge and would remain so throughout the war.[53] In the first six months after the coup, it confronted a gargantuan task in reconstructing the mechanics of government power and public order. Not only had these been ripped apart by the centrifugal blast of the coup, but this had also actively delegitimized the very concept of conventional political, judicial and military authority. As a result, the rate of restoring these things was painfully slow. But for the Republic nor was there any military respite. By October 1936 Madrid was under direct threat from Franco's armies which had swept up through the south laying waste to the civilian population. Under these conditions, with no reconstituted army yet to speak of, and internationally isolated, the Republic was seeking to defend itself against a rebel onslaught backed by the industrial might and military muscle of Nazi Germany and Fascist Italy. It was in these zero hour conditions of integral siege and isolation that there occurred the one major atrocity committed in wartime Republican territory in which forces ultimately responsible to the government were implicated.

This was a prison evacuation from a besieged Madrid in November 1936 that became a massacre. The government had already left for Valencia, not expecting Madrid to be held militarily. The city, caught in the vice of Franco and Mola's armies, was gripped by fear.[54] The sense of siege came from within as well as without. There was enormous apprehension about a "fifth column" – even alluded to by General Mola. The foreign embassies and legations were full of pro-Franco civilians who had sought asylum. The knowledge of what had happened in the killing fields of the south also underpinned people's fears, which were exacerbated by the clear threat issued by the rebels that they would take heavy reprisals against the civilian population of the capital. With Franco's African army encamped within sight of Madrid's main gaol, the decision was taken by the military and civilian leaders charged with the city's defence to evacuate to gaols further behind the Republican front lines some eight thousand pro-rebel prisoners, many of whom were army officers who had refused to fight for the Republic. But in the course of these transfers between two and two-and-a half thousand of the prisoners, those who had been classified as the most "dangerous", were extrajudicially executed by militia forces. These were drawn from several different sources – from Madrid's reconstituting police force, from the anarcho-syndicalist CNT-FAI, the Spanish Communist Party-controlled military unit, the Fifth Regiment, and also from the JSU which was the newly unified youth organization of the Spanish Socialist Party (PSOE) and the Communist Party (PCE) but by this stage firmly within the latter's orbit.[55] The rest of the prisoner evacuees reached their destination at other gaols. But the enormous pressure of the siege, and the sense of an endgame, had fuelled an exterminatory explosion that would further impel the retaliatory killing.

Known collectively as Paracuellos, for the village outside Madrid where the shootings took place, this was the clearest equivalent in the history of the Republic at war to the prison *sacas* (literally "taking out") in which thousands of civilian detainees lost their lives across rebel Spain. There the military authorities were accomplices. But there is no evidence that the Valencia-based Republican government knew about the killings at Paracuellos until after they had happened. It is, however, clear that executive officers of the Madrid Defence Council colluded in them, as did members of the reconstituting Madrid police force, while the logistics of the assassinations would have been impossible without the cooperation of the CNT whose forces at this point still controlled the capital's exit routes. The further damage done to the Republic's reputation and credibility internationally once the events at Paracuellos became known (via a multi-lateral diplomatic initiative which the Republic did nothing to obstruct), redoubled the government's resolve to recentralize political power and to prioritize the regularization of police and judicial authority in its territory. The Madrid Defence Council was brought under direct cabinet control and indeed disbanded as soon as was feasible – although the continuing lack of support from both Britain and France made the Republic's efforts to give teeth to its constitutional machinery much harder than it would otherwise have been.

Policy inside the wartime Spanish Republic nevertheless moved in a clear and recognizable direction: state political authority was gradually but consistently imposed in order to reduce the opportunities for extra-judicial/extra-constitutional forms of violence. In so doing the Republic sought, like any constitutional regime, to bolster its own legitimacy by exercising a monopoly over the use of violence.[56] Capital punishment, abolished in civilian law by the pre-war Republic, was reinstated for espionage and other crimes deemed to undermine wartime security or give succour to the military enemy. But it was used at a low level against civilians and even then most of these death sentences passed by the Republic's special wartime courts were commuted. The Republic continued to behave as a democracy, albeit one at war and in the most difficult of conditions. There were flaws in its constitutional fabric – the actions of the police were sometimes abusive, as were conditions towards the latter part of the war in some prisons and prisoner-of-war camps, as integral war weariness and demoralization intensified in proportion to what was by 1938 the Republic's almost total diplomatic isolation. But the re-established Republican judiciary did investigate abuses committed by the police, including the cruel treatment of prisoners and unlawful killings. The Republic defined these things as crimes – even if committed against the enemy. Whereas in the zones controlled by the military authorities such things were quite simply off the radar, and understood to be not crimes, but a prophylactic administered by power.

In the end, Spanish Republican democracy was cashiered by Britain and France in September 1938 as part of the same failed diplomatic gambit to appease Hitler that would obliterate Czechoslovakia, the last functioning democracy in central Europe. But Britain's dislike of the Second Republic dated right back to its birth in 1931. For not only did its proposed reforms set an example for the redistribution of domestic social and economic power within a capitalist democracy that was most unwelcome to the conservative political establishment in Britain, but the coming of the Republic in Spain also symbolized the democratization of political life itself, its opening up to a wider range of social groups. 1930s Britain, for all that it was a consti-tutional power, still retained a political class drawn from a very narrow social range, and since the Great War had changed the shape of politics, social and political conservatives in Britain had been fighting a rearguard action to keep its consequences at bay. In this the Foreign Office's respon-dents from Spain were at one with their diplomatic masters: there could be no clearer encapsulation of their mentality than a report in the course of 1938 which referred to the veteran trade unionist, Ramón González Peña, who was then the Republic's Minister of Justice, as a tinker from Asturias.[57] On the other hand, Britain's elites knew the Francoists socially. As a result there was throughout a double standard operating in the official evaluation of wartime events in Spain. The Second Republic at war was, in the eyes of British policy makers, damned whatever the state of its public order. In the early days it was "chaotic" and unable to keep control (this of course as a consequence of a military coup).[58] Later when it took a strong line in its (constitutional) wartime courts against those charged with acts of sedition, then the British criticized it for dictatorial tendencies. As for wartime violence against civilians, in Republican Spain it was murder plain and simple. In the rebel zone, however, it was a disagreeable but necessary process whereby the military authorities were imposing order. That Britain's political elites of the 1930s also saw violence against some social groups as a necessary measure rather than a crime should not, of course, surprise – especially if one remembers that in 1939 a British police chief was due to make an official visit to Dachau in order to observe "modern policing techniques" and was only deterred by the outbreak of outright war.[59] It was then as a result of these unspoken assumptions that Franco could credibly play to the gallery of their political fears and social snobbery in posing in September 1936 as the saviour of order in the propaganda films his office distributed after the relief of the garrison siege at Toledo in September 1936, days after his forces had taken the town in a "cleansing" operation which involved massacring wounded defenders in their beds as well as the doctors and nurses attending them.[60] Indeed the official British response to the coup-triggered political and communal violence in the Republican zone can itself be counted a signal and singular propaganda success for Franco's rebels, in that never once was it mentioned that the origin of the tidal wave of violence in both zones of Spain was the military rebellion itself.

What marks out the social and political uses of the violence in the rebel zone is the symbiotic relationship between grass roots violence and the emergent Francoist political order. The military authorities, as the supreme political authority in rebel Spain, could have stopped the extra-judicial killing, for there was no collapse of public order as had occurred in Republican territory. But instead they chose to harness the violence, and with it the idea of a crusade that had originally emerged from popular conservative milieux. We could define the kind of violence occurring there at the grass roots as a form of religious violence – in the sense that this usually has highly specific social and political goals. "The word 'pollution' is often on the lips of the violent", as the historian Natalie Zemon Davis has observed.[61] And the killings in rebel Spain were widely seen as a means of ridding the community of sources of pollution or defilement and the dangers they supposed. Priests played a prominent role here in justifying the killing – including to those about to die. But other priests were perpetrators, participating directly in the firing squads.[62] More common, however, the model of the radio priest in Córdoba who encouraged the killers and spoke of the cleansing as "the work of God".[63] And while anti-clerical killings in the Republic zone subsequently redoubled the zeal of conservative clerics, that this was not the crux of the matter is indicated by the fact that violence in the Republican and rebel zones was occurring simultaneously. More important was the *sui generis* desire of conservative clergy itching to impose a certain sort of social and "moral" control on Spaniards who were now daring to think and act differently. After 1939 the Church would regain enormous social influence in exercising new disciplinary functions on behalf of the Francoist state. Religious personnel played a key role *en masse* in the running of prisons, reformatories and other correctional facilities.

There was a strong element of ritual in the wartime violence too. There were mass public executions followed by the exhibition of corpses in the streets or the mass burning of bodies. Not infrequently there was a ritual component to the killing of local mayors or other Republican post-holders in the central square of the village or town. It is significant too that in central and northern Spain executions took place on established saints or feast days. There was an uncanny mixture of terror and fiesta – executions followed by village fêtes and dances, both of which the local population was obliged to attend.[64] The violence here served several different functions. First, it strengthened complicity; second, it served to exorcize the underlying fear of loss of control which was the subconscious linkage uniting the military rebels with their various groups of civilian supporters. But it was also the ritual aspect that *permitted the transgression* – by dehumanizing the victim and also by hiding from the perpetrators the full meaning of what they were doing. This was certainly true in the smaller communities of the centre-north where the killers were breaking a taboo in killing within their own towns and villages. Nevertheless, the presence of a ritual element serves to remind us that this violence was not a marginal or "asocial" phenomenon; it was not about a few psychotics rising to the surface in troubled times (even though there were some such individuals in the death squads). Rather the violence was part of a set of behaviours and goals being endorsed by considerable numbers of people and through which "society" was being remade.[65]

The kind of killing perpetrated by civilian vigilantes – often called the "hot repression" – tended to be what happened in the period immediately after rebels took control of a specific town or village. So given that their territorial advance was more or less constant across the war, then this scenario of violence repeated itself throughout the years of war across Spain. In each conquered territory the hot terror would then give way to a more systematic repression, the cold terror – in which the military authorities came formally to the fore and where those who had defended the Republic were court-martialled and executed *en masse* for "military rebellion", a punishment that would continue after 1939. As a form of killing it was barely "judicial" – in the sense that it was the result of summary justice. There were mass trials, sometimes of fifty or even a hundred defendants, with no due process, no case made beyond the bare charge of "military rebellion"; no legal defence provided and in which the accused could not intervene (all of which is discussed further in chapter 6 below). But whether the terror was hot or cold, the military were always in complete control. Terror could only happen because the military allowed it.

The military were unconcerned about the unconstitutional nature of extra-judicial murder *per se*. For those who had rebelled against the Republic, liberal politics, constitutionalism and the language of rights, were perceived as the problem not the solution. Moreover those being removed by the death squads were part of the same "problem". For the military too spoke the language of purification. Local ties, the bonds of friendship – occasionally even family – also linked the military to the vigilantes. And all saw the atrocities they committed not as atrocities but as a cleansing solution delivered by power.

The purpose of this violence – hot and cold – was, first and foremost, a way of "killing change" – in particular by undoing the language of rights, of constitutional political rights, that the Republic had permitted to be spoken. The violence was intended to teach those who had believed in the Republic as a vehicle of change that their aspirations would always be bought at too high a price. It was a way of shaking up society while staving off the redistribution of social and economic power heralded by the Republic. So here we have the "memory of murder" again, but in the different sense of exemplary mass murder putting those who survived it "in their place" and keeping them there – an exercise in what the historian Paul Preston has called "bankable terror". Second, the complicity created between the rebel authorities and those sectors of the population that engaged in or connived at the repression of their friends, neighbours and often even family members, also began to lay the foundations of a new rebel state and social order – which would be actively and explicitly consolidated from 1939 – above all via a regime-implemented policy of nationwide denunciation that played a crucial part in achieving mass repression and in constructing the prison universe in Spain.

3

Ghosts of Change
The story of Amparo Barayón

*Why add more words? To whisper for that which has been lost. Not out of
nostalgia, but because it is on the site of loss that hopes are born.*

(John Berger)

Franco's coalition was driven by a very particular desire: that of both the
colonial military elite and its civilian supporters to subject social change to
court martial and restore their ideal of a static society. In consequence, the
violence unleashed in rebel-controlled territory targeted those whose very
existence challenged that "ideal". This included dissenters from sexual or
gender norms, and most notably here, "new women". Many of them were
murdered by vigilantes. This chapter recounts one searing story, Amparo
Barayón's. It is emblematic of the human cost of Franco's bid to "kill" social
change, not least because it shows how the military coup detonated all
manner of private hatreds, as well as social fears and prejudice – all of which
were legitimized by the coup's pervasive rhetoric of "purification", to
become an integral part of the "crusade", with lethal results. What
happened to Amparo Barayón also belongs to an unfolding family story
which indicates the extent of the fear-driven social purification underpinning Francoism, as well as its long afterlife of violence

In 1989, the North American raised son of the Spanish Republican
novelist, Ramón Sender, published an account of his own and his sister's
search for the remains of their mother Amparo Barayón, and for the truth
about her imprisonment and extra-judicial murder. She was killed at the
age of thirty two in the early months of Spain's civil war, in rebel-held
Zamora in north-west Spain, the Catholic heartland of Old Castile. The
book, called simply *A Death in Zamora*, charts an extraordinary odyssey in
time, space and memory. On his return to Spain in the early 1980s, the son,
also called Ramón, discovers he has a whole extended Spanish family, which

This essay is dedicated to Amparo's two children, Ramón and Andrea (Sister Benedicta);
and to Amparo's niece, Magdalena Maes Barayón.

AMPARO'S FAMILY

First Marriage

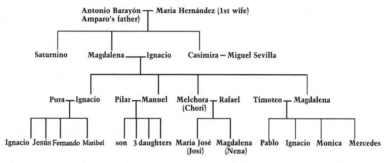

Second Marriage

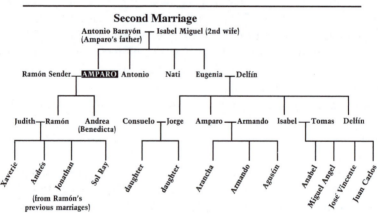

Barayón family tree

(Courtesy of Ramón Sender Barayón).

Amparo in cloche hat
c.1930.

(Photograph courtesy of Ramón
Sender Barayón).

emerges like a lost continent, bearing with it the history, the traces, the
unquiet ghost of his mother Amparo.[1] He meets Amparo's niece,
Magadalena Maes, who in 1942 at the age of seventeen had, in an act of
tremendous courage, physically with her own hands removed her beloved
aunt's remains from the common grave where they lay, reburying them in
the family tomb. "The bad thing [Magdalena tells Ramón] was they put
quicklime in with her. There was no coffin or anything, just the body and
the quicklime." For this act of temerity, even though Amparo's niece had
sought and received the requisite official authorization, she and her family
received anonymous death threats.[2]

A *Death in Zamora* is an extraordinary, richly-layered book that deserves
to be much more widely known. While compelling, it is not an easy one to
follow, because of its fragmented structure and allusiveness. But these qualities too arise from the very past it describes and are thus an integral part
of the story.[3] Its unfolding communicates in microcosm so many of the
profound things that future generations need to understand about the civil
war in Spain, as a *civil* war: its complex social and cultural causes and its
tremendous costs in the long aftermath of uncivil peace, up to, but also well
beyond the death of Franco in 1975.[4] Indeed the book's narrative is a crucial

part of the memory current that has paved the way for the long, slow and painful recuperation of Republican history and memory – the memories of the defeated that have been emerging in Spain since the turn of the millennium, the best-known of which are the campaign to open common graves to identify the remains of those who were extra-judicially murdered by the Francoist forces both during and after the war; the petitions for recognition and compensation by those used as forced labour by the regime; and bleakest of all, perhaps, the story (stories) of the lost children of Francoism, most notoriously those who were taken from their mothers, Republican women prisoners, and forcibly adopted by Francoist families – which for us now immediately recalls the shades of later violations in Videla's Argentina or Pinochet's Chile.[5] There are echoes of this too in Amparo's story, and although her own two children escaped the fate of the thousands whose names were illegally changed for adoption or who were institutionalized/abused in Francoist orphanage-"reformatories", they too bear other kinds of scars.[6]

In the title of this memoir – *A Death in Zamora* – *one* death stands for the many. Just as in Michael Ondaatje's great novel of a different civil war, *Anil's Ghost*, the Sri Lankan forensic scientist Anil struggles to give her "ghost", the anonymous victim of a recent and violent death, an identity and a history because he is "[t]his representative of all those lost voices. To give him a name would name the rest."[7] And in an important sense that is also true for Amparo Barayón in the case of Spain. For the tens of thousands of people killed in the Francoist repression – by the end of the 1940s the figure was at least 150,000 – had one thing overwhelmingly in common with each other: they had in some way or other benefited from the redistribution of power under the Republic, or from the cultural shift it represented. Local studies of the repression demonstrate quite clearly (see chapter 2 above) that those targeted the length and breadth of rebel Spain were those constituencies on whom the Republic's reforming legislation had conferred social and political rights for the first time in their lives. While a majority across Spain as a whole could be described as urban or rural workers – especially in the rural "deep south" where the indiscriminate killing was greatest – Francoism's victims came from a broader social spectrum overall and included many people of the middling sort. Indeed in conservative areas of the centre-north and north-west, such as Zamora, the rebels and their supporters displayed a special hatred for the more comfortably off who did not want to side with them, or indeed even to take "sides". Amparo's own immediate family contained people like this; her two brothers were small businessmen, relatively affluent, but open-minded and hopeful of change. Conversely, the many of similar social extraction to the

Barayón family group c.1913

Amparo Barayón, aged nine, with her father and siblings c.1913. Back row left to right: Casimira, Saturnino, Magdalena and Amparo. Front row left to right: Antonio, Nati, their father Antonio, and Eugenia on his knee. (Photograph courtesy of Ramón Sender Barayón).

Barayóns, but who supported Spain's military rebels, had in common a fear of where change was leading – whether their fears were of material or psychological loss (wealth, professional status, established social and polit-ical hierarchies, religious or sexual/gendered certainties) or a mixture of these things.

The assuaging of this overwhelming sense of fear was the deep energy which would drive and feed the Francoist repression in ways that meant it took on a life of its own. The trigger for it was the rebels' awareness of their precarious position in Spain as a whole, that the coup could fail, and thus there was a need to hit hard and fast[8] and to enact an exemplary repression: "It is necessary to spread terror. We have to create the impression of mastery, eliminating without scruples or hesitation all those who do not think as we do. There can be no cowardice. If we vacillate one moment and fail to proceed with the greatest determination, we will not win. Anyone who helps or hides a communist or a supporter of the Popular Front will be shot."[9] But behind this justification in political nomenclature there lay a whole social war.

This much is clear from the fact that a thoroughgoing repression occurred even in the territory which constituted the rebels' natural conservative heartland – of which Zamora was one part – where they were in control from the outset, where there was no real armed or even political resistance.[10] Nor is it feasible to argue that the violence stemmed from groups and entities which lay beyond the reach of the military authorities. For unlike what occurred in Republican Spain, where for a time, the rebellion capsized the government's ability to intervene, in rebel territory there was no collapse of public order. The fascist Falangist or clerical Carlist militia and other volunteers of the right could at any time have been disciplined by the military authorities that underwrote public order from the beginning. Not only did this not happen, but instead the military actively recruited thousands of civilian vigilantes to carry out a dirty war.[11] Thus military and civilian-instigated repression existed in a complementary relationship, as we have explored in chapter 2. This was the beginning of the "fellowship of blood", of the complicity of whole sectors of Spanish society, of "ordinary Spaniards" who became enmeshed in the murder of their compatriots.

Across rebel territory a powerful "moral justification" for the visceral violence rapidly enveloping society was publicly provided by the hierarchy of the Catholic Church. The Bishop of Zamora, Manuel Arce Ochotorena, was no exception, publicly endorsing the violence as a legitimate defence of "social order, country and religion".[12] While the bishop of the neighbouring province of León, at the beginning of September 1936 called upon the Catholic faithful to join the war against "Soviet Jewish-Masonic laicism".[13] This clerical war went well beyond the textual. All across Spain there were priests who blessed the flags of rebel forces and some, especially in Carlist Navarre, went to the front as fighters. Many were also directly involved in repressive violence against civilians, as happened in Zamora, as elsewhere in Spain.

The most frequent form of abuse was the extreme psychological pressure inflicted by those many priests who were called upon to confess prisoners before they were executed, the act of confession itself being converted thus into an act of war. In Zamora one warrior-priest, Miguel Franco Olivares, was notorious for his physically savage treatment of prisoners. It is likely he was directly involved in their killing too, as priests are known to have been elsewhere (see chapter 2 above). Those who were children at the time in Zamora remember Franco Olivares striding through the streets, wearing a pistol over his clerical garb, and thus contributing to the propagation of an atmosphere of terror in the town and surrounding area.[14]

Located on the other side of this "war" in Zamora, and across Old Castile, were all those who didn't "fit" traditional forms of order and discipline: those who "had ideas" and whose horizons stretched further, to whom the Republic's language of rights had given the opportunity to challenge their subordination and whose presence was gradually diminishing the distance between urban and city space and the "deep Spain" of rural servitude and hidebound provincial towns. In the latter, "new women" especially seemed to symbolize the changes in train, in that they were seen as a direct challenge to the verities of patriarchal power. Among the military rebels and all their immediate supporters there was an especially pathological fear and loathing of emancipated women which served as a very powerful motive force for the ensuing violence. Amparo Barayón was not merely killed in lieu of her husband the famous, and for the rebels "sacrilegious", Republican writer Ramón Sender, as commentators have previously assumed.[15] While those who condemned her knew who she was married to and would scarcely have been averse to taking revenge in this way, it is important to understand that the motivation for murdering Amparo went much deeper: that she was also killed *in her own right*.

For Amparo was a modern woman. In 1930, as Spain's monarchy crumbled, she had, aged 26, left the conservative provincial backwater of Zamora and gone to Madrid, the "big city", to become independent. A number of factors seem to have opened Amparo to the possibility of a life beyond the confines of her family and home town. The fact of her own mother's early death in 1911, when Amparo was seven, had resulted in a less rigidly structured upbringing than might otherwise have been the case.[16] Under the care of her older sister Magdalena,[17] she attended school and church, like any of her female, middle-class contemporaries, and indeed remained a practising Catholic throughout her life. She also took classes, including in piano, becoming sufficiently accomplished to later supplement her income by teaching others. But her formal education aside, she had time on her hands, some of which she spent reading and some listening and observing in the Café Iberia, owned and run by the Barayón family in Zamora's town centre, and which, in the Spanish tradition, was as much a centre for informal cultural and literary gatherings (*tertulias*) as a place for taking refreshment. The Café Iberia hosted what was a relatively eclectic clientele, culturally and socially. This background and the exposure to alternatives that it had offered, is at least part of what opened Amparo to the idea of other possibilities, a cultural preparation for later emancipation, and doubtless made her readier than many of her contemporaries to leave in search of what the capital city might offer.

In Madrid she found work as a telephone switchboard operator – a new

The Barayón family's Café Iberia in Zamora

Here as it looked during Amparo's childhood. It was part of the assets seized when her two brothers were arrested. (Photograph courtesy of Ramón Sender Barayón).

employment opportunity which was itself an indicator of Spain's burgeoning modernity. In Madrid she supported herself, she lived independently, educating herself both politically and culturally, and she met Ramón Sender and began living with him – which was quite something for those times, even in urban metropolitan Spain, for Madrid was not Berlin or Paris. Only her family knew about Ramón (Amparo was quite open to them in her letters home), whom she would marry in a civil ceremony in early 1936 when pregnant with her second child. Nevertheless, the very fact that she had spread her wings inspired horror among the pillars of provincial society and also among some of the more conservative members of her own extended family who saw her as on the road to damnation. And it would be some of these family members, determined to ensure the fulfilment of their own bigotry masquerading as prophecy, who were implicated in her fate.

These events transpired in Zamora in the late summer of 1936, after Amparo had fled back to her hometown with her two young children in the aftermath of the military rising. She, Ramón and the children had been holidaying in the verdant mountain region north of Madrid, in the province of

Segovia, when the military rebellion erupted. Caught in the crossfire in what was rapidly being turned into rebel territory, and after witnessing harrowing scenes of lethal violence and atrocity against civilian defenders of Republican legality, the decision was taken that Ramón should try to return to the capital Madrid, while Amparo would take two-year-old Ramón and baby Andrea (Andreina) and make her way home to her family in Zamora. She agreed to this on the assumption that home would mean safety – a mistake she shared with Federico García Lorca and also with many thousands of anonymous victims of the repression who went home to their deaths.[18]

The journey was a long one – as the coup had inevitably fractured the transport system. It was also fraught, because the train that a desperate Amparo had finally managed to board with the children to take them on the last leg of their journey was a military transport for rebel troops and was subject to bombardment by Republican planes near the town of Toro. But

The young Amparo with her sister Casimira (left) and Miguel Sevilla

The young Amparo in c.1916–18 (aged about 12) with her oldest sister Casimira (to the left in the hat) standing alongside her husband, Miguel Sevilla. To his left stands another of Amparo's sisters, Nati, whose health was very frail. (Photograph courtesy of Ramón Sender Barayón).

potentially far deadlier were the consequences of the suspicion-ridden atmosphere generated by the coup itself. The fact that among the belongings Amparo had rapidly packed for the journey was the Barayón family radio, one of several built by her technologically-minded younger brother Antonio[19] – and which she envisaged as a lifeline for getting news of Ramón – led to her being arrested en route as a spy.[20] Her release came only through the intervention of her brother-in-law, Miguel Sevilla, husband of her elder sister, Casimira. Sevilla, an ecclesiastical tailor with close links to the ultra right-wing Carlists, told Amparo over the phone that her older brother, Saturnino, had been arrested in Zamora.[21] From then on, Sevilla had Amparo too in his sights, but there was little she could do but continue her journey home, although now with a plan forming to get out swiftly via Portugal to France – something which was, in theory, a viable option, since Zamora was very close to the Portuguese border. Amparo eventually reached home in the first days of August (1936), two long weeks after her hurried departure from the rented holiday villa in San Rafael, Segovia, in the Guadarrama mountain range north of Madrid.

But the situation she found in Zamora was about as far from being a haven/respite from national political turbulence as it was possible to imagine. Just like the places through which Amparo had passed on the troubled journey back from San Rafael, home too now evidenced a rarified and literally dreadful atmosphere, with the townspeople in the grip of fear, or something worse. Arriving in Zamora, she was immediately detained by the new rebel authorities, but then almost straight away released.[22] Arriving at the family home, she discovered that not only Saturnino, but also her younger brother Antonio had been arrested. As a result, the family businesses had been closed down and their assets seized. The jewel in the Barayón crown, the elegant Café Iberia, near Zamora's central square, and emblematic of a more open and liberal culture, was now dangerously out of tune with the ultramontane ascendancy which had accompanied the military take-over.

The immediate cause of the expropriation, however, was the arrest of her brothers. Antonio, a reserved young man of twenty nine, well educated and with a lively curiosity about the world, was an engineer who had owned and run a successful electrical store. Heartened and enthused by the change he saw developing in the more hospitable climate of the Republic, and with a strong sense of social conscience, he had joined the Communist Party (PCE).[23] In earlier times, people of the middling sort seeking a political voice and some sort of purchase against the exclusive and clientelist order of old Spain had usually joined Spain's social democratic movement, either the UGT union or, more frequently, its party, the PSOE. But by the mid

1930s the PCE was increasingly an attractive option to people of Antonio's social background, and especially if they were young. The PCE was also boosted by the publicity attendant on its participation in the centre-left electoral coalition, known as the Popular Front, which had won the national elections in February 1936. But the party's appeal was not really an ideological one; few among Spain's socially aspiring lower middle classes knew much, if anything, about marxism. But they were attracted by the PCE's vigour, its appetite for change – which corresponded to their own, and also to the shock of the culturally new that they felt emanating from the party.[24] The PSOE seemed fusty by comparison, again, especially if they were young. In short, they perceived the Communist Party to offer a more effective instrument against the provincial and the sclerotic.

Whereas Antonio had been in contact with Amparo and Ramón while they were living in Madrid, Saturnino, Amparo's older brother, was rather more socially conservative. Amparo had clashed with him years before, as a teenager, when after the death of their father after the influenza epidemic of 1918, he had assumed his head of household duties with rather too much enthusiasm and rigidity for her tastes. Nevertheless, under the Republic Saturnino, already in his forties, had also taken advantage of the new political possibilities – for he too felt that the time for change had to come – joining the small progressive republican party founded by Manuel Azaña, the intellectual and politician who by 1936 was President of the Republic. And while the political right tended to prevail in Zamora province in general elections, Zamora city repeatedly returned a progressive majority in municipal elections across the Republican period. Indeed the justification for Saturnino's arrest was that he held a minor post of municipal political responsibility within the mayor's office in Zamora.[25] Under the terms of martial law established by the rebels, anybody occupying, or who had occupied, a Republican political post, however modest, was automatically deemed guilty of military rebellion, and would thus be subject to summary arrest.[26] The evident absurdity, not to say injustice of this, was masked at least formally by reference to existing public order dispositions, that the Republic had neglected to alter, and which not only placed the military in supreme control once martial law was declared, but also allowed them to declare it in the first place.

Both Antonio and Saturnino were extrajudicially murdered, Antonio on 28 August and Saturnino on 18 September 1936. The mode of execution was identical for each, as it was for hundreds of others "released" from the gaols of the locality – in the two brothers' case, from Toro gaol – in the weeks and months after the coup.[27] Those so released were usually placed into the hands of the Falange, as Antonio certainly was,[28] though sometimes too the collection squads included civil guards, and it is thought that the precise timing of Saturnino's death might mean it was a reprisal for the death of the son of a civil guard who had been killed at the front. Ostensibly the prisoners thus removed were to be transferred to other gaols in the vicinity (in the case of Toro, the destination prison was Zamora), but in reality they were to be killed.[29] In the case of both Antonio and Saturnino, their deaths were subsequently officially recorded as being of prisoners "shot while attempting to escape".[30] In other words Spain's historic form of extrajudicial murder, the *ley de fugas*, inherited from the long-lived Restoration monarchy, was now operating on an industrial scale against those who had sought a voice and a vote.

To this day both Antonio and Saturnino Barayón remain among the disappeared. It now seems very likely that Antonio's remains lie in a field within property still owned by the family of one of the area's principal landowners of the 1930s who was a major supporter of the military rebellion.[31] The Barayón family had some sense of this even at the time from information gleaned from agricultural labourers who had glimpsed the arrival of prisoners in this place. Saturnino was shot and buried a few weeks after Antonio and dumped in a mass grave that had been dug inside the cemetery at Toro, the town near to which Amparo and her children had endured an aerial bombardment on their tortuous route back to Zamora. His remains lie beneath those of other subsequent victims of extrajudicial execution. In later decades too, the area was developed to accommodate "official" graves, so an excavation is now not feasible.

At the time of Amparo's arrival back in Zamora in early August, family members were already withdrawing into themselves, in shock at the imprisonment of both brothers – that theirs was to be a worse fate the family did not yet know, although they already feared it. Amparo's niece, Magdalena Maes, then eleven years old, remembers her own father and mother (Amparo's sister, also called Magdalena) burning papers and books. They also destroyed the bust of a young woman adorned with a Phrygian bonnet (a well-known symbol of the Republic) which they had found in Antonio's study.[32] Amparo, horrified by the turn of events, feeling increasingly trapped, and anxious for news of Ramón in Madrid (who was lost to her as a result of the coup's fracturing of communication channels), made inconclusive attempts to secure a passport, something which only succeeded in concentrating upon her the baleful attention of the new military authorities. The final straw came when Amparo got news of her brother Antonio's "disappearance" on 28 August; she rushed impetuously to petition Zamora's governor, Colonel Raimundo Hernández Comes.[33] It would have felt like a tremendous relief after her time cooped up in the family house in the oppressive post-coup atmosphere. But the risk she was running was great, for Hernández Comes was the hard man of the coup. One of the leading conspirators in Zamora, after the triumph of the rebellion he had assumed both military and civilian control of the town.[34] It is said that Amparo accused him outright of responsibility for the killing of her beloved brother and the many dying in identical circumstances. We cannot know exactly what Amparo said, but given her strength of mind, and that she was grief-stricken over Antonio, it was probably not respectful, still less obsequious. If she did call what was happening by its rightful name, then she told no more than the truth. For it was the military coup that had unleashed the whole chain of killing, and Hernández Comes, on whose signed authority the prisoners were "released" into the hands of their killers, could not elude a primary responsibility for events. Whatever passed between Amparo and Hernández Comes, it was immediately after it that she was detained, on 28 August itself, the day of Antonio's execution and anonymous burial on a landed estate in the environs of Zamora. In the brother's and sister's demise were thus linked two of the key forces of old Spain – army and landed elite – whose power the Republic had sought to check. Only the Church's authority seems immediately missing from this family picture – but that would come later, for Amparo, in the form of cruel and unusual punishment.

We have no documentary evidence of any formal denunciation of Amparo being made to the rebel authorities in Zamora. But in these months of the "hot" repression, before the machinery of military trial and summary justice was instituted, much of the terror was paperless. There is strong circumstantial evidence of the implication of Miguel Sevilla, Amparo's brother-in-law, in that he advised Amparo that, when she went to the governor's office, she should on no account take along seven-month-old Andrea who usually accompanied Amparo everywhere. Sevilla also seemed to know of her arrest before anyone else. Amparo certainly blamed him.[35] And neither Sevilla nor her sister Casimira made any attempt to intercede on Amparo's behalf thereafter, even though Casimira taught French to Hernández Comes' children and was thus well-placed to have pleaded her cause. Casimira may have been afraid, for fear was a corrosive and paralyzing force born of the coup. But it is well known too that Casimira was strongly influenced by Miguel, whose fundamentalist beliefs meant he felt distaste for everything Amparo stood for. He was also likely entertaining certain social ambitions and saw the chance for financial gain in removing her from the picture, or at least in doing nothing to prevent it. Should the family assets – or any part of them – prove recoverable in the future, then he and Casimira would be well-placed to benefit as elements of proven loyalty to the nascent regime.[36] The Barayón family was riven. As Amparo was imprisoned, and Miguel Sevilla contemplated his future with Casimira, Amparo's other sister Magdalena returned traumatized from a visit to Saturnino in Toro gaol where, in addition to being forbidden under threat of her own arrest from communicating the news of Antonio's death, she was also obliged to share her taxi with a group of marauding Falangists who flagged it down and then, with brutal offhandedness, informed her that they were on their way to rebury the bodies of some "reds" that the wild boars had dug up.[37]

Amparo was imprisoned in Zamora gaol, accompanied by seven-month-old Andrea. What happened to her then takes us to the heart of what the rebel repression sought to achieve. She was interrogated with the express intention of making her "recant". In her case the objective was that she make a formal denunciation of her husband, Ramón Sender (her husband by a Republican *civil* marriage ceremony, even though Amparo herself was a practising Catholic). She was subjected to extraordinary pressure, including by a priest who visited upon her a torrent of abuse and, after she made her final confession, refused her absolution because she had not been married within the Church. In other words Amparo Barayón was subject to a form of sustained psychological torture the object of which was to humiliate her and ultimately to break her. So even though she had avoided the public forms of violent humiliation commonly visited upon Republican women the length and breadth of rebel-held Spain – the head shaving, the "purging" with castor oil and public parading – and even though Amparo Barayón was not physically tortured and raped, as many other female Republican prisoners were in the course of police interrogations, the object was the same: to break her. Then one day her name featured on the list of those the death squads came, by night to "take out" of gaol in the deadly *sacas*, exactly the same form of extrajudicial execution that ended the lives of her two brothers and of tens of thousands of others across Spain. On 11 October 1936 – nearly three months after the military coup against the Republic, just over two months since her return home to Zamora – Amparo Barayón was taken from the town gaol to the cemetery. There, by lantern light, they shot her and buried her, where she fell, in a common grave next to the cemetery wall.

We know of Amparo's fate from several specific sources – including from the priest in question, who gave an account to her sister Magdalena days after she had been killed. But most notably we know because, in the early 1980s, Amparo's son, Ramón, tracked down two of the women who had been in gaol with his mother. One of them, Pilar Fidalgo, also wrote her own contemporary account of her imprisonment, published in 1939 outside

Spain.[38] Fidalgo was arrested because her husband was secretary of the local branch of the PSOE in Benavente (Zamora), and she herself only escaped execution through a prisoner exchange. But before the exchange could happen, her newborn baby, who had been imprisoned with her, succumbed to illness and died. As many Republican women were imprisoned with their babies or young children – both during and after the war – in massively over-crowded and insanitary conditions, such deaths were not an unusual occurrence (whether inside gaols or in the transportations to or between gaols). Indeed this seems to have been part of the punishment for their gender transgression. One prison official remarked to Fidalgo that "red" women had forfeited their right to nourish their young, which is echoed in many other prison testimonies which recall how police interrogators and warders would observe pointedly that "red" women should have had more sense of respon-sibility than to have had children at all – because reds were without rights.[39] There were also cases of women imprisoned in an advanced state of preg-nancy whose executions were delayed until after their confinement.

Amparo's own children had a relatively more fortunate fate. Although

Amparo's two children

Amparo's two children, three-year-old Andrea and Ramón, four-and-a-half, in March 1939 in Washington Square Park, New York. (Photograph courtesy of Ramón Sender Barayón).

both Andrea and two-year-old Ramón spent three months in an orphanage after she was killed, they were then able to leave the rebel zone under Red Cross auspices, initially to rejoin their father whose petition for his children had instigated the Red Cross negotiations with the rebel authorities.[40] Thereafter both would begin an odyssey that took them from Barcelona through the refugee camps of France and eventually to a new life with an adoptive family in the United States. But for older child survivors who remained inside Francoist Spain, the price of nourishment (via Francoist social welfare organizations) often involved what Fidalgo herself described in her memoir as "moral suffering: obliging orphans to sing the songs of the murderers of their father; to wear the uniform of those who have executed him; and to curse the dead and to blaspheme his memory".[41]

If we can think past the sheer horror of these events, as historians, eventually, always have to do, we must ask what was going on here, what did these things mean? To answer that question we clearly need to focus on the purpose of the habitual physical and psychological torture. Why was there such a need to humiliate or to break the enemy, publicly or otherwise? All these forms of violence (in which should be included the humiliation and "moral suffering" inflicted on Republican children who came under the tutelage of the Francoist state) were functioning as rituals through which social and political control could be re-enacted. In murdering the "enemy", they murdered change, or the threat of change. In the same way, the widespread complicity of priests throughout Spain in the mass process of denunciation, killing and torture of those deemed opponents has to be understood in these terms – as a reassertion of control, rather than solely as an avenging response to the phenomenon of popular anticlerical violence in Republican territory. Indeed so strong was this desire to reassert control that even priests who got in the way of it, who tried to defend the "different" or the vulnerable, or who even spoke out against the killing, were themselves also murdered, often by Falangists.[42]

The Franco regime's imperative of "cleansing" repression borrowed heavily from an apocalyptic, manichean brand of Catholicism (harking back to the Counter-Reformation) with its dialectic of fire and sword, where the suffering of the "heretic", his or her "penitence" was a necessary part of the process. The expectation that the Republican population should suffer is repeatedly pronounced by rebel cadres and supporters of all kinds.[43] It was not for nothing that the post-war Francoist agency responsible for overseeing the labour battalions of Republican prisoners in 1940s was called the committee for the *redemption* of prison sentences through work.[44] This meant that people could reduce their prison sentences through labour. But note the word is not "remission", but redemption – so it becomes laden with

Catholic significance. But the interior landscape of the rebels, and of Francoism later, also contained more "modern" discourses of disease and impurity in which the Republicans' "marxist barbarism" was explained as a lethal virus, the germ of "anti-nation", a form of "degeneracy" which if not "cleansed" out to the last trace, would contaminate the healthy body of "Spain". Disease equalled disorder and, more significantly, disorder equalled disease. Francoist military psychiatrists carried out psychological tests on both captured International Brigade prisoners and Republican women prisoners. They were particularly interested, not to say obsessed, with the women.[45] This work, which has only relatively recently become the object of historians' attention, has often been billed spectacularly in press reports as uncovering how Francoist medicos were hunting for the "red gene".[46] Certainly their methodology was as crude as this suggests. But the "genetic backdrop" of Francoist social darwinism remained necessarily muted because of the evident clash with regime Catholicism. The circle was squared, however, by an all-embracing appeal to "purification" – which is an absolutely crucial word in Francoist Spain, as it usually is in all of the barbaric episodes – whether racial or political – that inhabit Europe's dark mid-twentieth century.

In the end, what the military, Falangists and other rightist volunteers did to Republican men and women responded to something other than tactical necessity in a military conflict. The startling uniformity of the degradation and objectification inflicted upon Republican prisoners both during and after the military conflict – and in particular the remarkable need of their captors to break (as in the case of Amparo) not only their bodies but also their minds before killing them, and, even where they were not killed, to leave them, as it were, psychologically "reconfigured" by their experience of prison/repression: all this was servicing the underlying rebels' project: to build (or "rebuild" as they saw it) a homogeneous, monolithic and hierarchized society. Francoist Spain was built, in effect, as a *Volks-gemeinschaft* and one which survived far longer than the German one. Nor was its foundational violence an "abnormal" characteristic – for all that there were clinically pathological individuals in the death squads. Segundo Viloria, the man regarded by the family of Amparo Barayón as the person who actually killed her, and who was also denounced by Pilar Fidalgo as guilty of many crimes including the sexual abuse of women prisoners, was one such. It seems that Viloria may also have conceived of a hatred of Amparo in particular when she refused his advances years earlier. According to Miguel Ángel Mateos, the official chronicler of Zamora, Viloria was a major perpetrator, the nature of whose atrocities was so extreme as to make him a case for psychiatric study. The Barayón family claimed that he "died insane in a mental hospital".[47] But this should not distract our attention from the central, and much less comfortable, truth that "cases for treatment" like Viloria do not in themselves explain the violence which ended the life of Amparo and of so many of her compatriots. That violence had its immediate origins in the military coup, and its development thereafter, because of what the coup unleashed, transformed it into a "normal" affair that would envelop and saturate mainstream society far beyond the end of military hostilities in 1939, as an accepted – and for many acceptable – means of disciplining and restructuring society in Spain.

This exclusion of the defeated was inscribed in all spheres of life – including the law,[48] education and employment. "The sins of fathers", in regime-speak, went on being visited on the children in various forms of civil death. Amparo Barayón's niece Magdalena, the one who reburied her, was denied access to higher education. The doors of the School of Journalism remained barred in spite of her long-cherished ambition to become a journalist (which Amparo had encouraged), her high marks and her evident promise: for she was the scion of a "diseased" family. Her anger and frustration at the realization that all her exits were blocked[49] came on top of

Magdalena Maes with her aunt Amparo

Three-year-old Magdalena Maes with her aunt Amparo and two young neighbourhood boys, c.1928. (Photograph courtesy of Ramón Sender Barayón).

years spent witnessing the tears and the terror of her own mother, Magdalena (Amparo's sister), who after everything else she had already gone through, was repeatedly called before the regime's tribunal of political responsibilities. In addition to threatening to fine her husband, or worse, the tribunal also enquired as to the whereabouts of Amparo herself, as if she were still alive. Magdalena, mindful of her own family responsibilities, and well aware that Amparo's own fate had been triggered by her very attempt to call the authorities to account over Antonio's death, did not enlighten them, beyond stating that Amparo had been taken away one day by the police and was never seen again. This scene of denial before the tribunal was played out many times across Spain as the relatives of Republicans had to omit all reference to what had happened to their loved ones in order to protect themselves.

So crushed by worry was Magdalena senior that she went to the extreme of renouncing voluntarily and in perpetuity her share in the seized Barayón inheritance.[50] In the lines of her legal testimony the fear is evident, as she renounces not only her claim to the family legacy but also virtually abjures the connection with her lost siblings – Amparo, Saturnino and Antonio. (Indeed she necessarily speaks of Saturnino and Antonio as if they were still alive.) There are shades here – albeit attenuated ones buried in legal formality – of Pilar Fidalgo's description of Republicans being required to "blaspheme the memory" of their dead. A further twist to the story suggests that Magdalena may have been encouraged in her renunciation by malicious tongues, which illustrates the multi-layered, *social* component of the repression triggered by the military coup.[51] Conversely, the fact that her husband, faced with the threat of economic or physical repression, felt obliged to mobilize his own, very Francoist, father to intercede on his behalf, is an example of a resurgent clientelist mode so typical of the regime, but which, more than a mere reconstruction of the pre-Republican era, was pivotal in reconfiguring a new postwar social and political hierarchy.[52]

Faced by this accretion of terror and injustice, the spirited young Magdalena's response was, in contrast, an increasing rage and frustration which led her to participate in political resistance,[53] as a result of which she was arrested, brought before a military court (*consejo de guerra*) and imprisoned in 1946 at the age of twenty one. Unlike Amparo, Magdalena survived her incarceration, serving three of a six-year gaol term in Zamora and Valladolid.[54] But just like her aunt, Magdalena too endured the hallmark of the Francoist prison experience, the determination of the "victors" to break the will of those who thought differently and, whether or not they succeeded in this, to ensure the lasting humiliation of those they subjugated through the rehearsal of extravagant public displays of conformity. Branded on the memory of those who knew Magdalena Maes is the image of her, newly released from prison, and with her head still shorn, standing on the family balcony during an official public holiday, and next to her, her husband-to-be, wearing the blue shirt of the Falange, the price he paid for entry to a successful career as a journalist in the tightly controlled media universe of the regime. This scene encapsulates both the Franco regime's direct coercion and also the more insidious, but equally pernicious, ways in which it exacted the high price which all totalitarianisms demand from those obliged to live through them. Only their mortal victims have even a chance of escape. The perpetual fear, the everyday defeats, the many and repeated acts of ugliness enforced upon the "defeated", through which the regime ensured compliance and over which there was rarely a choice, if those who were largely powerless wanted to salvage any kind of a life.[55] This was not something easily understood by those who left Spain, or who did not have to live through it as adults.

The journey made by Ramón Sender and his sister, and told in *A Death in Zamora*, ends with knowledge of the dense web of reasons for their mother's death, and, through it, of the complex dynamics of the civil war itself. That knowledge could not expunge for them the enormous moral responsibility of those implicated. But worse, nor could it bring them solace. For the conditions of Spain's transition to democracy, after Franco's death in 1975, required that Amparo remain, in the words of her son Ramón, "an unshriven ghost". Unshriven in both senses – denied absolution, as she, a practising Catholic, had been by the priest in Zamora gaol. (On his return to Spain in the early 1980s Ramón wrote of wanting to wrest her from "the clutches of the three entities that had killed her, her family, her church and her town".[56]) But also metaphorically in the sense of unrelieved of her burden of wrong (the wrong done *to* her) which made her a "ghost", if we understand by that one who has been denied voice and memory, and thus denied a space. Amparo had, thanks to Magdalena, been reburied in the family tomb in 1942 – in itself an extraordinary outcome for someone extrajudicially murdered.[57] But her name was not inscribed on the tomb until the 1970s. Even then the adding of her name would cause unease among some members of the Barayón family. Three decades of Francoism had done their work: for even among sectors of the population who were not ideologically Francoist, the regime had managed to impart an amorphous sense of the guilt of its victims, as if they themselves were the embarrassment, and somehow responsible for their own fate, so the best thing was simply not to make a fuss ("incordiar") by raising such "awkward" and "inconvenient" issues.[58]

No one could be brought to account for Amparo's murder. First, because Franco had won not only the civil war but also, in the end, the Second World War. In spite of Franco's close political identification with the Nazi new order in Europe, he did not align Spain militarily with the German–Italian Axis and thus never directly threatened Allied imperial interests. The Allied liberation of Europe stopped at the Pyrenees. And Franco's dictatorship was left in place by Western powers increasingly preoccupied with cold war divisions and prepared to turn a blind eye to mass killing and repression inside Spain in return for Franco's repeated affirmation of crusading anti-communism.

Given this scenario, and especially the enduring effects of the Cold War, then there was no outside force powerful enough to query or challenge the Franco regime's highly tendentious view of the civil war as a war of liberation against those without ethics or value – a mythology on which Franco never ceased to stake his legitimacy. In 1964, as Spain's beaches began to fill up with mass Euro tourism, the Franco regime – which was still executing people for "war crimes" – celebrated its "Twenty-Five Years of Peace". In the public ceremonials and the millions of posters plastered over walls in towns and villages the length and breadth of the country, the war was still portrayed as a religious crusade or war of liberation (never a civil war, the words were never used) against the hordes of anti-Spain in thrall to the "judeo-marxist-masonic conspiracy"; a war for national unity against separatists, of morality against iniquity. So even in the mid-1960s what was being celebrated was not in fact "peace", but "victory". And even ten years later, with the physical disappearance of Franco in 1975 and the beginnings of superstructural political change, in important respects the "postwar" – that is to say the "war" – was still not going to be over.

Why was this so? The most obvious reason was because the return of democracy (Spain's transition) had been agreed by the Francoist elites in return for an amnesty, the law of October 1977, a legal provision (though many now question its legality) which duly became embedded socially and culturally as the "pact of silence". No one would be called to account judicially, nor would there be any equivalent of a Truth and Reconciliation Commission. This was the agreement – and for fear of the army and the considerable residual firepower of the civilian extreme right, it was accepted by the regime's democratic interlocutors as the lesser of the available evils. But the disadvantage was that those who had been obliged to be silent for nearly forty years were once again being told that there could be no public recognition of their past lives or memories.

Yet one of the most remarkable features of the 1980s onwards in Spain was an explosion of detailed empirical works, often by local historians, or others without a university affiliation, which have minutely reconstructed the repression on a province by province basis. This work has constituted the necessary memorialization of the civil war and its long aftermath. Most crucially it means the public recognition of all the stories that could not surface under the dictatorship, nor under the very special and precarious circumstances of the democratic transition in the 1970s. This new history of the repression, told with real names, and counting the dead from municipal registers and cemetery lists,[59] is, in a very real sense, the equivalent of war memorials for those who never had them, for those who were not liberated in 1945. Such empirical historical research and the ensuing publications are, then, an act of commemoration for whole groups of Spaniards who could never be mourned publicly when they died; a memorial for people whose lives and memories were traduced by a totalitarian state.[60] In short they are an act of reparation, of democratic and constitutional citizenship.[61]

But for this remembrance to happen then fear had to be overcome[62] and that has taken until the twenty-first century. Since 2000 there has been an explosion of Republican memory: with the success of civil pressure groups who have petitioned the Spanish government to exhume the remains of those executed by Francoist forces, both during and after the military conflict, from common graves so they may be identified and reburied by family and friends.[63] Likewise, those who were forced labourers have been part of these civic petitions, demanding that what happened to them be acknowledged publicly before they die – this irrespective of the more complex (ongoing) battles around issues of financial compensation.

There has been a flood of books on prisons, labour battalions, the guerrilla and most recently of course on the most emotive subject of all the "lost children" of Francoism.[64] They were the babies and young children who died inside prison – many nought to three year olds were born and died there, like Pilar Fidalgo's child. There were also those young children of prisoners whose names were changed so they could be illegally adopted by regime families. And the thousands who were sent to state institutions because the regime considered their own "red" families to be "unfit" to raise them. There were also (though more unusually) refugee children who were kidnapped from France by the Falange's external "repatriation" service and then placed, not with their families, but in Francoist state institutions.[65]

The explosion of Republican memory now occurring constitutes an outpouring – before the generations who suffered what it remembers pass for good. And here, of course, the comparison to be made is with Holocaust memory in its broadest sense – in that one of the crucial triggers is the end of "biological memory", and the tremendous sense of sadness, loss and danger that engenders. But the return of Republican memory is necessary not just for those who must tell their story, but for all living Spaniards of whatever generation. Because democracy in the end cannot anywhere be constructed on an unacknowledged hecatomb. With the current opening up, the return of Republican history and memory, Ramón Sender and his family can at last shrive Amparo and not so much lay her ghost as bring it home, give it space: thus recuperating both voice and memory – in Spain as in Michael Ondaatje's Sri Lanka, the one ghost and the many.[66]

This chapter stands as an illustration of the scale and intensity of the "social cleansing" operation unleashed and justified by "the war". In the last analysis, this *was* the war. The level and nature of the violence visited upon the Barayón family was not unusual, not even in its gothic strain, though many who suffered these things had neither the resources, nor the inclination, to preserve the memory explicitly and determinedly in the way that Magdalena Maes has done all her life. In this regard, she is less typical, for there never was a silence – at least not within her personal and family space.[67] In exploring these events here I have sought to reflect upon the redemptive power of certain kinds of remembering – themes that weave through the entire book. In the telling, "Ghosts of change" advocates a mode of history writing which embeds itself in the stories of real human lives, both to communicate the enormity of "History" as a process, while also discharging an ethical – and democratic – debt to those who paid its price. This is a discussion which, in a slightly different key, also threads through the next chapter.

Republican cavalry, February 1939

Republican cavalry, February 1939, photographed by the artist Manuel Moros at Collioure as they rode into exile in France. (Photograph courtesy of Jean Peneff, nephew of Manuel Moros, for the Moros Estate).

4

Border Crossings
Thinking about the International Brigaders before and after Spain

Caminante, no hay camino, se hace camino al andar . . . Caminante no hay camino, sino estelas en la mar. {"Traveller, there is no road, we make the road by walking . . . Traveller there is no road, only the wakes on the sea".} (Antonio Machado)[1]

Obscure like everything that's true. Formulas can be transparent, but reality is not. (Victor Serge)

The thousands of foreign volunteers who fought for the Republic in the International Brigades in many ways offer an external reflection of the individuals and groups struggling inside Spanish society to achieve progressive change. What I highlight in this chapter, through an exploration of the social and cultural histories of the volunteers, is how they represent hybridity and heterodoxy of various kinds: they embodied it, often fought for it (in Spain and elsewhere), and those of them who survived the Spanish battlefields frequently suffered for it too. What they were "about" – consciously or unconsciously – was crossing the lines, which is probably as good a definition of how social change happens as one can find.[2] As stormy petrels of social change, the brigaders refused, destabilized and complicated supposedly fixed, homogeneous categories of identity – whether national, racial, cultural or sexual – in ways that link them inextricably and inexorably to radical forms of cultural change, though these rarely proceed in a straight line, as historians well know, and contradictions abound. At the level of individual lives, this is not a happy story, since it is about struggle of various kinds. The brigaders' lives embodied what the Russian dissident revolutionary Victor Serge described in 1940 as history unfolding "in spite of us, through us, with us, even if it crushes us."[3] The verdict remains apt, even though we in the twenty-first century no longer believe in historical progress in the way that many of the brigaders did. From the perspective of today, we can see that much of what was they struggled for later passed into Western social and cultural norms. But at the level of individual lives lived at that time, against the grain, enduring forms of cultural and existential displacement and "exile" of different kinds, theirs was a searing experience. So in considering these lives, we need to resist the late twentieth- and twenty-first century tendency to gloss over individual difficulty and defeat, in search of some comfortingly upbeat "resolution" or "closure". We may resist this in part to commemorate them honestly, to write as they lived, against the grain. But we do it too because something about their experiences of defeat and survival, the facing up to loss with dispassionate honesty, an absolute refusal to mythologize, speaks powerfully to the needs of the current moment.

In the course of this chapter, three interrelated themes are explored. First, the history of the International Brigaders, which will be located where it belongs, but is still relatively infrequently found, in the context of "diaspora", that is to say the process of internal exile and migration within Europe that followed the Great War. For it is impossible to comprehend the International Brigades as a historical phenomenon without first taking into account their origins in this earlier diaspora. Second, the chapter will examine certain reductive state and establishment narratives of the later cold war period as they subsequently shaped public and collective memory of the brigaders – both "East" and "West" – providing evidence for us (just as for the brigaders themselves it confirmed) that those with the habit of line-crossing as a mode of being would never and could never fit the requirements of any state narrative. Third, the chapter will also explore the social and psychic impact of "Spain" – that is, Republican defence and ultimately defeat – upon individual brigaders, what the novelist Henry James once described as the crucial "reverse of the picture".[4]

The International Brigaders as a symbol of European diaspora

One man's imagined community is another man's political prison.[5]

Among the approximate 35,000 International Brigaders who fought in Spain (12,000 to 16,000 at any one time) there were volunteers from all over the world. But most had their origins in Europe: even in the two North American contingents from the USA and Canada – some 3,000 and 1600-strong respectively – the great majority were either European migrants or the children of migrants.[6] Moreover, a very high proportion of these

European migrants were already political exiles: not only Germans, Italians and Austrians, but also those from many other European countries dominated by right-wing nationalist dictatorships, autocratic monarchies and the radical (fascist) right – including Hungary, Yugoslavia, Romania, Poland and Finland. The brigaders were part of a mass migration of people – mainly from the urban working classes – who had already left their countries of birth at some point after the First World War (sometimes before) either for economic reasons or to flee political repression – and frequently both. Among the Canadian volunteers, for example, there were many Finns who had fled the repression unleashed by the nationalist leader Mannerheim after the civil war of 1918. One Canadian Finn even spoke of going to fight in Spain to avenge his sister who had been killed by the whites (nationalists) during that war.[7] Or all those restless, radical refugee boys from rural Italy or from the towns and villages of what had been the Austro-Hungarian empire who, when they fetched up fighting against Franco's nationalists wanted to get even with those narrow-minded, good – and proto-fascist – burghers in their own home towns, drilling "national guards" on the public squares and humiliating and marginalizing anyone who did not conform, or who wanted something different.[8]

In fighting fascism in Spain these exiles and migrants were, then, explicitly taking up unfinished business that went back at least as far as the 1914–18 war. Its dislocations had brutalized politics, inducing the birth of the anti-democratic nationalisms that had physically displaced them. In the resulting flux, labour activism or "being a communist" offered them a place, and protection too in a hostile environment.[9] These forms of left internationalist politics dovetailed with their own diasporic condition, signalling a powerful corrective to the other, literally murderous, forms of politics inhabiting their own countries. In a sense, the brigaders can be identified with the border-crossing revolutionary spirit of an earlier time: "what has become of that nineteenth-century universe where we paid in sous and crossed every frontier where we liked and as we liked?" After the failure of the 1848 revolution, the national idea in Europe was increasingly co-opted into outright conservative state-building agendas. But the idea of travelling hopefully, of bearing change across borders, lived on. And this is clearly visible in the International Brigaders' own "border- or line-crossing" potential in terms of social change related to race, gender and sexuality: "I am that exile from a future time", as the radical American poet, Sol Funaroff, expressed it. Born in Beirut in 1911 of a family of impoverished Russian-Jewish exiles whose own odyssey through many European countries ended in New York, Funaroff threw himself into solidarity work to support the Spanish Republic. Seriously ill from childhood, and always eking out a material existence at the margins, he nevertheless burned bright in his life and his work, dying in 1942, aged 31, of rheumatic heart disease – an affliction referred to by one unflinching slum doctor as "poverty heart": "I am that exile from a future time . . . from shores of freedom I may never know".[10] But, politically, the brigaders' own times (1918–45) were running against them. It was a world that, far from opening up to hybridity, was closing down ethnically, culturally and nationally – both during this period, but also after 1945. It was this which would fix the position of the International Brigaders everywhere, as political, and indeed very often existential, outsiders.

As Sol Funaroff had seen, the political stakes were raised for all the exiles and migrants of 1930s Europe, as a result of the economic depression. Mass unemployment and deprivation – particularly in urban areas – accelerated political polarization by seeming to announce the collapse of an untenable economic order (capitalism) whose maximum defenders were, in the eyes of those who became brigaders, the very same people who sought a return to, or the reinvention of, the rigid political and social hierarchy of the pre-1914 world. The fact of that world having gone forever was nowhere more visible than in the new *forms* of politics which were erupting, quite literally, onto the streets. Absolutely new too was the fact that it was young people who were taking politics to the streets.[11] This represented a sociological shift – as the young suddenly became political actors and cultural protagonists in their own right – something that was also strongly reflected inside Spain itself.

For the mobilization of young people was another singular feature of the Republican era. In the early 1930s, many middle-class university students had become Republican activists. Among them were Carmen Parga, who was studying history, and Manuel Tagüeña Lacorte, a student of medicine. There is a photograph of Parga, taken in 1930, where she is standing among a group of smiling nineteen-year-old activists in front of Madrid's brand new University City on the western edges of the capital. When the civil war erupted the campus would be destroyed in the major battle for the city fought against Franco's besieging armies during November and December 1936. The International Brigades, thrown into the breach of Madrid's defence, engaged within the new university buildings in bloody hand-to-hand combat against the Army of Africa, the professional core of Franco's troops, in a fight and upon a terrain whose symbolic charge was not lost on an international audience.[12] There is also a much less famous photograph of Carmen and Manuel in 1930 on the "playa de Madrid" (Madrid's "beach"[13]), wearing discreet but pared-down bathing attire – an image that speaks subtly but clearly to a world of other losses which would be sustained along with political defeat. By 1938 the twenty-five-year-old Tagüeña would be leading a major detachment of the new Republican army into battle at the Ebro (July–November 1938). The "reverse" eventually suffered by the army was not a military but a political one, triggered by what happened half way across the continent in Munich where, in late September, Britain and France agreed to Hitler's dismemberment of Czechoslovakia. The final Republican defeat in March 1939 saw Manuel Tagüeña Lacorte and Carmen Parga begin a lifetime in war and exile in Moscow and Mexico where Tagüeña died in 1971, aged fifty-eight. His memoir, *Testimonio de dos guerras* ("A witness to two wars"), first published in Mexico in the early 1970s, is one of the most serious and honest of any produced by Spanish protagonists about that time, and by far the best of those written by the Republic's military leaders.[14] Although of course Tagüeña had *become* one because of the war, just as it was the war too that created a generation of young political leaders in Republican Spain – representing a transformation within the politics of the country, even if rapidly eclipsed by defeat. One only has to recall the twenty- and early thirty-year-olds who were appointed to positions of major responsibility on the Madrid Defence Council, the body appointed in November 1936 to organize the defence of the capital when the government evacuated to Valencia. Indeed some of the Council's youngest members, those charged with the security and running of a city struggling under massive aerial bombardment, were under twenty five years-of-age.[15] A major source of Republican defence too came from those very young men (often teenagers and unskilled labourers), usually without any history of political activism, who surged into the militias that constituted the emergency resistance to the military rebellion in Spain's cities and towns.[16] This was the generation which would be scythed by the Francoist repression, a repression that in Madrid was begun in March 1939 by a Republican army commander, Colonel Segismundo Casado, whose affiliations and precise objective in rising against the Republican government remain to this day a matter of dispute.[17]

There were young International Brigaders too – in their middle twenties, occasionally younger. Some of them would rapidly bear weighty responsibility. The Latvian-born Len Crome (Lazar Krom), who had trained as a doctor in Edinburgh, was only twenty-eight when he became head of the medical services of the 35th Division which served the XI Brigade (mainly German-speaking) and the XV Brigade (primarily English-speaking).[18] Bill Aalto, the Finnish American boy from the Bronx whose story encapsulates so many of the themes of this chapter, as we shall see later, was close to his twenty-second birthday when he was recruited from the Brigades to join the Republican guerrilla forces. But for the most part the brigaders were somewhat older, at least in their late twenties – although

Bill Aalto as a teenager

A photograph of the teenage Bill Aalto, dating from before he left for Spain, aged 21, at the start of 1937. It was reproduced in a pamphlet on Finnish and Finnish American brigaders published in 1939: K. E. Heikkinen and William Lahtinen (eds), *Meidän Poikamme Espanjassa* (Our Boys in Spain), (n.p. [New York]: Finnish Workers' Federation, USA Inc., 1939). Tamiment Library and Robert F. Wagner Labor Archives, New York University. In 2002 an English translation of the pamphlet was made by the Lincoln brigade veteran, the late Matti Mattson, a copy of which is also available in Tamiment.

still usually too young to have fought in the Great War, if not to have lived through its street-fighting aftermath in many places across Europe. The brigaders felt that by going to fight the military rebels and their fascist backers in Spain they were also striking a blow against economic and political exclusion across the whole continent. They were thus quite conscious of themselves as political soldiers in an ongoing European civil war.

They were soldiers in a deeper sense too. For this European civil war was, like Spain's own, also a culture war. The brigaders were the direct counterparts of those social sectors inside Spain who were now challenging head on an older political order rooted in social deference. This was a form of politics, and of political struggle, that everywhere in 1920s and 30s Europe derived from an acute clash between values and ways of life: fixed social hierarchy against more egalitarian modes of politics. In Spain, those who supported the Republic, either in arms or on the home front, did so because they were people who aspired to some form of social and cultural opening and who perceived the Republic as offering a more hopeful future, the possibility of a more fluid form of society.

As we have already seen in earlier chapters, these were the groups whom the military rebels and their supporters were seeking to "cleanse", discipline and subjugate, in order to kill the threat they posed. By the same token, the brigaders' defence of the Republic was, then, a defence of its right to challenge this murderous, backward-looking rage. In Spain the brigaders were fighting against the very forms of society and politics already inhabiting many of their own countries, and to stop Franco from constructing his own variant of a brutal and exclusionary national community.

As a European civil war of culture, Spain's was also a race war. But again this was not simply about German Nazism: so many of the European regimes from which brigader-exiles had fled after 1918 developed forms of politics and desired national "order" based on ethnic segregation and "purification" – aimed both at racial and other kinds of minorities (see chapter 1). In the traditional, rural-dominated societies that were then still the norm in much of central, east and south-east Europe, these "minorities" included the urban left – although in Germany itself, the social democratic labour movement that constituted the Nazis' first target cannot be described as a minority; it was a mass social force.[19] But it is also true that the first German concentration camps set up in 1933 did incarcerate and persecute German outsiders, the different, the marginal, the heterodox – whether politically, socially, culturally or sexually – that culturally hybrid Germany represented so magnificently, for example, in the photography of Auguste Sander.[20] And the German International Brigaders took to Spain at least one song, *Peat Bog Soldiers* (*Moorsoldaten*), written by inmates of the first Nazi camps.[21] The song was adapted by Bertold Brecht and Kurt Weill's musical collaborator, Hans Eisler, in conjunction with Ernst Busch who later also sang it, accompanied by a chorus from the Thaelmann battalion, in a recording made in Barcelona in 1938 during the heavy aerial bombardment of the city.

And while these first Nazi camps inside Germany did not target Jews especially as Jews, nevertheless many Jewish people were among the incarcerated and once they were confined then their treatment was always among the worst. That there were so many Jewish volunteers among the International Brigaders – around a quarter of the total – is unsurprising if one considers two things. First, the long history of antisemitism in the European continent and the way in which it was directly shaping the "purificatory" and social darwinist politics of the European right after 1918. By the 1930s this was quite explicit in Spain too, even though there was no indigenous Jewish population. The discourse of the Spanish right was nevertheless resolutely antisemitic, and indeed the idea of a "judeo-masonic-bolshevik" conspiracy against "eternal Christian Spain" was one of the Franco regime's founding myths.[22] Second, the strong Jewish presence in the Brigades also reflected the longstanding and strong radical political tradition among Jewish migrant communities who had fled the pogroms and endemic discrimination in Russia and east Europe.[23]

Among the Polish brigaders in Spain a high proportion were Jewish and a specifically Jewish company was formed within the Polish battalion where it attracted an international membership – including Jews from various European countries, and Palestine, but also others, including a Greek, two Palestinian Arabs and a German who after deserting from the Nazi army insisted on serving with this Jewish unit. It was named after a young Jewish communist, Naftali Botwin, killed in Poland in 1925.[24] The Botwin Company's flag bore the words "for your freedom and ours" in Yiddish and Polish on one side and in Spanish on the other, and its members would later fight, along with many other International Brigade veterans, in the French resistance and in other partisan conflicts, for example in Yugoslavia – confrontations which comprised the ongoing European civil wars of 1939–47 (see chapter 1 above). Most Jewish brigaders in Spain, however, fought in other units than the Botwin and many saw their antifascism as a more important mark of personal identity than their Jewishness – which, in an important sense, is anyway better defined as their Yiddish cultural identity since it was inseparable from their *secular* internationalism (Zionism being too close to the other forms of nationalism they eschewed as a part of the original, European segregationist political malaise).[25] Yiddish was in fact the nearest thing there was to a common language within the International Brigades – as British nurse Patience Darton once recalled when she spoke with devastating sadness of how three Finnish brigaders, mortally wounded at the battle of the Ebro in 1938 and transferred to her care in the nearby cave hospital, had died, for lack of a common language, *untranslated*.[26]

In fighting fascism in Spain all the brigaders were resisting many forms of violent social and political exclusion simultaneously. Nor is this "meta" interpretation of the Brigades' significance gainsaid by the indubitable fact that some individual brigaders were themselves antisemitic, or otherwise nationally chauvinist. Given the nature of the dominant culture, it is inconceivable that some would not have been. But neither does social change occur in a smooth or linear fashion. It is the fact of the Brigades and their structural position in this story is which provides the key to what they meant.[27] In racial and cultural as well as political terms, then, the heterogeneity of the Brigades made them a living form of opposition to the principles of purification and brutal categorization espoused by fascism and, above all, by Nazism. Nor was this just about doing battle with the European demons manifest in forms of brutal social categorization. The

Abraham Lincoln Brigade itself, in which around ninety African Americans fought, was the first non-segregated American military unit ever to exist – the US Army itself continued to operate segregation throughout the Second World War. Indeed the Lincolns numbered black officers among its commanders too. Viewed through this optic, what the International Brigades symbolized is a certain spirit of future possibility. They were – though very imperfectly and by no means fully consciously – the soldiers of cosmopolitan cultural modernity.

This idea of "social change in action" linking through from Spain to the Second World War and beyond is evocatively suggested in Javier Cercas' epochal, best-selling Spanish novel of 2001, *Soldados de Salamina* (Soldiers of Salamis), where he discusses the role of a group of politically and racially diverse soldiers who fought for the Allies in the ranks of de Gaulle's Free French in North Africa: exiled Spanish republicans, assorted International Brigade veterans and other European antifascist exiles and refugees – many of whom were escapees from Vichy France's concentrations camps and forced labour brigades – came together with ex-members of the French Foreign Legion in order to participate in January 1941 in an offensive against the Italian oasis of Murzak, in south-west Libya."Just imagine . . ." as one of Cercas' characters remarks, and the narrator continues, "as if he [the character speaking] were himself discovering the story, or the meaning of the story, as he told it. 'All of Europe controlled by the Nazis, and in middle of nowhere, without anyone knowing it, there they damn well were – four North Africans, a black guy and that old cuss of a Spaniard . . . raising liberty's flag for the first time in months.'"[28]

By this telling, the multi-ethnic and cosmopolitan composition of the free French forces thus becomes central to the meaning of the war. Those who plant the Allied flag at Murzak were Hitler and Franco's "mongrel soldiers" who with their anti-heroism saved Europe from fascism's idealization of racial purity and martial virtue. It is "anti-heroism" because, significantly, in Cercas' telling they "volunteer" for the Murzak mission by drawing lots and losing. This same story of hybridity and difference played out too in resistance movements inside Europe, for example in France. It is now becoming much more widely appreciated that Spanish Republicans and International Brigade veterans played a major role in both the rural and urban resistance. Indeed the urban-based MOI (*Main d'oeuvre immigrée*, or migrant labour front) whose cultural cosmopolitanism and racial heterogeneity as much as its political radicalism made it the living antithesis of Hitler's new order, traced its origins to International Brigade veterans – mainly escapees from the prison camp of Gurs – and to the tradition of left internationalism that had underwritten their involvement in Spain. As well as French and Spanish Republican fighters, MOI included Italians, Rumanians, Armenians, Poles, Austrians, Czechs and Hungarians. As in the International Brigades themselves, so too in the MOI, a great many, perhaps more than half, were Jewish. This profile put the MOI under greater psychological pressure than any other resistance organization. Not only were the risks already greater in an urban environment, but a majority of its members were on the wanted list three times over: as leftists, as foreigners and as Jews.

In February 1944 in Paris the occupying forces sentenced and executed twenty three MOI fighters from a group led by the Armenian poet Missak Manouchian, who had lost his own family in the Armenian genocide. Among those executed from Manouchian's group in 1944 were also several International Brigade veterans and a Republican Spaniard (Alonso). The Nazi occupiers then plastered the walls of the city with the famous *Affiche Rouge* [Red Poster] from which there stared out the images of numerous of the group, including Alonso, Manouchian himself and two brigaders, Shloime Grzywacz and Ferenc Wolff (*nom de guerre* Joseph Boczov).[29] Unrepresented on the poster was the only woman among the twenty three executed – Olga Bancic, a Romanian communist who had also been involved in solidarity work for Republican Spain during the civil war. She was not executed in Paris with the rest of the group but taken to Germany and beheaded in Stuttgart prison in May 1944. The Red Poster was a clear attempt to delegitimize the resistance through an appeal to French chauvinism – something that would certainly have struck a chord. For the Nazi "war against hybridity" was not waged "against the European grain" at all. Though Hitler certainly pushed it to the limit, ethnic homogeneity as supposed political "coherence" and psychological "integrity" was an idea shared by very many people in European countries east, south, west and north. Indeed the myth of the ethnically homogeneous European nation state had in a sense been most powerfully represented and re-scripted by the *western* peacemakers of 1918–19, for example in the not so subliminal message beneath all the elaborate and ultimately unworkable machinery of League of Nations' "minority protection" which intimated that normality and assuring a "conflict-free condition" required ethnic homogeneity.[30] Certainly in 1944 the French communist party understood the broader social and cultural currency of the Red Poster, and in a bid to build a national coalition around the resistance, played up its antifascism but *played down* its multi-ethnic composition. The heroes of the French resistance simply could not be represented as Armenian Jews or Spanish *guerrilleros*. Although, if we were to engage today in making a hierarchy of the inassimilable and inarticulable, then one would have to say that "foreigners" in the French resistance are relatively more assimilable, whereas still much further out on the edges of representability are the tens of thousands of Spanish Republican refugees and refugee International Brigaders who were incarcerated in the early months of 1939 in France, that is to say in *Republican* France, in what was, and what can now only be described as a camp universe, whose mushrooming was itself facilitated by the rise from 1938 of a strong current of ethnic nationalist sentiment which was increasingly directed against migrant workers, naturalized French citizens, and needless to say, anyone who was Jewish.[31] In France as elsewhere in Europe, this was also an anti-city discourse, evident, for example, in the burgeoning criticism of the Popular Front government reforms of 1936 in favour of urban workers as somehow "contaminated" and, above all, "unFrench".[32]

Questions of race and ethnicity within Europe, as forms of potentially brutal categorization, are thus ever present when discussing the ramifications of International Brigade intervention in Spain. But so too are these ideas in other geographical contexts. The defence of the Spanish Republic was a major magnet for very diverse writers and fighters; thinkers, activists and revolutionaries who were linked by a common desire to work towards the breaking down of such brutal categories. For example, the Indian writer and social critic, Mulk Raj Anand, a close friend of Nehru, who wrote the classic anti-caste novel, *Untouchable* (1935), immediately recognized his own cause in the defence of Republican Spain which he publicly supported and visited in 1937. Race, for evident reasons, also threads through the ongoing cultural border-crossing among North American brigaders. The black Lincoln veteran, Eluard Luchell McDaniels, sailing home from active service in 1941 and on leave in Durban (South Africa) led his fellow sailors in a sit-down protest at a Woolworth's segregated lunch counter.[33] And Irving Goff, who had fought with Bill Aalto in the Republican guerrilla, was in the late 1940s a freedom rider *avant la lettre*, when as an American communist party organizer in the south he violated the laws of Louisiana by arranging racially mixed political meetings during presidential campaigning in 1948. And as the party's district organizer in New Orleans, Goff, in his work to encourage black voter registration, jeopardized his life on more than one occasion by ignoring southern racial customs.[34]

Goff was of course a highly disciplined party operative, but that is not the whole story of his line-crossing and risk-taking — for these things are intrinsically tied up with the experience of "Spain". The perfect illustration of this comes in another episode just after the war involving Goff and his comrade in the Republican guerrilla, Bill Aalto, the working-class Finnish-American boy from the Bronx, the tough, intelligent, street-wise kid who became a guerrilla captain and came out of Spain with the highest

commendation of any awarded to a Lincoln brigader. In the spring of 1940
Goff and Aalto were on an agitprop tour of college campuses, touring the
Northeast and upper Midwest to speak on behalf of Republican Spain and
its prisoners and refugees. One day while they were parked in a car awaiting
their driver near the campus of Ohio State university, quite suddenly Bill
told Irv Goff that he was gay.[35] That he should tell Goff with whom he had
a close bond from the war in Spain – they had shared a near death experience after the famous Carchuna gaol break of May 1938, had remained
friends and still shared a life of political activism – perhaps seems less than
surprising to twenty-first century readers. But this was 1940, not the 1970s
– it was nearly thirty years before Stonewall, and Bill was revealing something that made him vulnerable, not because he was uncomfortable with
his sexuality, but because it made him illegal. So the revelation has to have
been a kind of dare or challenge.[36] Bill was refusing to play by the rules,
refusing to accept the need to compartmentalize his life any more. The
timing here is significant: these thoughts had cohered immediately after,
and, I would suggest, directly as a result of his experience of the war in
Spain. The rationale which held supremely for Bill, but which also applied
to many other brigaders in different circumstances, including the in almost
all other things diametrically opposed Goff, was that for the war they had
all fought to have meaning, then life had to change – it had to go beyond
the sterility, colourlessness, "inauthenticity", not only of the political status
quo but also of social convention. Ohio State was a crossover moment. Ever
afterward Bill Aalto was a searcher – asking hard and remarkably modern
questions about the politics of the personal, about the social construction
of particular categories of public and private. For the rest of Bill's far from
easy life, his chiding refrain to friends would always be "you see life steady,
but you see it small".[37] After Spain he was determined not to. His friendship with Goff cooled but did not break – even in spite of what would be,
three years later, a major act of betrayal by Goff himself.

   The Ohio State moment in Bill Aalto's life also stands, I would argue,
as a clear example of the caesura through which a human subject comes to
be made, in which the moment of "truth" is defined by a radical break. This
occurs when someone goes with an intuition founded apparently on
nothing, an indefensible wager, an "unjustifiable" commitment. As more
than one philosopher has indicated too: "thought changes the world more
than it understands it".[38] What this story also serves to remind us of more
generally is that gender and sexuality were one variety of border crossing
that the "old" left of the 1930s generally baulked at – a frontier or line-
crossing too far.[39] When the American Evelyn Hutchins applied to be sent
to Spain as an ambulance driver, she came up against entrenched prejudice

inside the American Communist Party (CPUSA).[40] The political left, though keen to further racial equality, could only conceive of recruiting women to Spain as nurses or support staff. In the end Hutchins won. But hers was an isolated victory. Women were not generally recruited for volunteer service in Republican Spain except in functions considered appropriate to the mainstream, and thus socially conservative, gender norms of the times. Indeed when Hutchins later applied, along with other male brigader veterans, to serve during the world war in the OSS (*Office of Strategic Services*) – a force of irregular operatives being recruited by US authorities for service in occupied Europe – she was turned down flat. Bill Aalto too came up against the rigidities of gender culture when in 1942 he was stood down from active OSS service because of his sexuality – although in his case it was not the organization itself that vetoed him (indeed OSS head, General Bill Donavan would have been happy to have him serve) but the intervention of other International Brigade veterans, Bill's co-recruits to the OSS, who, alerted by Irv Goff himself, saw fit to block him from active service. Their decision would lead to an event which would change Bill's life forever, thereby completing the process of sea-change that had begun in Spain and made itself manifest in such singular fashion near Ohio State campus.[41]

While Bill's difficult post-war journey would never cease to be political, it traversed a highly personal terrain which allowed him, at least for a time, a degree of latitude. But for many other International Brigaders from continental Europe, the defeat in Spain left them without any place to be in the world. Unable to return to their countries of origin under pain of imprisonment, and not infrequently death, they passed from Catalonia (after its fall to Franco's forces in February 1939) to French internment and punishment camps or labour battalions and, as already mentioned, thence (after the fall of France in 1940) to partisan and resistance movements. They fought on in the belief that this was a continuation of "Spain". But in the world order that emerged after 1945, they would find their cosmopolitan and heterodox spirit and cultural difference to be, once again, surplus to the requirements of the new political and social order – West and East. If in the West, brigaders were persecuted and sanctioned as subversives, many of the East European brigaders who made it back after fighting the war for the Allies would subsequently disappear into prisons or the gulag.

Crossing the Lines

What has become of that nineteenth-century universe where we paid in *sous* and crossed every frontier where we liked and as we liked?

The question was posed by Louis Aragon, the French poet and communist activist who was a major figure on the cultural front which defended the Spanish Republic. He formulated it early in the second half of the twentieth century, in 1965,[42] and thus at a point when the writer's assessment was loaded with an acutely painful nostalgia derived from a knowledge of the depradations wrought by the political cultures of Stalinism to the utopian projects of the left. But even Stalinism was a variant, if a particularly brutal one, of something else – namely the rise of a more complex surveilling and measuring state, particularly after 1918.[43] This development was evident too in the increasing intensity of the surveillance abroad of political exiles by police and intelligence agents. Modern states had of course always policed politically "unruly" exiles. But by the late 1920s and 1930s "subversive" nationals were rapidly coming to be seen in not dissimilar terms to Hitler's derogatory description of European Jews – *Luftmenschen* ("people of the air") – that is, surplus to the requirements of the homogenizing state which sought compliant, standard "subjects". Thus as the exiles crossed borders, with them crossed the agents charged with protecting the order of states – Italian, German, Soviet and other – to surveil, discipline, return them, sometimes to kill them. Border crossing was here inspiring much greater levels of fear, distrust and watchfulness – which erupted in Spain too as a signal component of what happened during the Barcelona May Days of 1937. But this was not just the story of Stalin's intervention via the NKVD, as is still widely assumed, courtesy of Orwell's *Homage to Catalonia*.[44] For Mussolini's secret police was also active and was probably responsible for murdering the leading Italian anarchist thinker Camilo Berneri and his secretary during the May rebellion in Barcelona, just as a few months later they also assassinated two prominent Italian antifascist exiles, Carlo and Nello Rosselli, in France. Nor is the reference here only to authoritarian or totalitarian states. This state work of harsh control and censure was soon evident in the postwar USA too. Bill Aalto himself was forced back to New York from Italy in 1952 when the State Department removed his passport and suspended his disability pension. He would fight court cases for the few remaining years of his life to recover his passport, achieving this only in the year he died, aged 42 in 1958.

In the postwar West, International Brigade veterans were, as is well known, viewed either implicitly or explicitly as restless subversives, politically untrustworthy and malcontent, unpatriotic, potentially traitorous – the antithesis of a settled, demobilized, compliant population from which they were repeatedly excluded in various ways and silenced. In the East too, in spite of the apparent differences, things were startlingly similar for many veterans. In the countries of the communist bloc, as this had emerged by

1949, the fight against fascism was the foundational myth of the new socialist order – and thus too was the defence of the Spanish Republic. But as such state devices are wont to be, it was a very controlled and pared-down political narrative, rigorously policed. Many "real" International Brigaders did not fit its requirements. Thus, ironically, what occurred in East Germany, as Josie McLellan's thoughtful study indicates, was the obsessive surveilling of brigader cadres (the *Spanienkämpfer*), the very group which was supposed to be the antifascist aristocracy of the DDR.[45] They were surveilled as they wrote, and rewrote to order, their official "biographies", destined for public consumption and edification. This death by editorialization, the bid to reinvent and reduce every *Spanienkämpfer* to a two-dimensional socialist realist hero was, of course, another means of silencing them. This was the fate of any account that sought to render the pain of war *per se*: the grief at the death of comrades, or the huge stress that all officers and troops worked under in the Spanish Republican army given the sheer inequality – compared to the Francoist armies – of infrastructure and military equipment provoked by Non-Intervention itself. Any representation of brutal military discipline – itself integrally linked to those self-same stresses – was also *verboten*. A particularly ironic case of such censorship saw the bowdlerization of the memoirs of the German communist writer Ludwig Renn,[46] who was one of relatively few brigaders with serious military experience prior to Spain, having been an officer in the German army during the Great War. Renn, who came from an aristocratic family in Saxony, published a savage critique of German military incompetence in his huge novel *Krieg* ("War") and joined the German Communist Party (KPD) in 1928. He was arrested in 1933, went into exile in Switzerland and then to fight in Spain where he commanded the Thaelmann battalion, later becoming chief of staff of the Eleventh Brigade. But even as a military heavyweight, he was not allowed to depart from the East German state script – no pain, no fear, no feeling could impinge upon the narrowly inscribed approved male war hero of the 1950s DDR. It is, then, scarcely surprising that in 1955 the authorities airbrushed out of Renn's memoirs any reference to beautiful boys – as if his sexual difference somehow impaired his credibility as a fighter. It is, however, noteworthy that then authorities were still censoring this kind of material as late as 1981, when the posthumous publication of the memoirs of a comrade of Renn's, Bodo Uhse, had an amusing wartime anecdote excised in which Renn waxed lyrical about the beautiful underwear worn by a young man he had once picked up in a Valencian cinema.[47]

Far more destructively, the DDR's narrow script led to half a lifetime of limbo and marginalization for another dissenting *Spanienkämpfer* – the prickly, difficult and rather wonderful Rudolf Michaelis whose story is so complex that it would require a chapter of its own to do him justice. To borrow the words of another famous International Brigader exile and dissident, the Czech Artur London, when Michaelis died in Berlin in 1990, he "had so many prisons behind him".[48] An anarchist whose original profession was as an archaeological restorer at the Berlin state museum, Rudolf Michaelis' life was traduced by every state. First he was thrown into Nazi "preventive custody", where his life was saved only by the intervention of a senior colleague at the museum who had influence with Goering.[49] In exile in Spain when the military coup occurred, he joined an anarchist column to fight the uprising and in May 1937 was imprisoned in a Spanish Republican state gaol after the May Days rebellion involving anarchists and dissident communists in Barcelona in 1937.[50] On release from prison he joined the Republican army, having taken Spanish citizenship, and fought in it until the Republic fell in spring 1939, at which point Rudolf crossed the border into France and joined the resistance. Crossing back into Spain shortly after (in the autumn of 1939) with a group of *guerrilleros*, he was caught and imprisoned in a Francoist gaol in Barcelona where he spent five years and during which time he was regularly tortured. From 1944 he was detailed to live under *libertad vigilada* (a punitive form of parole) in Carabanchel, near Madrid.[51] In 1946 he was repatriated to Berlin where he stayed with his family. With few other options available to him in that time and place, he made a peace of sorts with the new state order of the DDR as it emerged in 1949 – although in joining the SED, the official state party of the DDR, Michaelis was cut dead by his anarchist comrades in the West. He was expelled from the SED in 1951 for being politically too heterodox. Nevertheless, the DDR still afforded him a liveable life, both in material terms and, crucially, in that it still offered him a means of participating in a collective memory of what Spain had signified – which while reductive, *was not a lie*. Nor did Michaelis suffer trial or imprisonment in the DDR, as some other dissident veterans would eventually do in late 1950s.[52] But inevitably he was confined to the margins: his life could not be articulated, was unspeakable and *un-representable* within either the state *Spanienkämpfer* script or the Western cold war narrative of the "eastern victims of Stalinism".[53] Rudolf Michaelis' story overflows these in every direction. His memoirs were eventually published under a pseudonym in West Germany – but not until 1980. And in East Germany too, it was only in the late 1970s and 1980s that he was actually able to begin speaking about his experiences, as part of the multiplicity of anti-fascist traditions – albeit in private talks only – as non-official, semi-public spaces for debate began to appear.

Elsewhere in the East, however, the whiff of cosmopolitanism that adhered to "Spain" was a death sentence, very often literally. So many of those who were consumed in the trials and purges – above all in Hungary (1949) and Czechoslovakia (1952)[54] – had been in Spain. Indeed the very fact of having been there opened them up to charges of being "restless subversives, politically untrustworthy and malcontent, unpatriotic, potentially traitorous" – just as they were seen in virtually identical terms through a McCarthyite lens in the United States. The political purges, initiated in Hungary in September 1949 with the Rajk trial, were sparked by spy panic after the arrest in Prague of Noel Field, a former State Department official and active antifascist turned refugee relief organizer, who had worked in a humanitarian capacity in Europe during the war and who had been in contact with many European communists – either because the organization he worked for (the Unitarian Service Committee) had provided them with humanitarian aid and visas, or in some cases, because Field had acted as an informal link between European communists and the OSS. The premise of the Rajk trial was that Field was really a US intelligence operative and the panicked question was: who else had he turned?[55] (Rajk himself would confess to "holding conversations with Trotskyites in a French internment camp for Spanish civil war fighters".) Yugoslavia too had been gripped by a similar fear – in 1946 the Yugoslav–American Lincoln Battalion veteran George Delitch, who, parachuted in with the OSS, had been a powerhouse of the Yugoslav partisan war effort, was executed by Tito as an American spy.[56] In Czechoslovakia too the Slansky trial of November 1952 focused on communists who had been western emigrants, again many of them International Brigade veterans, who were seen as a dangerous factional group and accused of collaboration with Western espionage agencies during their internment in France. Artur London, the brigade veteran who had been through Mauthausen was, when arraigned, the Czech under-secretary for foreign affairs. In his account of the trial what emerges very clearly is the link between border-crossing and "contamination".[57] The state authorities were obsessively concerned that exiled communists had been "turned" – by everyone, so it seemed: the Gestapo, and both the French and US intelligence services. Just what had they really been up to in the cities of western exile or the prison camps of France and Africa? The MOI was uniformly seen as compromised and "contaminated" because of its contact with OSS, and thus its surviving veteran fighters were suspect. And while this was at some level about real fears born of a sense of political vulnerability, there is also something else here – an echo of submerged social darwinist anxieties, the fear of difference, of things which challenge the state script, and therefore also (perceivedly) its stability, by the challenge posed to social uniformity and homogeneity, all of which is expressed as a fear of contamination. And, as a crucial element here, one should also note the intense antisemitism which inhabited much of the onslaught against communist exiles and veterans of the International Brigades during these purges and trials – Jews being then seen in the official Soviet optic as the epitome of untrustworthy, heterodox communists, untrustworthy *because* heterodox.[58]

Fear of the International Brigades thus represented here a fear of social fluidity and cultural heterodoxy: not each and every brigader represented this,[59] but certainly the collectivity and the memory were signed as inherently other and unstable. Thus state agendas excluded and silenced many brigader veterans, pathologizing the selfsame progressive, questioning dynamic that epitomized their way of seeing the world and their understanding of change – the very things that took them to Spain in the first place. As Ludwig Renn commented in utter perplexity in 1952, it seemed that "everything connected with it [Spain] is cancelled. Supposedly this is happening because there were too many traitors in Spain. I don't understand such points of view."[60]

What can be glimpsed here is not very far removed from what was perceived as "dangerous" by postwar Western political establishments – and especially evident perhaps in the US where an army of social scientists was deployed to find applied ways of stabilizing society, of cutting through the flux and closing down the mobility that had been generated by the war. And of course, as we know well, the Cold War everywhere was in part about stabilizing internal political and social arrangements in the postwar – East and West. This is not to suggest that the dynamic was purely top-down or exclusively statist. This closing down of things was a process that involved ordinary people, and which in important ways co-opted the post-war desires of some of them for comfort, composure, simplicity. These dynamics met, for example, on the juries trying HUAC (House Un-American Activities Committee) defendants which were always packed with federal employees. This phenomenon had a clientelist dimension of course, but was about the popular imaginaries of the jurors too.

McCarthyism itself was, of course, not as directly deadly as the East European trials – though it did certainly cause deaths, including some suicides. But state repression always takes its form according to local political culture and, after all, there are many ways of "killing" people without physically executing them or putting them in gulags – which is to say that one can kill someone by making them totally unemployable (as happened in some cases), or else unemployable in anything remotely approaching what a person felt called to do by virtue of his/her talents. Reducing people to poverty, making life unliveable, getting them thrown out of their homes

and thus indirectly often breaking up their families and their personal relationships – all of these things did follow, as we know only too well, from
McCarthyism's legal repressive practices. The forms of state repression and
civil and political discrimination endured by International Brigade veterans
in the US in the 1950s were many – under a "McCarthyism" which, in all
but name, went back to the 1930s, if not to the 1920s.[61] McCarthy also
sought to make a high profile victim out of the Spanish composer-turned
Republican military commander, Gustavo Durán. A contemporary of
Lorca, Dalí and Buñuel, Durán had, like many International Brigaders,
"faced his situation" and engaged practically to defend the possibility of
change in Spain. Having escaped barely with his life in the wake of the
Casado coup, Durán would weather the McCarthyite storm. But his life was
changed irrevocably and, after Spain, he would never compose again.[62]

The legacy of McCarthyism runs deep not least because of the psychological and cultural dislocations it induced. Mexico, for example, while in
some ways providing a refuge (though not a haven) for persecuted American
radicals, as recounted in Diana Anhalt's 2001 oral history-cum-memoir *A
Gathering of Fugitives*,[63] also posed many fundamental existential problems,
especially for the cultural workers who loomed large among this particular
exile. Anhalt's account itself is absolutely honest about the pain and

Gustavo Durán on the Aragón front, spring 1938

Gustavo Durán on the Aragón front, spring 1938. (Photograph courtesy of Cheli and Jane
Durán). (A copy of it [and of the series from which it comes] is held by the Archivo
Histórico del Partido Comunista de España, Madrid).

personal cost involved in refusing to conform – that is, in *needing* to refuse to conform – as is the writer Howard Fast. The son of a Ukrainian migrant, Fast himself served a prison term in 1947 as a member of the Lincoln veterans' (VALB) Spanish refugee relief committee for refusing to reveal to HUAC the names and address of its donors and supporters. He also wrote luminously about the significance of the Lincolns' leave-taking of Spain in his exquisite short story *Departure*,[64] which captures indirectly yet perfectly that central feeling that so many brigader veterans (including support staff and medical workers) shared, along with many of those who had worked in Spanish Republican solidarity roles across Europe and beyond: namely that feeling of being burned by Spain, or transfigured, but never being the same for sure, and not being able to fit again, anywhere, ever – another kind of exile, to add to the territorial and political. In Fast's superb autobiography, *Being Red* (1990), he relates his encounter with his friend the screenwriter Albert Maltz, one of the Hollywood Ten – the filmworkers indicted for contempt during the late 1940s witch-hunt in Hollywood, facilitated by the President of the Screen Actors' Guild, Ronald Reagan.[65] Fast encountered Albert Maltz later in Mexico; Maltz was so terrified by the potential effects of the draconian Communist Control Act of 1954 that he felt unable to leave – in spite of deep feelings of cultural alienation. "I have no roots here", he told Fast, "our lives are our language". But he had been so seared by his experience of prison that he just could not risk it again: "I have to live, I have to find love. I have books that I must write."[66]

While the devastating experience behind those words is at one level far removed from Europe's concentration camp universe, it nevertheless shares something vital with the sentiment expressed by the Hungarian poet Miklós Radnóti, who invoked Republican Spain and the friends who had died in combat there as symbols of what made the fight still worthwhile. He was writing in July 1944, while imprisoned in a Nazi-controlled labour camp near Bor in Serbia and only months before he was himself killed by Hungarian guards on the prisoners' forced march in the wake of the retreating German army:

> Among false rumours and worms, we live here with Frenchmen, Poles,
> Loud Italians, heretic Serbs, nostalgic Jews, in the mountains.
> This feverish body, dismembered but still living one life, waits
> For good news, for women's sweet words, for a life both free and human.[67]

"Spain" haunted them all because it was a site of possibility, of becoming. That is why it haunts us still. One has only to think of Alvah Bessie's image of Ernst Toller (haunting because haunted), as he visits the

Ernst Toller with Walter Hasenclever,1928

Ernst Toller (seated) with fellow poet and playwright Walter Hasenclever in 1928. Like Toller's, Hasenclever's work was banned and burned by the Nazis. Living in exile in France, Hasenclever was interned as a "foreign enemy". He took his own life in the French prison camp of Les Milles in June 1940, to avoid falling into the hands of the occupying Nazi forces. (Photograph: Ullstein Bild, Berlin).

Ebro battlefield in 1938 and stands out in the open against a blaze of fire, ignoring all their frantic warnings that he should take cover. Toller is indifferent to the chances of death; he stands in the landscape of the Ebro, but is also surrounded by his Bavarian ghosts, the dead comrades of 1919. As if emerging from a long despair, Toller would make a superhuman personal effort in 1938 and the early months of 1939 to mobilize governmental humanitarian aid for Republican Spain, touring Britain, the US and Scandinavia for the purpose.[68] The fall of the Republic was for him quite literally unbearable and ended with his suicide in a New York hotel room in May 1939.[69] For others – including, in their very different ways, Bill Aalto, Gustavo Durán and Rudolf Michaelis – the end of the Republic was still a situation to be faced: "when the light faded I went in search of myself".[70] For all the bleakness of its aftermath, "Spain" stands as a reminder of the possibility of becoming: of the "journey without maps" made by the protagonist in Michael Ondaatje's *The English Patient*, who was not only *not* English but had also renounced the very category of nationality and national identity because of the damage these had done;[71] and of Machado's own reminder that the road does not exist; we make it by walking, by crossing borders – that doing so hurts, but that it is also necessary, a human(e) imperative.

5

Brutal Nurture
Coming of age in Europe's wars of social change

Where did they go, the unshakeable ones?
The lost ones, last ones,
{ . . . }
After the camps at Argelès-sur-Mer,
St Cyprien, at Barcarès, after the barbed wire
in what places did they choose
or not choose to live, upstairs rooms
so swept by roads and travelling?[1]

Photographs { . . . } enact a reckoning with history that takes the measure of
the residual effects of the past in the present, as well as in the future. Here the
photograph serves not only as a historical document or source, but also as a
reflexive medium that exposes the stakes of historical study.[2]

A photograph could be the subtle light that unassumingly helps us to change
things. (W. Eugene Smith)

This brief photo-essay links chapters 4 and 6 by reflecting upon the huge
social cost of Republican defeat and also the links between it, the subsequent diaspora/exile (including in its internal forms) and the post-war
migrations of the 1950s and 60s which remade Spain, just as they also
provided crucial labour power for the "economic miracles" of northern and
western Europe.

❋   ❋   ❋

The photographs by Robert Capa featured in this chapter are from the *Mexican Suitcase*
exhibition (http://museum.icp.org/mexican_suitcase/) and are included by kind permission of the International Center of Photography, New York. Manuel Moros' images (Fond
Peneff) appear courtesy of his estate, and I would like to thank Manuel Moros' nephew,
Jean Peneff, for his generous assistance here.

Robert Capa Photographs

Republican soldiers visited by dignitaries on the Catalan front, late December 1938–January 1939. (© International Center of Photography/Magnum Photos).

Their faces are points of light against the dark of greatcoats and the penumbra of the meeting space. Capa records almost tenderly this moment of respite, of intimate engagement, on the Spanish Republic's final front. Gazing watchfully, they are absorbed by the visiting dignitary's words, yet reserved, until the sharing of cigarettes breaks their circumspection. The visitor's task is to boost morale, to convince them that, against all the odds, the defence of Catalonia is viable as well as vital, that there is still time to turn the diplomatic tide, avert the continental deluge. His audience is composed of Republican troops of the 5th Corps, some of them veterans of the blistering Ebro battle waged against the combined might of German and Italian airpower between July and November 1938, across the lunar escarpments of neighbouring Aragón – a battle in which the Republic's defeat was not military but political, decided far away as Britain and France took appeasement to its "logical" conclusion and accepted Hitler's dismemberment of Czechoslovakia, the last functioning democracy in central Europe. This final front in Catalonia was more than only Spain's.

The boy soldier whose clear-eyed gaze draws us in might easily be one of those Ebro veterans – young enough to have volunteered for the youth brigade of the Juventudes Socialistas Unificadas,[3] or to have formed part of the "baby draft" (*quinta del biberón*), the seventeen-year-olds whose conscription in spring 1938 provoked the public protests of mothers, as the Republic cut into bone to defend itself, siege conditions eroding the

Republican boy refugees

Republican boy refugees, Collioure 1939, photographed by the artist Manuel Moros. Some of the Moros images, like other key photographic testimonies of these times, spent years hidden or buried to maximize the chances of their own survival and also those of their creators. (Photograph: courtesy of Jean Peneff, nephew of Manuel Moros, for the Moros Estate).

Republican boy refugees

(Photograph: courtesy of Jean Peneff, nephew of Manuel Moros, for the Moros Estate).

promise of egalitarian social reform it once bore. His gaze is gentle, expectant, focused on the speaker. Our own reading of that gaze takes in the inevitable knowledge that this is a moment at the end of things: behind them, the punishing battles fought since 1936 against the odds; ahead, the hurt of history.

But what might it mean that Capa's own focus is so resolutely upon the young soldier? Muffled against the cold, above the photographer's lens, the smooth plane of his face is safe in this moment from the projectile bombs. The mildness of his gaze belies the past and future of a war from which, even if he survives, there will be no "coming home" – because this military conflict is also an inexorable instrument of social change; a battle to decide who will speak through politics. The boy will be made by the war, whether he's a volunteer, or a war orphan like the lone boy sentinel also photographed by Capa,[4] or the conscripted son of war-weary Catalan small-holders. He will be made by it just as surely as were the militia boys of 1936 and the thousands of adolescents who joined up to defend the Republic, many of them unskilled workers, with no previous political affiliation, but who were subliminally aware that something was changing. Though less aware, perhaps, than the restless refugee boys who crossed a continent to fight for the Spanish Republic, just as Capa did by photographing it. But like those young International Brigaders from Hungary, Poland, Yugoslavia, Austria and other European lands, the Spanish boy soldiers were refugees too, in their own way. Capa's sympathy for them all was sympathy for those who no longer fitted Europe's waning neo-feudal rural order – these boys chipping at the rigidities of social deference, in search of a place, a voice. In Spain too the old power seemed to be dying, but slowly and viciously and, as it turned out, not yet. Nor would it depart in the way scripted by Republican reformers, and not before in its passing it claimed from that generation a barbaric tribute, exacted in the coin of "national cleansing" and the camps: the adolescents who died before Franco's firing squads in the exemplary mass killing of the 1940s, the teenage slave labourers who built roads, dams and the dictator's mausoleum, or the youngsters in the anti-Franco guerrilla, and the Spanish boys who passed from French internment camps to forced labour battalions, onto to the "irregular resistance", or were deported with Franco's acquiescence to Nazi camps – thirteen-year-old Spanish Republicans breaking stone in the quarry at Mauthausen.[5]

Perhaps hardest of all for the twenty-first-century viewer, no less than for the reader of this episode of history, is to understand what politics meant for the young Republican soldiers who gaze out at us from a historical frontier far nearer chronologically than it is culturally. Politics in the 1930s was not a "personal option", not something they could take or leave, be or not be. It was a molten flow engulfing the world to remake it, taking possession of personal lives, whether their owners willed it or not, the unforgiving medium through which history unfolded, in Victor Serge's words, "in spite of us, through us, with us, even if it crushes us".[6] For a time, there was nothing outside it. By this reading, political activism was itself a way of acquiring human agency, and a form of body armour too, donned by the least powerful in the hostile climes of vertiginous social change.

Even for those young Spanish Republicans who survived this war in all its extended forms, survived the reordering of the European continent that came through the experience of the camps, the legacy still became a permanent facet of their lives, "swept by roads and travelling". Above all, it was a legacy of learned precariousness: from them the "tribute" would be exacted in the heavy cost of a different model of social change and in the tenuousness of their future survival therein. They would become the migrant labourers who made the "economic miracles" in Spain, France, Germany, Switzerland, having learned to expect little and make do with less. All of this is there already, prefigured in the sudden vulnerability of a raised canvas sandal.[7]

6

Franco's Prisons
Building the brutal national community in Spain

La gente decía en la posguerra, "El que no está preso, lo andan buscando".

All of Spain is a prison. (Marcos Ana)

Franco's was the brutal national community that got away. It was, of course, far from being the only one that survived long term to inflict violence on its population. (Later in this chapter there is a discussion of certain similarities between Francoism and Stalinism.) But the sense of "the one that got away" is intended to highlight the longstanding, cold war-derived failure internationally to condemn, or even to recognize, the scale of the abuses committed by the Franco regime – a failure whose past and present implications are discussed in chapter 7.[1] Unlike Hitler's, Spain's brutal national community was not dismantled by military defeat. General Franco, instead of being tried as a war criminal at Nuremberg, was able to shelter beneath the Western canopy – endorsed by the USA and the Vatican as an anti-communist bulwark and a geopolitically significant component in the Cold War. Thus a Western order that retrospectively mythologized its opposition to Nazism as opposition to the camp universe, and which denounced this too as the ultimate offence of Stalinism, patronised a regime in Spain that was, like the Soviet Union's, based on mass murder and its own gulag. For Francoism, like Stalinism and Nazism, can best be defined as a regime that was at war with its own society.

This chapter offers an analysis of long-durée Francoism, intended by its progenitors as the antithesis of social change. It begins with an exploration of how and why the brutal national community was built – starting after the coup of 17–18 July 1936 and continuing throughout the 1940s – and then examines its consequences for Spain's polity and society in the medium term. Francoism is understood here to be a particularly violent and long-lived "solution" to managing conflictive change, tightly controlling the population as Spain converted at breakneck speed to an industrial economy in the later 1950s and 1960s. The end, when it eventually came for the dictatorship, lay not in the political revolution its supporters had always feared, but in an anthropological one: symbolized above all by the mass migration from countryside to city which generated not only industrial transformation but also a cultural shift of vast proportions. But that mass migration looked back as well as forward, being in important regards the last act of the civil war. For the hundreds of thousands of rural poor who undertook the route, many with a Republican past, it was also a violent experience, and one whose social history remains to be written, just as its social consequences still remain to be reckoned properly by scholars today.[2]

The Prison Universe

After Franco won the military phase of Spain's civil war on 1 April 1939, his victorious regime was able to extend its new order to the entirety of national territory. State and society were to be brutally remade – "homogenized" by the violent exclusion of the defeated. Pursuit of this goal would see the regime murder and incarcerate its own nationals on a scale that outdid anything that the Nazi state undertook within its pre-1938 borders. All those who had supported the Republic were demonized as "anti-Spain". Placed beyond the nation, they were deemed to be without rights. Up to a million men, women and children spent time in prisons, work camps, forced labour battalions and reformatories where, ostensibly, they were "re-educated".[3] Extra-legal forms of persecution were rife, including preventive detention. This exclusion of the defeated was inscribed in all spheres – the law, employment, education and culture, including the very organization of everyday life and public space. To understand properly the integrated nature of the repression one would have also to compute the effects of punitive economic policy (autarky) and social welfare policy, the purges of the professions, educational debarment, as well as the regime's discourse and ideology.[4] But this chapter will concentrate specifically on the machinery of direct repression. At the heart of this was the operation of a state of war/exception (*de jure* till 1948, *de facto* till 1963).[5] The Franco regime reduced the judicial process to a branch of state terror: though, just as in Nazi Germany, it retained juridical *forms* because these were seen as legitimating and strengthening the Francoist state itself.

But these were very much forms. For the 1940s in Spain saw the application on an industrial scale of the abusive form of summary justice

Prison column of captured Republican soldiers

Prison column of captured Republican soldiers, Peñarroya, early 1937, framed against a wayside cross and telegraph poles which also resemble crosses (Photograph: Fondo Serrano, Hemeroteca Municipal de Sevilla).

described in chapter 2. Continuing with the practice present in rebel-con-quered zones during the military phase of the civil war, this saw those who had defended the Republic court-martialled and executed *en masse* for "military rebellion". This process often saw mass trials, sometimes of fifty or even a hundred defendants, with no due process, no case made beyond the bare charge of "military rebellion"; no legal defence provided and in which the accused could not intervene in any real way (they were permit-ted neither to call witnesses nor present evidence).[6] Indeed defendants were usually only able to identify the "defence" lawyer in court because he would be the one asking for the death penalty to be commuted to life imprisonment.

Potential targets included anyone who had Republican connections (indeed even those who had simply benefited from Republican social reforms): those who had been volunteers in the Republican army (as opposed to conscripts), or who had visibly supported the Republic in any way, could come within the purview of the military courts: from military officers through political post-holders right down to village officials, even women who had run the *colonias infantiles* for refugee children. Thousands of death sentences were handed down as well as huge prison sentences. The regime was thus redefining Republican political activity, or even identity, as criminal, which is to say, it was redefining crime *per se*.

The scale of these "cleansing executions" – judicial murder after summary trials – alarmed even Himmler who was visiting in October 1940, though obviously he was concerned not with the humanitarian issue but the wastage of much-needed "Aryan" labour. Himmler had come to set up a Gestapo consultancy for Franco's political police, the *Brigada político-social*, to advise them on surveillance and interrogation techniques and also to help convert Franco's files on political opponents into a workable instrument of repression.[7] We now calculate that the Francoist repression which erupted with the military coup of 17–18 July 1936 and which continued in hot (extrajudicial) and then cold terror right through to the late 1940s, saw the killing of at least 150,000, a figure which includes the c. 30,000 who were disappeared in the dirty war of 1936–39.[8] This is a baseline figure: first because for some areas the tabulation is still in progress (including for post-1939 Madrid). Second, there is the sheer difficulty of tracking and identifying those who died in the killing fields of the south, and especially those who died there who were already refugees from elsewhere and who carried no documentation;[9] third, the same is true for those refugees from all over Spain who had taken refuge in Barcelona only to die in the flight to the French border in 1939 or those who committed suicide after waiting in vain for evacuation from the Mediterranean ports; fourth, there is the question of "hot" (extrajudicial) repression in the wake of Franco's final military victory on 1 April 1939 in the third of Spain (out and down from Madrid to the eastern and south-eastern seaboards) that had remained Republican territory right up until then; fifth, there were also extrajudicial murders in and near concentration camps and then, later, inside work camps, and sometimes in prisons, all of which inevitably remained undocumented. Even in any cases where prison executions did leave an administrative trace, then much of this was subsequently lost in the deliberate destruction of prison records in the final years of the Franco regime. A comparison with political executions under the Third Reich, Francoism's brutal tutor, is even more difficult – given that from 1938 there was a huge expansion in the territory and population under Nazi control through annexation, conquest and occupation, with the cumulative radicalization of the Nazi project through external warfare, as the racial blueprint was implemented. But within Germany, for the period 1933–38, judicial political executions, largely of communists or social democrats, numbered probably fewer than 500.[10] Extrajudicial murders from January 1933 – on the streets, in police stations, in the early concentration camps and sometimes in prisons themselves – are harder to quantify, but an estimate would be in the low thousands for the period up to 1939.[11]

In addition to widespread summary justice in Francoist Spain, there was also large scale administrative detention in the post-war years – i.e. people were detained without judicial intervention of any kind. The regime itself estimated 60,000 such cases in 1940.[12] This was the reality behind Franco's constitutional window dressing, such as the 1945 *Fuero de los Españoles* ("Spaniards' Charter") – designed for international consumption in the wake of Nazi defeat. But inside Spain many individuals were repeatedly subject to re-arrest, brutalization, and administrative detention, after being released from prison. One case in Valencia serves as an example: there the parents and other family members of one recently released prisoner were imprisoned and beaten up by the local Falange until he gave himself up to what was a second period of administrative detention; and this cycle was repeated again following his second release.[13] There could have been fewer more effective ways to teach people their powerlessness than by ridiculing thus their hopes for constitutional protection, as part of the language of political rights once spoken by the Republic.[14] Indeed most of the regime's practices, whether via direct repression or the punitive dimension which autarky inserted into everyday life, can be encapsulated as teaching the defeated the meaning of their defeat.[15]

Franco's use of the military justice system also developed one fatal new twist after it had achieved total control of Spain on 1 April 1939. This was the regime's deliberate decision systematically to use mass denunciation. It declared open season by exhorting "ordinary Spaniards" to denounce their compatriots, denunciations for which no corroborating evidence was required and which, in the first phase (lasting some two years, up to September 1941), could even be anonymous.[16] These denunciations were henceforward what triggered and drove prosecutions en masse within the nationwide system of military courts.

What this meant was that the regime was legitimizing itself by mobilizing (indeed creating) a social base of perpetrators, tens of thousands of them across the land. Thus it was building on the complicity already established earlier by social fears and personal losses sustained during the war, thereby locking these people and their futures into the fate of the regime itself. This would be endlessly toxic: not only did it create victims and mobilize perpetrators at a specific moment in the 1940s, but it maintained the perpetrators mobilized for three and a half decades through a set of public policies/social practices that consistently discriminated against the defeated and those who "inherited" that defeat. Integral to this was the regime's unchanging manichean discourse – i.e. its ideological and cultural discourse of the civil war as a battle of "morality vs. iniquity", of "martyrs against barbarians". That is what marks Francoism apart – the lasting toxicity of its original legitimating strategy, a binary discourse which gave rise to an "afterlife of violence" that still burns the social and political landscape of twenty first-century Spain.

When the regime first launched that nationwide policy back in 1939–40 it was not hard to find denouncers. As is usual with denunciation in any socio-political frame, into the denouncers' own motives were meshed a mix of the personal and the political. Indeed, the Spanish case is a text book example of the personal becoming political. Many of those formed up in the ranks of mass crusade Catholicism under the Second Republic were already mobilized/configured by abiding social fear – even *before* they suffered the actual wartime losses of family and friends or the violent deaths of those close to them; or else were subjected to coercive/abusive behaviour post-rising as a result of being defined as belonging to "them", the social and political constituencies supporting the coup. Once all of this came together, then the Franco coalition would have a social base with which to work. Indeed in environments which had seen decades of increasing social tension before the war, and in which intra-communal relations were particularly fraught, such as the village cluster of Los Pedroches in Córdoba in Spain's agrarian south, investigated by Peter Anderson, there arose a number of cases of serial denouncers who both satisfied their own need for revenge as they also provided a useful supplementary resource for the investigating and judicial authorities, hard-pressed by the sheer volume of "work". For, even though the charge of military rebellion against a defendant was usually brought automatically, nevertheless they were always desirous of finding a real person to point the finger.[17] More than a few of these serial denouncers, their passions vented courtesy of the opportunity proffered by the regime, ended by feeling remorse and discomfiture at the extreme consequences of their actions. But by then it was too late – indeed some who attempted to retract their assertions or to suggest that the swingeing outcomes imposed by the military courts were not at all what they had had in mind, were given short shrift subsequently by the Francoist authorities. This dense climate of complicity irrevocably generated by state action is also an important motive force explaining the appeal of "silence"/"oblivion" during the years of Spain's democratic transition in the 1970s.

It is important to underscore here too that the role played by such individuals within the military trial system of the 1940s was as denouncers rather than witnesses – an important distinction. Much of the extra-judicial killing in Republican territory – that is to say, what occurred in the state-imploded months immediately following the military coup – left, by its very nature, very little viable trace of exactly who had perpetrated it. Certainly the military trials involved no investigative process, and no corroborating evidence was required. Quite frequently the basis of a case was the originating denunciation plus hearsay – nothing more. But the fact that the link between actual crime and actual defendant was so frequently unsafe was almost irrelevant. For the function of the military courts was not to ascertain the *individual* guilt of any accused person. What mattered was the general context of Republican violence during the war, what one might term the Francoist generalized discourse of "barbarians and martyrs" – that was the supreme *incrimination* and all the corroboration or credibility these charges needed in the eyes of many of the military judges. Franco himself is on record as admitting, very revealingly, that given the "work of archangels" the regime was undertaking, then there could not be an exact fit between those punished and those who were "guilty".[18] But ultimately that didn't matter because Republican guilt was intrinsic – it was perceived as a form of collective contamination. So here there is a clear parallel between Francoist judicial practice and that of the Nazis – in that both, unlike the Soviet case, overturned previous liberal jurisprudence/practice. No longer was it an *act* that was to be punished but rather a *person.* Hence the low priority given to corroborating evidence, and hence too the category of "preventive", or "administrative" detention itself. The scale of state-encouraged denunciation in Francoist Spain also far outstripped its dictatorial contemporaries.[19]

Massive prison sentences were handed out. Twenty to thirty years was not unusual and twelve years was considered a light sentence. In the immediate post-war years there was a huge increase in the prison population. The figures remain fragmentary, with official statistics widely seen by specialist historians as underestimates – not least because of the explosive phenomenon of administrative detention which left only a very imperfect trace in the statistical record. In 1940 the official tally was over 270,000, the vast majority of whom were political detainees – a category deployed by the state authorities, even though they refused to recognize it publicly.[20] (The total prison population for January 1936 had been around 34,500.) This means that at its high point the Franco regime was imprisoning 1,158 prisoners per 100,000 inhabitants. In November 1936 Nazi Germany had had a prison population (including those in the early concentration camps) of 178 prisoners per 100,000 inhabitants.[21] The rate of imprisonment in Spain remained, proportionally, much lower than in the Soviet Union. On current figures, just under a sixth of the Soviet population spent time in a gulag, while just over one seventeenth of Spaniards did. But given the vastly different legal and social contexts, there is also a crucial qualitative question to be underlined here: in a country where the rule of law was, relatively speaking, significantly more firmly implanted than in Russia, imprisoning – even if "only" for a few years – one-seventeenth of the population had a searing psychological impact, as well as a practical one, among "suspect" non-imprisoned sectors over whom the regime was keen to exert tight social control. As popular wisdom had it: "el que no está preso, lo andan buscando" (anyone who isn't yet a prisoner, is on the wanted list). In 1942 Spain's prison population was still, even by the official tally, 124,423. This explosion from 1939 saw a huge increase in the physical space of prisons. All sorts of buildings were deployed – derelict warehouses, farms, seminaries, schools – whose capacity varied greatly. But in almost all there was horrific overcrowding.

Beyond the prisons themselves there also existed a constellation of labour battalions, work brigades and other instruments of slave labour such as military penal colonies that ran the length and breadth of Spain. The military forces detached to organize these referred to themselves as "the army of occupation". Forced labourers undertook the construction and also the reconstruction of war-damaged roads, railways, dams, towns and other public infrastructure, as well as the building of Franco's own mausoleum outside Madrid. They were also loaned out to private industry and mining and construction companies. While the revenue generation of the Spanish

Prison Gallery, Barcelona 1941

(Photograph: Carlos Pérez de Rozas, Arxiu Històric de la Ciutat de Barcelona/Arxiu Fotogràfic).

slave labour system never produced the serious financial returns of the SS universe, it nevertheless constituted a crucial source of free labour for the state, just as it boosted the profits of numerous Spanish companies.[22] But its major function remained disciplinary and over the long term. The largest such project was the Canal del Bajo Guadalquivir, an immense irrigation project involving over five thousand slave labourers and which took twenty years to complete, in the interests of the same landowners who had backed the military coup of 1936.[23] The underlying philosophy was that "work" offered a route to "redemption" through penitence and expiation. But in fact the Francoist notion here was very close to far less Catholic examples in the same time period, for example the slogan used in relation to the Soviet gulags: "Work in the USSR is a matter of Honour and Glory" suggests a not dissimilar "rationalization" of how work – the substance which epito-mized the huge changes supervening after the Great War – was being offered/put into service as a practical and even a metaphysical "solution" to the reconfiguration of societies and polities. Indeed Soviet Russia was grudgingly admired by the Franco regime. The problem was not the intense suffering being imposed on Soviet workers in the name of national economic development, but the fact that they had "lost god".[24] In hard-edged terms, in Spain the Catholic rhetoric of expiation through suffering ("freedom" from guilt) was legitimizing the extraction of surplus value (free labour). So the old (traditionalist values) impelled the new (industrial moderniza-tion from a low capital base). To compare Nazi Germany's cynical concentration camp "logo", "Arbeit macht frei" ("work will set you free") is probably a step too far – although it nevertheless reminds us that the historical question still remains over the nature of the subliminal (libid-inal?) investment in "work", including in obscene and nonsensical forms within concentration camps, as part of a perceived "solution" to the ills of European society.

Often inmates went from prison to penal colonies – and sometimes back again. Many young men were administratively detained and placed in the penal brigades without even the pretence of there being a judicial process to be gone through: they were thus being detained not because of any specific act, but because of who they were – someone with a defined Republican past or who had been associated with any of the Republic's political, social or cultural initiatives. Often too it came down to the arbi-trary power of the local mayor or Falange boss who didn't like one's "attitude". Prison and prison camp conditions in Spain were acutely dangerous up to c.1947 in terms of overcrowding, lack of hygiene, medical attention and food. They were condemned by the International Commission against Concentration Camp Regimes (CICRC) which conducted an

enquiry into the Spanish penal system in 1953. The Commission also
pronounced that while the Francoist prisons and camps of the 1940s were
not extermination camps – in the sense that the Nazi death camps had been
– nevertheless, the disciplinary regime that obtained in Spain during the
1940s put the lives of the inmates at the total and arbitrary disposition of
the prison/camp authorities and that, as in a concentration camp regime,
inmates suffered dire material conditions and *extreme forms of arbitrary
violence that frequently led to their deaths.*[25] The CICRC interviewed scores of
prisoners across Spain and their testimonies include accounts of arbitrary
shootings and beatings to death by guards; the extra-judicial executions of
prisoners after minor (or sometimes invented) infringements of prison discipline; the machine gunning of prisoners in camps. Ciano, when he visited
Barcelona in July 1939 as Italian foreign minister, had already summarized
the situation: on being taken to visit a labour camp, the state of the inmates
prompted him to remark that "Franco did not have prisoners of war, but
slaves of war".[26]

But nor was it a case of the Franco regime prosecuting only civil war
"crimes". From 1939 a whole raft of additional legislation massively
extended the definition of what constituted crimes of resistance to the
state[27] and thus brought in a new wave of prisoners. As a result, there
occurred periodic pardons (*indultos*) for civil war-related offences (though
never for anything defined as post-war "crimes against the security of the
state"). Tens of thousands of people were released by the mid 1940s. These
pardons were necessary or the gaols would have caved in under the pressure
of the incomers (the newly incarcerated). They also permitted a closer
control of those remaining. But a pardon did not mean a simple return to
society, it meant entry to another penal regime, that of conditional liberty
(*libertad vigilada*) – an exceptionally punitive form of parole via which the
regime's control was extended further. Those subject to it could only engage
in certain sorts of work which in practice meant manual work. One's place
of residence was also designated – usually far from home and family – which
in the punitive environment of the post-war meant being distanced from
the personal networks without which it was impossible to find any kind of
job however lowly. The requirement to report regularly to the police further
increased prisoners' impoverishment by interfering with their employa-
bility even in menial jobs.[28] Everything conspired to make prisoners
exceptionally vulnerable in the labour market. Conditional liberty was then
an extreme system – although freedom of movement in 1940s Spain existed
only as an exceptional political or social privilege: very few ordinary people
escaped surveillance in a society in which travel anywhere required a safe
conduct or pass from the authorities.[29]

And prison proper – what purpose did it serve in eyes of the regime? Incarceration means civil death – embracing social, sexual and emotional dimensions. And the regime's intention was to ensure that the selves, the "I's" that went in to prison would cease to exist – whether or not they died physically. What is remarkable both during war and after was the desire exhibited by those operating the Francoist system to break and remake Republican prisoners psychologically. This was to be achieved, quite explicitly, through forms of orchestrated/choreographed humiliation within gaol. (This also occurred in daily life outside – but that is another story.) Imposing suffering in gaol was decidedly part of the process – and integrally linked to notions of penitence and expiation. It was implemented first by highly Catholic army psychiatrists who – Catholicism notwithstanding – ran crude quasi social darwinist psychological tests on Republican prisoners, especially the women; and second by religious personnel who were a key component of prison and reformatory staff throughout postwar Spain, and a veritable mainstay in women's gaols, and who everywhere exercised new disciplinary functions on behalf of the Francoist state[30] – though no doubt this willingness also responded to *sui generis* desires of conservative clergy to re-impose their own preferred forms of social and "moral control".[31]

It was often the religious personnel in particular who waged brutal forms of psychological warfare against inmates by applying intense forms of personal pressure – for example by sadistically leaking selected family details from the prison files (one has to remember that war, prison and myriad other forms of social surveillance fractured normal communication channels and thus redoubled the power of those in authority). Everything was consciously reduced to a battle of wills. In women's gaols too issues around female physiological functions such as menstruation and menopause were manipulated to distress prisoners. Many women politicals – not infrequently serving sentence of fifteen years or more – were taunted by religious warders who "reminded" them that by the time they got out of prison they would be too old to have children.[32] Warders also enforced religious observance as well as certain sorts of political observance on the inmates whose impact was magnified by the panopticon effect and highly choreographed space of gaols. More obviously, though no less effectively, they could deprive prisoners of basic rights – such as a daily walk in the quad – or could consign them to isolation cells for weeks or even months on bread and water for the most petty and arbitrary of acts – even for making an insolent or indirectly "political" remark. The religious orders running the gaols also had the power to exclude prisoners from meliorative mechanisms (such as access to the scheme that reduced the length of sentences against prison labour performed)[33] if they considered them insufficiently "contrite". Food too was used as a weapon to enforce obedience. Accepting confession and regular religious instruction brought food "privileges" within a system where the basic ration was well below subsistence, and not everyone could receive the parcels from hard-pressed families on the outside which were the only way to stave off malnutrition. Every mechanism and procedure was discretionary in order to promote prisoners' dependency. One female prisoner described it, eloquently, as requiring them to abjure their past and blaspheme their own dead.[34] In short, it was a means of murdering people without killing them – though the psychological pressures did also lead to prison suicides.

In one notorious case, that of Matilde Landa in Palma de Mallorca gaol in autumn 1942, the suicide was triggered by the sustained psychological siege to which she was subjected by regime personnel, and most notably, the representatives of the powerful lay Catholic association, Acción Católica. Landa was an educated professional woman, "of good family", a former pupil of Spain's famous Institute of Independent Education (*Institución Libre de Enseñanza*), founded in 1876 by liberal educationalists and university professors expelled from state universities for refusing to teach in accordance with Catholic dogma. Sensing the opportunity for an important propaganda victory, the Franco regime sought to turn Landa into a trophy, by making her "recant" and agree to public baptism. This intense pressure also turned her into a symbol for the community of political prisoners. For Matilde it meant an intolerable situation in which the relief of regime pressure could only come through reneging on who she was and betraying her comrades. On 26 September 1942 she took another route out, throwing herself off the edge of an internal prison gallery. She did not die immediately and during the forty-five minutes this took, she had forcibly imposed upon her the religious rites that she had continuously refused throughout her incarceration.[35]

Other forms of assault against prisoners were common too. The rape/sexual assault of women prisoners was systematically perpetrated with impunity by the servants of the Franco regime – in police stations and interrogation centres prior to incarceration – just as it had also been used as a weapon of war during the military phase of 1936–9, discussed in chapter 2. Transfer to prisons and concentration camps was no guarantee of safety. At night, Falangists took young women away and raped them. In individual terms, rape is an act of violence, a form of psychological warfare through humiliation, but in macro terms it is also about what the woman's body means within the national ideology/culture of the male policeman doing the raping: "the body of a woman represents the whole community from which the woman comes, so rape signifies victory over the whole community" – in this case the Republican nation.[36]

Nor was it only adult men and women who inhabited the prison universe: as we glimpsed in chapter 3, children did too. They came to it in numerous ways – those that survived did, at any rate, for there were very high perinatal mortality rates both inside women's gaols and between gaols during transportation by cattle truck. Children were kept with their mothers in gaol until the age of three at which point they were legally required to be relinquished – sometimes to family members, but in many cases to state institutions, even though they may have had an extended family willing to take them. Many thousands of working-class children were placed in orphanages because the regime deemed their Republican families "unfit" to raise them. (There were also the cases of illegal adoption of prisoners' children by regime families, discussed in chapter 3. Certain, arguably related, criminal continuities in present-day Spain are also discussed in chapter 7.) The institutionalized children, of whom there were many thousands, were in their turn abused.[37] The Franco regime spoke of the "protection of minors", but this idea of protection was integrally linked to regime discourses of punishment and purification. In theory, the punishment was of the parents, the "redemption" or "rehabilitation", of the children. But the reality, as experienced by Republican children, was of an ingrained belief in state personnel (religious in particular, but others too) that the children had actively to *expiate* the "sins of the fathers". Yet, at the same time, the children were repeatedly told that they too were irrecuperable. As such, they were frequently segregated from other classes of inmate in state institutions and mistreated both physically and mentally in other ways. The Francoist fixation on retribution here, as in other spheres, meant they projected their own obsessions onto the defeated, and thus could only think of the "enemy" in terms of the revenge that he or she might take. Thus victory was brutalizing the victors too.[38]

One child who endured both a Nazi concentration camp and a Francoist reformatory in 1940s Barcelona has written of their fundamental institutional similarities as factories of dehumanization,[39] while another "lost child" of the Francoist institutions, interviewed in his seventies for a television documentary, spoke of the real "him" as having died during his incarceration in the 1940s.[40] It is no wonder that so many children preferred life on the streets, for street children forced into petty theft and prostitution were also a singular phenomenon of 1940s Spain – as famously evoked in Juan Marsé's seminal novel, first published in Mexico in 1973, *Si te dicen que caí* (The Fallen).

The conclusions to be drawn here are clear. The Franco regime was killing (and incarcerating) for control, that is, to establish control. This was supposedly for the sake of older ways of being and thinking of which the Spain of the Catholic Kings, Imperial Spain, hammer of heretics, and "Spain one, great and free", were all emblems projected by regime ideology/discourse. But in reality what was emerging was – inevitably – something new. It is often claimed that, while Francoism may have been brutal, it was nevertheless just an old fashioned, demobilizing authoritarianism and that this is "proved" by the subordinate role of the explicitly fascist Falange and, conversely, by the protagonism of the Catholic Church.[41] In other words, the Franco regime abolished mass democracy, but it did so without recourse to any novel or modern means. But in view of what has been outlined in this chapter (and also in chapters 2 and 3 above) that seems an entirely insufficient definition of Francoism – insufficient above all in relation precisely to the Church's role.

All of the political forces that made up Francoism explicitly rejected parliamentary democracy and the rule of constitutional law as vile symptoms of the liberal age. But, unlike traditional conservatives, Francoists did *not* view these things as external political forms that could simply be banned. Rather they were seen as having already been incorporated into a large part of the Spanish population, as having, in short, "infected" it. The issue was no longer the body politic, but the biological body of the "nation" and the total control thereof. This was the crux of Franco's strategy both during and after the military conflict of 1936–39: the internal colonization of the metropolis, in order to destroy the "alien" Republican nation/culture therein. The Franco regime constructed its political practices and goals in the light of this key belief in the need for "purification" – something which, by definition, meant it had to go much further than old-fashioned authoritarianism in order to remedy the "problem". The regime went furthest, as we've seen, in its treatment of the defeated whom it excluded socially and politically.

The Franco state nourished itself on a backward-looking ceaselessly perpetuated myth of violent retribution and for decades waged a war daily against huge swathes of its own population. *It carried out a massacre with the object of achieving a rational, circumscribed political community*: Hannah Arendt's formulation fits perfectly here. Massacre and the creation of a homogeneous political community were two sides of the same coin.[42] The regime also used the civil death of incarceration to the same end and both, ultimately, as a means – a monstrous means – of (re)making memory, which was of course another crucial form of exerting control.[43]

Francoist developmentalism and the ghosts of the past

The real result of brutal state-making/the prison universe was not, of course, a static society, but a particularly violent and long-lived "solution" to managing conflictive change, as Spain converted at breakneck speed to an industrial economy in the 1960s. For, while the idea of a static society had been a powerful mobilizing force in the realization of what was perceived as "necessary violence" during the 1930s and 40s, the Franco coalition understood that its own survival into the future depended on its ability to harness economic change in order, in the immediate term, to resolve the crisis of near state bankruptcy caused by its own economic policies (autarky), as well as to ensure, in the medium term, and through a modicum of prosperity, a sufficient social base to support the regime. Indeed this latter would become more important as time went on and it became increasingly difficult to control society via repression alone – as a result of the increasing economic complexity brought about from the late 1950s by accelerating industrialization and urbanization, the spin offs of post-Second World War European economic boom which played a large part, along with the Cold War, in salvaging Francoism.[44] So the possibility of creating an ultra-conservative model of modernization in Francoist Spain came to depend less on overt repression – although this went on existing into the 1960s and 70s and always retained its capacity to be qualitatively extreme, symbolized par excellence by the regime's use until the very end of *garrote vil* as a mode of capital punishment. It now came to depend more on the ways in which the *memory* of an earlier repression filtered through and *informed the reception* of development – its possibilities and limitations – among both Spain's urban and rural worker constituencies and by the 1960s also among its burgeoning new urban middle classes, the child of Francoist development itself.

The massive internal demographic transformation that accompanied the shift of Spain's economy to an industrial base, in the process broke up what had historically been the reservoirs of social support both for revolution and traditionalist reaction – respectively the rural landless of Spain's deep south and the smallholding peasantry of the centre-north. Both were atomized to become the new urban workforce that fuelled Spain's second industrial revolution/thoroughgoing industrial transformation. The scale and speed of this process in Spain effectively meant that the landscape of the 1930s was "abolished", thus ending the very terms and substance of the most intractable economic and socio-cultural problems that had confronted the reforming Second Republic – namely mass landlessness and an increasingly frightened

Camp de la Bota shanty town, Barcelona

Camp de la Bota, Barcelona's shoreline and port-front shanty town, photographed in 1966, close to the time of its demolition. Camp de la Bota is an urban terrain which unites the overt terror of the early Franco regime with the structural violence of the later dictatorship. In the immediate "post-war" years it was the site of both a concentration camp and execution ground for Republican prisoners; then, later, it was the location of this shanty town where, under the ultra laissez-faire industrialization pursued by the Franco regime, the urban and rural migrant poor who fed the process were themselves warehoused (incarcerated?). (Photograph: Arxiu Històric de Poblenou).

and fundamentalist smallholding peasantry of the rural interior, ripe for ultra-nationalist mobilization. The scale and speed of this change was brutally disorienting for all those who had to live through it at the sharp end.

The migration of some sectors of the rural poor to the towns and cities had in fact begun right back in the 1940s, as those survivors with a Republican past fled villages where their lives were made unliveable; they did so clandestinely, dodging the police and disembarking from trains outside the city limits to avoid security controls – for there was no free movement for defeated constituencies in the 1940s. By the next decade, however, this political diaspora was absorbed within an accelerating economic migration to the cities, now tacitly accepted by the regime as necessary to feed developing industry. The lines between political exile and economic migration in the context of 1950s Francoism, however, were often blurred, and certainly it is true to say that this rural migration of hundreds of thousands of Spaniards constituted both the last act of the civil war and the beginning of a new époque, although one still saturated with the subliminal, yet controlling "memory" of murder.

By the 1960s, the "time of the poor" was an accelerated "flight forward" to "better times" and away from a stagnant present of labour and sacrifice, however much this "present" was celebrated in the rhetoric of the regime. For those rural and urban workers who still had some Republican heritage – although many did not, as breaking those links and reconfiguring the memory of the 1930s through the penal regimes of the 1940s had been one of Franco's primary objectives – the flight forward was also an escape from an ideological past which the regime now intimated, as much as taught,

Laundry day, Camp de la Bota, 1967

(Arxiu Històric de Poblenou).

was dangerous for them. Indeed that sense of danger in the past underscores one of the key functions of later Francoism: to inflect any remaining memories of the Republic, as an earlier egalitarian project for social change, with a sense of ineradicable danger and risk for those who even "remembered" it.

But for all poor and socially marginalized constituencies, which included the sons and daughters of the impoverished smallholders of the Castilian heartland who had once been the foot soldiers of "crusading" Francoism, the regime's unwavering commitment to laissez-faire modernization constituted the loss of a present as well as a past. Instead there was economic modernity, the "opportunities" of the market, as an escape forward and to "fill" the void of a lost culture – whether that culture was Republican or of the traditionalist and localist hue that once fed the religious visionaries of northern Spain in the 1930s. For all the uprooted, the changes of the 1960s were to an extent alienating, this notwithstanding the dangerous or straitened circumstances they left behind.[45] The fear-induced autism that resulted was perhaps the Franco regime's most generalized cultural product.[46] The "culture shock" of second-wave industrialization weighed heavy too among the peasantry of the Basque rural interior, where, mediated by other forms of binary nationalist belief, it would play an important part in shaping what ETA later became, as the singular child of the Franco dictatorship.

Bleak and stultifying too for many urban professionals, if not actively alienating, were the effects of the regime's utter cultural and intellectual mediocrity, and especially its obsession with ensuring a rigid outward conformity to its neo-traditionalist values in public life. For people like Magdalena Maes Barayón who had lived the terror of earlier decades in her own family and personal history, it was something worse – though she too remembers the cultural desert – with libraries laid waste, having to read classic European novels "under the counter", and to this day she cannot throw away a book, not even those she considers mediocre.

The Maes family moved away from Zamora in the early 1960s, settling in Málaga in 1964. In this they exemplify the national pattern – for by 1975 one in every four Spaniards was living in a municipality different from that of his/her birth.[47] But, as Magdalena's daughter Mercedes recalls, there was no escape from the past under a vindictive regime that predicated its core political legitimacy upon maintaining a certain idea of *Volksgemeinschaft*. Any of Mercedes' interactions with the state – over a driving licence or passport or university entrance – elicited a response that underlined that she was from a family with a dubious past (two great uncles and one great aunt extrajudicially murdered and a mother who had been a political prisoner) and that she should never forget it. Indeed although she would be admitted

Maes–Barayón family photograph, Zamora c.1963

Amparo's niece, Magdalena Maes, is third from the left (behind the front row of children) and her mother, also Magdalena (Amparo's sister) is second from the right in the same row. (Photograph courtesy of Ramón Sender Barayón).

to higher education, unlike her own mother, Mercedes also remembers being the only member of her class at an affluent girls school in Málaga who, at the beginning of the 1970s, was obliged properly to fulfil her six-month "labour duty" (*Servicio Social*) to the regime as the price of her university entrance, while the rest of the girls simply followed what was by that time the standard practice of delivering to the local women's section of the Falange the requisite baby basket of goods for distribution to needy families.[48] Instead Mercedes did her six-month tour of duty running a ragged school down on the shoreline in Málaga. This story in many ways encapsulates late Francoism: the extravagant bureaucracy easily circumvented by insiders; the clientelism and conformity encasing the long and vindictive memory of the regime, all lying below the thin surface of new material wealth, but this a model of laissez-faire development with low public spending and little state provision that perpetuated extremes of wealth and poverty, against a backdrop of sun, sea and sand – the screen through which most of Europe still looked at Francoism. Mercedes' life experience was a world away from the children who attended her ramshackle and poorly equipped schoolroom and who called her "la señorita hippy" (Miss hippy). But her past made her indelibly an outsider. It was an identity forged both by her interactions with the Francoist authorities and also in the contemplation of her mother's own life spent down among the ghosts, always imagining what might have been.[49] Mercedes found a way out for herself by leaving Spain, immediately after finishing university in 1975. She picked the UK as her destination because it was a country in which the police did not carry guns. But hers was an individual solution rather than a collective one, just as it was, writ large, for all those Spaniards who undertook the same route.

In retrospect we can see that internal migration from countryside to city, combined with outward migration to Europe and the emergence of a urban managerial lower middle class (mostly) loyal to Franco all worked – temporarily at least – to stabilize the regime. To be sure, a new industrial union movement had also emerged by the early 1960s and its mobilization in the economic crisis-ridden early 1970s would play a part in cashiering the Franco regime. But of far greater immediate import was the politically de-radicalizing effect both of that economic stabilization, and of mass migration and emigration themselves – emigrant remittances too being a crucial component of economic development under the Franco regime – which in turn atomized any radical collective awareness of what might then come after in place of dictatorship.

Indeed, when it came, the crisis of the Franco regime was a different kind entirely to that envisaged by the clandestine opposition. Catalyzed by an international economic crisis that crystallized with the oil crisis of 1973, in essence it was a crisis of the dictatorship's domestic political legitimacy. The effects of economic downturn hit hard because those affected were not only the poor or worker and dissident constituencies which had always borne the brunt of repressive state action, but also socially conservative urban and white-collar middle classes, previously the object of regime preferment and privilege, and even domestic power elites who were experiencing the effects of international commercial recession. By 1973 for the first time, the Franco dictatorship could guarantee neither internal social order nor economic prosperity for its own base. The political situation was blown open, quite literally, by the assassination in December 1973 of Franco's closest confident, the acting head of government, Admiral Luis Carrero Blanco, who was blown up by an ETA bomb in Madrid. Given Franco was already seriously ill, this immediately plunged the continuity of the regime into huge uncertainty. The situation was especially barbed because the regime still had the backing of the majority of the army. Moreover 100,000 members of the Falange were still permitted to carry

guns.[50] Francoism's power here was reinforced too by the effects of the uneven development that had always characterized Spain, whose force was further concentrated by nearly four decades of toxic propaganda that had maintained an apocalyptic vision of civil war divisions. This was dangerous for the present because it fed the fears of provincial conservatives, including small business sectors, now facing economic recession and thus even more dependent on regime patronage to survive.

In the event, a favourable – if also fraught – international conjuncture, plus the presence within Spain of some powerful commercial sectors looking for regime change as the necessary prerequisite of European political and economic integration, tipped the balance in favour of a successful transitional process. After the death of Franco himself in November 1975 removed the crucial symbolic impediment, this process was impelled by reformist Francoists who understood that dismantling dictatorial structures dating back to the civil war and 1940s was the price of continued prosperity in new economic times. They were supported by the democratic left – Spain's socialist party and its communist party, now pursuing a highly cautious, reformist line in keeping with its new Eurocommunist mode.[51] Their leaders saw Europe not as a marketplace but as a symbol of cultural openness and political freedom, echoing the position "Europe" had long occupied in the imaginary of the left in twentieth-century Spain. But far more present in their thinking was that political change would perforce be the art of the possible in a country where the bulk of the army was still unconditionally Francoist, not to mention the ranks of fearful pro-Franco civilians in small town Spain. This was the iron reality which underlay the powerful conditioning myths of "the memory of murder" perpetuated for nearly forty years by the Franco regime. For fear was the great unspoken protagonist of the transition process in Spain. Fear most of all of another civil war: the demise in Chile of Salvador Allende's reforming government killed off by the army in a US-backed military coup in September 1973 and unleashing a similar "cleansing" violence against Chilean citizens, was also a sharp and painful reminder of the limits of the possible in 1970s Spain. The transition thus remained, on the one hand, a highly controlled process, choreographed by reformist Francoists who were regime insiders, yet nevertheless unpredictable throughout. It succeeded in bringing about successful institutional transition in dangerous circumstances in which the possibility wasn't so much of another civil war – for the structures of 1930s Spain that had generated the conflict were now gone – but certainly of a bloodbath. The transition which occurred in Spain between 1975 and 1982 encompassed a formidable range of superstructural changes that delivered a constitutional polity based on the principle of universal suffrage – against which the military rebels had originally risen in July 1936. It was thus no small thing that was achieved, and against significant odds – odds that are often forgotten by critics in retrospect. But it was also, and precisely because of the risks, a process that focussed on superstructural change, agreed between political elites and leaderships, in some ways resembling the nineteenth-century "politics of notables" that long dominated Spain into the twentieth century. This process was thus, almost by definition, silent on the subject of the civic values and *content* of democracy – not unsurprising as the architects of change were themselves Francoists and thus schooled within a system suspicious of the very notion of civil society, the Francoist project itself having been born in opposition to the expansion of civil society evident by the 1930s, as the product of accelerating socio-economic change. The transition of the 1970s in Spain was thus a feast of change, but also a civic famine, in that it left unresolved the huge weight of forty years of violent dictatorship, addressing none of the vast accumulated social hurt, the damage done.

This unfinished business – the elaboration of a cohesive civic culture and of a democratic practice – remained thus, pending, awaiting the consolidation of Spain's formal constitutional system. Or at least, that is one way of arguing it – that a constitutional system is not enough to guarantee democracy, which in the end depends upon more than a state system, and crucially requires a participatory practice both by servants of the state and by citizens. So the key is the cultivation of an active civil society. One can also argue that an important prerequisite for such a society is an open and non-fearful attitude to its own past. In this regard the growth of a civic memory movement in twenty-first century Spain could appear as one indication of civic maturity. But this movement continues to be highly contested. As we explore in the next chapter, it has produced a backlash – the so-called "memory wars" – which have in turn fed off the rise of ultra-nationalisms elsewhere in Europe. What these memory wars indicate above all else is the extent to which the categories of meaning produced by the Franco dictatorship still dominate twenty-first-century Spain's epistemological and cultural landscape. The field of memory is still mined.

7

The Afterlife of Violence
Spain's memory wars in national and international context

For the state, the political revelation of its guilt is a difficult task; the memo-rialization of its victims is even harder. Almost all the projects of memorialization of the Soviet victims have been initiated by private persons. Without private initiative, no book and no monument in Russia would describe the terror.[1]

The past is never dead. It's not even past.[2]

This chapter draws together the themes of the book to explore the lasting legacy of brutal state- and nation-building in Spain. More than thirty years after the death of Franco and the end of his dictatorship, many of its most damaging effects endure inside the constitutional polity, just as they continue to take their toll within society in twenty-first-century Spain. There are some remarkable "quirks in the optic" too, if we consider how Francoism is perceived beyond Spain. Why, in spite of our now over-whelming empirical historical knowledge of the scale and intensity of Franco's repression, and of the apartheid society he constructed, has he always somehow resisted classification with his logical, contemporary comparators – Hitler and Stalin? Franco never ruled over a real territorial empire, of course (notwithstanding the fact that empire remained the unifying obsession of the entire Spanish right), nor was Spain militarily or technologically powerful enough to unleash a Europe-wide war of occupa-tion in pursuit of such an empire – for that reason, Franco and Francoism were constrained within a single national canvas. But, within that space, Franco's extremely violent assertion of a narrow notion of "national com-munity" – involving the outright murder and mass imprisonment of those deemed "beyond" it, a proportionately very substantial section of the Spanish population – as well as his unequivocal and consistent support for the brutal organizing principles of the Nazi new order, all place Francoism squarely in the frame with Hitler. The wellsprings of hate in Spain were not ethnic in origin (not even when directed against regional nationalists), but they were still "xenophobic": after all, Franco's war – both on and off the battlefield – was conducted as a "reconquest" against what was deemed alien. And like Stalin, Franco pursued an intransigent political idea of "purifying" state and domestic order with extreme levels of brutality and coercion. In Franco's Spain, as in Stalin's Russia, the surviving population of the excluded had no recourse other than to labour and be silent. In the end, it is the Franco regime's blistering and enduring ideological and physical assault against the excluded, those it killed and those it reduced to bare life (the subject of this chapter), which places it in the same bracket as the other major totalitarian dictatorships of the twentieth century.

A reluctance to classify Franco and Francoism in this way remains to this day, however, and can be found in jobbing historical exchanges between contemporary Europeanist historians, but even more in the popular media and general Western public opinion. There is still a failure to grasp the scale of the brutality beneath the burlesque of "southern European dictatorship". This phenomenon is the result of two things: first, the asymmetry of cold war outcomes and second, the way in which, as a result of this asymmetry, we still inhabit – as do Spaniards themselves – a framework of meaning composed and projected by the Franco dictatorship whose longevity permitted it an unparalleled opportunity to shape its own "record". It is this which, still today, renders somehow "invisible" (while in full public view) the originating mechanism of war inside Spain – a military and paramilitary attack launched against the civilian population.

The work of uncovering the violent consequences of that originating mechanism, by researching the detail of Francoist killing and repression at a local level, began in small and symbolic ways back in the early 1980s on the margins of society in Spain, among those affected directly or indirectly, but also among the otherwise civic-minded who had not themselves experienced the loss of those close to them. This movement gathered pace in the 1990s, boosted in some ways by the post-1989 "return of history" across Europe. As the mythic post-war narrative of "nations united in antifascist resistance" came apart elsewhere, then the significance of the Franco regime to the convulsive history of the twentieth-century continent, of what was done to citizens and compatriots everywhere, and by whom, began to be glimpsed.

But the deconstruction of Francoism's frame of meaning inside constitutional Spain has always been up against formidable obstacles – including notable resistance within the state apparatus, irrespective of the shade of political incumbency. In this regard, and notwithstanding other differences of political culture and experience, there are some striking similarities with the post-Soviet experience where a heterogeneously configured and relatively marginal civic memory movement also struggles against a state that neither properly recognizes, still less commemorates the unlawfully murdered.[3] And even in spite of the "return of history", other powerful countervailing forces have also emerged since 1989. As a result, forms of sociological Francoism[4] continue to this day to shape collective memory inside twenty-first-century Spain, as singularly evidenced in the enduring institutional and social opposition to the civic campaigns to find and identify the extra-judicially murdered in the unmarked graves where they still lie. Most recently this "Franco effect" has been apparent in the unprecedented – and largely successful – bid inside Spain to gag the judge who sought to challenge the impunity of the dictatorship. The democratic deficits in both state and society which have produced this situation partly originate in the nature and circumstances of Spain's transition to a constitutional parliamentary system in the late 1970s. But the afterlife of Francoism glowing at the heart of Spain's continuing memory wars – which have a particularity and a vehemence arguably unsurpassed in Europe[5] – has also become a component of very present politics. For sociological and "nostalgic" Francoism – which never really went away – is now grist to the mill of a newly ascendant populist conservatism of ultra-Catholic hue that takes sustenance from the rise elsewhere in post-1989 Europe of intolerant forms of populist nationalism, usually with their own adjunct of moral fundamentalism. In this way, Spain's memory wars are becoming increasingly interlocked with other similar (and similarly visceral) conflicts elsewhere – particularly in central and east Europe – which are, in turn, giving a new lease of life to many Francoist myths. In this sense, Spain once again lies at an international crossroads, a crucible of "primitive" conflicts over the understanding of its own and Europe's past.

The wages of fear: Spain's transition to a constitutional order

At the time of Spain's transition there could not be any explicit political or social reckoning with the crimes against citizens committed by the Franco state and its personnel. Fear was the predominant mood right across the period – generated by "the memory of murder" in all its dimensions, and by the continuing power of armed Francoism – but also by a looming international recession. Although the economic crisis crystallizing with the 1973 oil shock had itself been an important factor triggering superstructural political change in Spain, its continuing unfolding across the transition period of the late 1970s and early 1980s meant that, as unemployment rose, popular attention came to be concentrated not on politics, still less on the politics of memory, but on the economic hardships to come. Industrial and service sector workers feared for their jobs. Mass political mobilization on the streets still continued at key moments, successfully ensuring that the pressure for constitutional reform was maintained. But, in the medium term, the net effect of the economic crisis was to undermine the politics of local activism and civic engagement that had earlier defined grassroots anti-Francoism in urban Spain. Trade unionism had been an integral part of this, but its membership was decimated by the onslaught of deindustrialization at the heart of the harsh neo-liberal "adjustment" (the so-called "ajuste duro") of the 1980s. Anti-Francoist workers were offered, and accepted, political change in the form of a constitutional parliamentary system. But this could not and did not save their jobs in the heavy industrial sector. And with those jobs, so too there disappeared a social fabric which had contained the memory of a different possible future to the one we have today, with its atomized social base in a liberal market economy dominated by the service sector. Anti-Francoism as a political strategy, rather than as a visceral position, may also have been made more fragile among urban workers as a result of the very nature of the dictatorship's postwar project of obliterating even the knowledge of a politically and socially plural past. This disarticulation of consciousness, another of the dictatorship's lasting legacies, more or less isolated the activists of the 1960s from half a century of pre-civil war labour culture, politics and practice. The impact of this rupture is open to argument, but the atomizing effects of deindustrialization were clear.

Nor was there any compensatory repository of civic consciousness among commercial and professional middling constituencies. Ambitious and materially aspiring, many in these sectors had previously been at least passively accepting of Francoism because of the preferment and prosperity the regime had guaranteed. By the mid 1970s they were anxiously focused on encouraging economic overhaul in Spain, to assure their own future in the face of worldwide economic crisis. So, recession and economic "adjustment", coming on top of the very forms of society generated by Francoism, has meant a continuing lack of any *majority* investment inside Spain in the idea of "society" as a set of common civic values – something which has consistently limited, and is now actively undermining, any serious political reckoning with the violent past.

Further reducing the potential here has been the longstanding agreement, made and remade from the transition onwards, among Spain's mainstream political class – whether social democratic,[6] centrist or on the right – to keep the lid on that difficult past by ruling it off limits for public discourse. They have also sought to enforce the same rule on ordinary citizens, although that has been increasingly less successful – in spite of cyclical recession since the 1970s. But even in the attempt to gag an emergent civil society, we can discern another Franco effect – the strong belief that political matters are the exclusive affair of a professional political class, accompanied by an intense, if latent, suspicion of civil society and the enduring belief that citizens' behaviour is potentially destabilizing. Thus citizens' interests have *legitimately* to be kept subordinate to those of the state. This too is manifest in the Garzón affair, where a judge who was also part of that state system was brought down for expressly seeking to shift the balance in favour of civil society. The backlash against him is not only classically rightist, however, since it derives from an unspoken assumption held across virtually the entire post-Franco political class that it has a common interest, almost irrespective of "ideology", in not exposing itself, or the state apparatus, to the uncertain political consequences of exorcizing the violence of the recent past. In part this assumption stems from a seemingly tacit understanding that the legitimacy of the state today, and by extension its political personnel, is inseparable from continuity across the transition. While this does not amount to an endorsement of Francoism *per se*, at least not on the centre-left, some of the state attitudes and forms of political behaviour that derive from this assumption have, nevertheless, contributed to making the memory wars even more acute, once they erupted (almost inevitably) within civil society, and indeed have probably also escalated them.

But before explaining what this means and where it has led in twenty-first-century Spain, it is first important to recognize the overwhelming extent of the continuities in political and social life across the transition. To start with the most obvious and tangible aspects, the very logic of the transition, as a pact between reformist Francoist sectors and the democratic opposition, meant that there was no departure of Francoist state personnel from either the executive or the judiciary, nor any root and branch renovation of the political class.[7] This has ensured that certain attitudes remain, including towards the state as a system of patronage and access to a spoils system.[8] The presence of the past is evident in visible and direct ways too – in Spain today there are startling continuities in the national political class, with the presence of Francoist "families" both in the literal sense and in the sense of the ongoing influence of currents and tendencies that map onto the dictatorship's political interest groups. One very important example here in regard of the memory wars is the presence of powerful conservative Catholic lay associations which have, since the turn of the century, gone onto a major offensive to rehabilitate the foundational myths of Francoism, bankrolling cultural initiatives – whose products reach newspaper kiosks and neighbourhood stationers more or less nationwide – and pressing into service the considerable media resources of the Catholic Church, including its radio network, COPE. Another weapon here has been that of commercial book distribution and promotion. Now that every level of the book industry is highly commodified, internal bookstore displays are effectively "for sale" too – the most highly prized and expensive being the central islands. It is noteworthy that the most meretricious of the Francoist propagandists always have their books prominently displayed in these positions – precisely because the propagandistic networks and entities into which these authors are embedded pay premium amounts for a privilege that few, if any, individual jobbing historians could afford – university professionals, or otherwise.

Conversely, there have been for many years, and are still, strange elisions and reluctance – amounting to censorship by other routes – whenever Spanish television and radio, whether public or private, is confronted with themes appertaining to Francoist violence and civil rights abuses. For example, the Catalan documentary, *Els nens perduts del franquisme* (2002), which broke the scandal of the children of Republican political prisoners abducted by the Franco regime, was made at the very start of the twenty-first century by a team of investigative journalists who then had considerable difficulty getting it broadcast on Spanish television – indeed it took some five years before a nationwide screening was achieved and even then it was broadcast on the less 'popular' second channel.[9] Nor has the issue of surreptitious indirect censorship gone away since then. The prize-winning 2008 documentary, *Mari-Carmen España: the End of Silence* (Martin Jönsson and Pontus Hjorthén, Sweden, 2008) is a road movie which follows one woman's attempts to exhume her extrajudicially executed grandfather in southern Spain. With superb production values that convey both the historical and current political complexity of the undertaking, it is by far the best piece of documentary work on the subject. It has been fêted internationally and is now commercially distributed as a teaching resource in schools in Germany and the USA. But it remains without a taker in Spain, the numerous attempts made by its director to find a distributor or to agree a deal for it to be broadcast nationally having so far come to nought. The same is also true for the pathbreaking and emotionally acute documentary *Death in El Valle*, made in 1996 by the New York-based Spanish-American photographer, Cristina M. Hardt, which deals with the extrajudicial execution of her grandfather in 1948 at the hands of Francoist security forces.[10] In the case of Spain's private media companies and their reluctance to broadcast material about the difficult past, it has to be borne in mind that many were created in the wave of privatizations initiated after 1996 by the incoming government of Spain's conservative Partido Popular, in many regards the ideological heir of Francoism. It was notorious that the sell-off became a process whereby the party's business clientele was allowed to make a killing in return for allowing the party to position its political appointees as the chairs of company boards, thus maintaining a strong measure of control.

But there are also other, related, Francoist continuities which are just as insidious – probably none more so than the existence in some parts of Spain to this day of a public sphere in which Francoist values can still prevail – most particularly in the form of a set of social and cultural assumptions about hierarchy, due deference and "rightness", and which put one strongly in mind of the culture and atmosphere of the "gentry pact" discussed in chapter 1. The structures it once sustained have now gone – swept away everywhere in Europe in the long aftermath of the Second World War – but its mentalities and prejudices live on in Spain in what we can term the sociological Francoism of many small provincial worlds of nineteenth-century social attitudes, where the idea of pluralism and cultural *aggiornamento* is still more or less alien. This is strongest, as one might expect, in parts of the centre-north which was always the Francoist heartland and where less social change has occurred – other than in the form of people leaving, which by definition has left older structures and prevailing attitudes and prejudices intact and unchallenged, or, more accurately, as we shall see later in this chapter, apparently unchallengeable. But for the moment let us consider why this situation still exists. The explanation is of course the singular trajectory of Francoism itself, which has produced a remarkable political continuity from the originating military coup of July 1936 all the way to an "afterlife" within constitutional, twenty-first-century Spain.

Franco won the civil war with the aid of the Axis. He remained throughout the Second World War entirely politically committed to the triumph of the Nazi New Order in Europe, and he contributed a great deal materially to that end and all the time without the "alibi" of occupation. Yet through a series of favourable historical circumstances he also survived its collapse. This set of circumstances made for a political "career" unique in Europe. Franco was never defeated in any war. Under the changed Western priorities of the cold war world, Franco's Spain took its place (in the days before inter-continental missiles) as a "sentinel of the West" with an international veil drawn over the regime's murderous "past" (which was, as we have seen, very much its "present" too). Inside Spain there would occur a profound economic transformation but never a process of political renovation, *not even in the explicit sense of a public recognition of what Nazism had done.* This happened at no point in the post-war decades – obviously not while Franco ruled, nor indeed during the transition, for the reasons already explained. Nor was there ever real pressure applied by the Western establishment for Spaniards to engage in this publicly, because to have placed Francoism under serious scrutiny – after, just as before, 1989 – would have made it rapidly apparent how the Spanish regime had replicated exactly the structural violence and coercion/repression of the cold war enemy, thus undermining notions of the West's political and ethical superiority and begging questions about what exactly it was that had "won" that war. Western European historians were not necessarily bound by these rules or this narrative, of course. But something seems to have rubbed off, otherwise it is difficult to explain the mile-wide blind spot – even to this day – whether internationally in the media or in academic historiography, when it comes to understanding and explaining the nature of Francoism.

The ghosts of the transition

For as long as the cold war division of Europe held, there was no "problem" in Spain. The settlement that had been agreed by its political elites as the basis for transition to a constitutional order remained in force. The Cold War itself, even in its final stages, impeded any serious discussion of the unreckoned past in mainstream politics and the media in Spain, just as it did generally across southern Europe. Not that this prevented those constituencies which had borne the brunt of this violent past through having suffered it in their own lives from enacting commemoration, as many had been doing for years, either in private spaces/ceremonies, or indeed in other countries and hemispheres – for the Spanish civil war produced an exile that crossed the European and American continents. But the ideological freeze generated by the Cold War did block any wider dissemination or understanding of the experiences of these memory communities within Spain itself – for that required a pool of willing interlocutors, something which only became feasible after 1989. It was the fall of communism which, by destroying the symbolic charge of cold war discourse, created at least the potential for such interlocutors.

For a time after 1989 the political and media focus was on the overthrow of communist regimes in central and east Europe and the exposure of their thoroughgoing and everyday tyrannies. But as soon as this lens began to extend to southern Europe and Spain, where many of the same political and social dynamics had obtained (including the substantial deployment of citizen-informers throughout the Franco years, the files appertaining to which remain sealed), then a conservative revisionism started to appear, which, in Spain as elsewhere, undertook direct comparisons between "fascist" and communist dictatorships, representing them as analogous types of regime and, thus, by this sleight of hand, sanitized "authoritarian" regimes, and the atrocities committed by them, without ever confronting or properly analysing what the actual fascist pasts of many European countries had meant, and at whose cost.

This revisionist discourse blended imperceptibly into another familiar one, which urged people to "move on", to "overcome the past" by resolutely not looking back. Such discourse resonated strongly with earlier notions in Spain, especially among politically and socially "defeated" constituencies, of the necessary "flight forward" into economic development and away from "terror". To this end, the old fear was still sometimes pressed into service too: in 1986, for example, when the incumbent prime minister Felipe González, leader of the social democratic PSOE, which had inherited power in 1982 from the reformist Francoist coalition, sought to turn around the national vote and bring in a referendum result in favour of Spain's full membership of NATO. To achieve this González virtually constituted a new national audience *in fear*, as he conjured unquiet memories in warning that the cost of not "moving on" would be civil conflict, national failure, apocalypse.[11]

In spite of this continuing discourse of fear "spoken" by the entire state/political class, there was still, on the social margins, some civic progress in the recuperation of the memory of a difficult past. (The concept of "memory" remains a controversial one for historians, of course. But in this chapter the term is intended to describe something relatively uncontroversial – in definition, if not in content – namely, that memory is a reasonable shorthand or figure of speech for thinking about why, in what context, and with what stakes, certain moments in the past are spoken about in the present.) As early as 1977, the now iconic comic strip *Paracuellos* appeared. It was provocatively named – for Paracuellos, the village outside Madrid where the Republicans shot over two thousand prisoners during the wartime siege of the capital,[12] lay at the heart of regime martyrology. But in the comics, Paracuellos is a state orphanage in the same location, where a group of impoverished children, sometimes from Republican families, but always from the urban and rural poor, endure the petty tyrannies and everyday barbarism of Franco's new order, as it taught them their station in life.[13]

Already by the early 1980s, too, a few local historians, usually working as citizens, or, at any rate, outside the academy, began the work of the primary recovery of the repression, even though there were still formidable political and bureaucratic obstructions as well as many practical ones.[14] From forgotten and often mouldering documentation in local archives, they produced a record of the Francoist repression, naming the dead from municipal registers and cemetery lists, thereby recreating a history for which the analogous sources in state repositories no longer existed. There also occurred the first tentative commemorations of the extrajudicially murdered victims of Francoism.[15] In small runs by engagé and/or obscure publishers, or in some cases, self-published, there also appeared the memoirs of political prisoners and the first accounts of Spanish deportees to Nazi concentration camps – books which it had been very hard if not impossible to publish in Spain much prior to 1980.[16] Many thousands of people were already involved in this recuperative and commemorative work. But it was still unreflected within the mainstream, unreported by the national media, and over it a veil of silence was drawn by state functionaries and the political class.[17]

During the 1990s the excavation of this past accelerated, also becoming more visible in the publishing and media mainstream. One of its most remarkable features was an outpouring of detailed, empirical works by historians – an important minority of whom were now university historians, but many more who were still working entirely on their own account. By the new millennium this expanding historical record was both driving, and being further driven by, the labours of an ever more dynamic memory movement rooted in civil pressure groups nationwide, which demanded the exhumation of the Republican "disappeared" from the common graves that lie all across Spain, so that the remains could be identified and reburied by family and friends.[18] This was now a populous movement, with many young people involved – Spaniards both from Spain and elsewhere, as well as a set of young international volunteers drawn from NGOs and mobilized by a burgeoning politics of human rights.[19] But just as, or indeed because, the international tectonic shift of 1989 was slowly but surely bringing all this into the mainstream in 1990s Spain, expanding the audience nationwide, it in turn provoked a Francoist backlash and through this a series of increasingly fierce memory wars which continue to rage as we enter the second decade of the twenty-first century.

Although one can accurately describe the backlash as a "nostalgic" Francoism, it is far from backward-looking. Rather, it has begun to mobilize seriously in response to a raft of progressive social reforms tabled by the incoming social democratic PSOE administration from 2004. Some of this opposition has also had to do with a 2006 educational reform which reduced the special privileges of Catholicism and made religious education *per se* an optional subject for pupils. But the high profile hysteria of those mobilizing was heavily projected onto those of the PSOE's reforms relating to gender and sexuality, especially the legalization of gay marriage and adoption.[20] Its sociological base is a fearful populist conservatism, provincial in the main, and mostly rooted in the centre-north, but with an urban and nation-wide component too. As in the 1930s, the organizational forms, strategies and discourse of this movement owe much to Spain's Catholic Church whose hierarchy today is more intransigent and fundamentalist than perhaps at any point in the last half century – certainly unrecognizable in it are the liberal currents of *aperturismo* which appeared in the years leading up to and during the transition. Beyond the specifics of the PSOE's social reforms, in their sights is a whole progressive politics of civic engagement and indeed the very principle of the social inclusion of *difference*.[21] What they want is a return to a world that accords with their own traditionalist values and moral conservatism – in the telling encapsulation of one of their spokesmen, they want "social peace" – an expression reminiscent of the search of social conservatives in 1930s Spain for an impossible "static society", but which in the twenty-first century also comprises a refusal to reflect truthfully upon the recent past. The increasing economic anxieties that nowadays also attend the moral agenda are scarcely likely to reduce the political shrillness of this emergent populist conservatism.

The assault on the memory movement in all this is emblematic. For what is being targeted is the danger posed to social conservatives that they will have to face up to a knowledge of Francoism that is incompatible with their own belief in their moral certitude. They would have to confront a story of Francoism that is not "scripted" to allow them to live with themselves.[22] Indeed any assimilation of what Francoism actually did would diminish its efficacy as a mobilizing myth (except perhaps through *ressentiment* and anger at those who "expose" these uncomfortable truths), thus undermining it as a serviceable political model for the new conservative populist nationalism. There are numerous other cases in Europe, central and east, where murderous nationalists have successfully been recycled. But what often makes this possible is some kind of interposing frame or filter via which "blame" can either be placed on Nazi occupation or, alternatively, a Stalinist enemy – or sometimes the permutation allows for both.[23] In Spain there never was any "screen" or "alibi" of foreign occupation or control to miti-gate or dilute what happened ("between nationals") in the 1930s and 1940s. The aggressor was known to be Spanish – notwithstanding the key mili-tary support provided by Nazi Germany and Fascist Italy for Franco's war effort. Thus if what was inflicted on compatriots then cannot be justified now, it throws a serious shadow not only over Francoism as a historical phenomenon, but, given the underlying continuities, also on the credibility of the state and of the new and intransigent forms of nationalism now emerging within it.

What is ultimately at stake in the memory wars between different currents in Spanish society is the need to repress the memory of Francoist state violence as the necessary price of renovating and legitimating conservative nationalism, versus the need for a full state and public acknowledgement of the depth of the damage done and social hurt inflicted by the dictatorship over four decades. There is a not inconsiderable international civic support for those inside Spain seeking to end the "impunity" of the Franco dictatorship – from the strong support of Garzón offered by associations of jurists internationally, to the young volunteers who have participated all over Spain in the digs to exhume the war graves. Politically, however, the tally is more ambiguous. There have been some significant symbolic measures by the European establishment, notably the Council of Europe's condemnation in 2006 of Franco's human rights abuses: this the first such international pronouncement of this kind since the UN's statement of diplomatic sanction in 1946. But, now as then, there exists an underlying political tension in Western political attitudes towards Franco, given the crucial and consistent support the dictatorship received into the 1970s, especially from successive US administrations. This civic–political tension beyond Spain is important because its knock-on effect within the country is to edge the political advantage towards a mobilized moral conservatism, thus allowing the maintenance of dictatorial "impunity". While these conservative sectors do not represent a majority inside Spain, it often seems as if they do because of the effects of another facet of slow-release Francoism. The longevity of the dictatorship, the unparalleled opportunities it had to shape cultural memory and public perceptions for forty years, as well as the strong retrospective sense of the smoothness of Spain's "pacted" transition, have all created for the Franco regime an amorphous air of political legitimacy among Spaniards who, while not themselves ideologically Francoist, did not experience within their own families, or otherwise directly, the dictatorship's violent and socially exclusionary policies – or who have, in some (albeit rarer) cases, actively suppressed the memory of it under the impact of Francoism's long reconstitution of public memory.

But there is more here too. Those who speak for the new populist conservatism reiterate the (old) Francoist canard that "nothing happened here [in Spain]" (*aquí no pasó nada*) and, contradictorily with the former, assert too that the victims of Francoist violence also got what they deserved because they were, *per se*, morally iniquitous. (During the papal visit to Spain in

August 2011, the ecclesiastical authorities in Madrid saw fit to distribute
to the young faithful gathered for the event a handbook in which the political and religious conflict of the 1930s in Spain was described in terms so
crude and manichean – the 'martyring' of the Church and the Catholic
faithful – as to be indistinguishable from Francoist propaganda.[24]) In
behaving thus, not only do ultramontane conservatives continue denying
the legitimacy of the civic memory movement and its claims to speak for
those dead traduced by a dictatorial state, they also implicitly cast doubt
on the idea that a primary function of the state in Spain today is to guarantee the civil rights of all its citizens, irrespective of their differences. What
is taking shape here is an ascendant political fundamentalism, operating
within a constitutional order and counterposed to a movement which
understands democracy differently – as necessarily including a symbolic
pact between the living and the unquiet dead, a pact that by definition
invokes a notion of solidarity across time, but which also has the potential
to generate tangible benefits of social empathy and cohesion for today's
society in Spain.

The sheer intensity of these present-day memory wars in Spain is only
properly explicable, then, in terms of their high stakes for current and future
politics – both as a specific social agenda, and as a vision of the values that
should inhabit the state. The *substance* of the wars, however, is only intelligible in the light of the Franco regime's singular historical trajectory as "the
undefeated". The temporal disjunctures this has continually produced from
the 1980s to the 2010s are striking although, in fact, these could already
be glimpsed before the end of the dictatorship, as for example in the case of
Spaniards conscripted by the Franco regime in the early 1940s and sent to
Germany as labourers for the Reich's war effort, who were subsequently paid
compensation by the West German government – a compensation which
arrived to them in their villages where they were still subject to a regime
that had never publicly admitted the error of Nazism, still less engaged in
any process of social and cultural denazification or anti-Nazi public
discourse.[25]

Strange times: temporal disjunctures in "post-Franco" Spain

In a summer long ago, far longer than the chronological distance suggests,
and at the height of the process of constitutional change in Spain in 1977,
the then newly-appointed Bishop of Zamora met with the niece and
daughter of Amparo Barayón who had been murdered by a Francoist death

squad in October 1936 (see chapter 3 above).[26] The occasion of the meeting was a visit to Spain by her daughter, Andrea Sender Barayón, who as a baby had been incarcerated along with her mother, but who since the 1940s had lived in the US. In adult life Andrea had taken religious orders, returning to Zamora in 1977, in her early forties, as Sister Benedicta of the Order of Saint Helena. In this meeting the bishop apologized to her and to Amparo's niece, Magdalena Maes, on behalf of the Spanish Catholic Church, especially for the additional misery which had been caused to Amparo in her final hours by the priest who had refused her absolution – for although she was a practising Catholic, her marriage to Ramón Sender had been in a civil ceremony. This encounter spoke to a spirit of *aggiornamento* that had inhabited the Spanish Church at the time of the transition, evoking too the final residues of the Vatican's own in a process that reached back to the briefly liberalizing influence of the Second Vatican Council.[27] Exchanges such as these give a sense of the atmosphere, allowing us to glimpse the openness and possibility, which also permitted the first few tentative exhumations in the late 1970s and early 80s of other victims of Francoist extrajudicial murder. But this was rapidly brought to an abrupt halt by the brute force explosion of the past in the form of the attempted military coup of February 1981, the *Tejerazo*. Even though it failed in its attempt to reverse the constitutional order in Spain, like the at once distant and near coup of July 1936, relative failure would also mean success by other means. For a long time after the *Tejerazo* many things lay broken – among them the possibility of a more open public attitude to the recent past, which lay trapped beneath a powerful recrudescent fear.

Emblematic of this crushing fear, as well as of what turned out to be the loaded political dice of the transition, is the story of the film director Fernando Ruiz Vergara (1942–2011) and his ill-fated documentary, *Rocío*. Made in 1980 and originally selected by the culture ministry of new constitutional Spain for the 1981 Venice Biennale, it offers an oblique but also mercilessly forensic dissection of the power structures, both religious and secular, behind one of Spain's most famous popular Catholic festivals – the *Romería* of Rocío, in Huelva (Andalusia) in the rural south, which was – and is – symbolic of that "folkloric Spain" so vaunted and exploited by the dictatorship. Ruiz Vergara's film took on, then, the sacred cows of the Spanish right. As if this was not challenge enough, *Rocío* was, in effect, also the first documentary ever made on the Francoist repression. For it named and displayed both the victims and perpetrators of the "cleansing" violence following the military coup of 18 July 1936 in the small town of Almonte, which was the neighbouring town whose municipality owned the hamlet of El Rocío. In spite of ministerial imprimatur and critical acclaim, however, the film and its director were both about to become notable victims of resurgent Francoism, and in ways that endure to this day. On 23 February 1981, the very morning of the *Tejerazo*, the sons of an ex-mayor and landowner identified in *Rocío* as bearing a major responsibility for the killing, filed a case against Ruiz Vergara for defamation which they would in due course win – courtesy of judges who had been trained and appointed by the dictatorship – and which saw the director heavily fined, imprisoned, and professionally wrecked.[28]

But even more devastating for democracy in Spain was the fact that alongside the director in the dock was the resident from Almonte whose oral testimony, as someone who had lived through the period of vigilante terror in the town, had named the ex-mayor as being among the perpetrators. On trial here too, then was the very use of (a necessarily indirect) oral testimony as evidence in cases of extrajudicial killing. "Hearsay" is of course a problematic commodity, and we have seen how it was systematically abused in the Francoist military courts when they tried thousands of Republicans. But *Rocío* was not a court of law – an option that was indeed closed to Republican victims by the terms of the October 1977 amnesty law, fruit of the transition, which protected all servants of the Franco state, or those acting in its name, from prosecution for any act committed in its service. *Rocío* was then serving as a forum for a survivor of a victim group to speak publicly of what had happened – and no one at the trial, prosecution included, ever disputed the facts of the case – that one hundred local civilians had been killed by Francoist vigilantes in Almonte in July 1936. This was simply never discussed, a matter of no "relevance" to the court case. The judges ruled inadmissible seventeen corroborating testimonies from other villagers, opining instead it was exceedingly "inopportune" that the film had raised any of these matters at all.[29] Time and again – for the case went through more than one court and then to appeal – the judges found in favour of plaintiffs whose clear objective was to close down discussion of the events. That this was more than a personal matter too is clear from the coded wording of the case filed that February day in 1981 and which referred to the film as having insulted the Catholic religion and outraged public sentiment.

As a result of the verdict, delivered in 1985, *Rocío* was censored to remove references to the alleged perpetrator. It was even seized by the authorities – the first film ever to be so in democratic Spain – after a southern television station screened it *in its censored form*. For many years thereafter it was also subject to a *de facto* ban – a ban that still haunts the public sphere today, as we shall see later in this chapter. The outcome of the *Rocío* case, in the army-invigilated democracy that followed the *Tejerazo*'s "failure", meant, in effect, that the mortal victims of the Franco state were as if killed again, as the pall of silence was redrawn. After nearly half a century of the victors' justice, how else could what had happened in Almonte in July 1936 have come into the public domain except through a piece of courageous oral testimony? For if the testimony-giver had indeed been a direct observer of the events he recounted then he too would have been among the murdered. As it was, he was judicially sanctioned for speaking out. The afterlife of Francoist violence which had, for many decades, wrought its effect by remaining "unspeakable", emerged here again to reimpose its vicious discipline – but this time in a democratic court of law.

It would take the best part of another decade, and the wave of obstinate, snail's pace local historical research to create the *empirical* potential for a re-emergence of the victims' voices. Unjust though it was in view of the broader context, sociological Francoism could dispute oral testimony if this was the only evidence of its crimes. But it could not dispute the contemporary written record of murder that fortunately still remained – in the lines of the civil (death) registers, as well as in more than a few other local and provincial archives, often buried long forgotten in their remotest recesses.[30] It was this steady work by historians that would provide a solid base from which to launch the memory movement of the 1990s. Under the impact of European change from 1989, Spain's civic memory movement also took a step forward into the relative mainstream, as a new generation – the grandchildren, and in some cases the great grandchildren – standing further removed from the fear, took up the task of recovery. Indeed the largest and most prominent of Spain's civic memory associations, the Asociación para la Recuperación de la Memoria Histórica (ARMH) itself grew out of one person's search for the remains of his own grandfather, shot, like Amparo Barayón, in October 1936 in the military rebels' heartland of León.[31] By the early years of the twenty-first century it was already a nationwide initiative and an internationally recognized one, although inside Spain still dependent on the financial and physical support of a myriad volunteers in the face of the frequent suspicion, if not downright opposition, of the state and public authorities of whatever political hue.

Within the broad civic memory movement, differences of emphasis have arisen over what constitutes an adequate politics of commemoration. Not everyone has been convinced of the need for exhumations, arguing instead for a process limited to naming the victims through historical investigation and via the ceremonial placing of physical forms of commemoration (sculptures, memorial stones or plaques etc.); and indeed sheer economics, among other logistical impediments, will inevitably mean that only a tiny minority can or will ever be exhumed. Nevertheless, the very strong desire of many relatives for the physical retrieval of the remains of those they have lost is noteworthy. As Mercedes Kemp, the great-niece of Amparo Barayón, expressed it recently in regard of her two great uncles, Antonio and Saturnino (both of whom, as we saw in chapter 3, remain among the disappeared): "naming the lost is important for sure, but I want those bones . . . I want those bones".[32] The power of the civic memory movement in Spain today derives in large part from its singular ability to *name* things, to call extrajudicial murder by its rightful name, to exorcize the sinister euphemisms written on falsified death certificates or in Francoist police reports. One can also read this desire to retrieve the physical remains as a historical effect in itself. For the driving desire is, in some measure, connected to reversing what Francoism did – which was to disappear these people and to consign their dead bodies to unmarked ground (albeit often well "marked" in the minds of the local population) – intended as a symbolic measure of their exclusion from the nation; of their "worthlessness", of their reduction to bare life: those who can be killed, but not sacrificed.[33]

The singular power of naming is of course also strongly attested to by the fact that this was exactly what the Franco regime itself had done with those dead it made its "own" in 1939–40, indeed precisely through the action of naming (those "who fell for God and Spain", *los caídos por Dios y por España*), continuing to "own" them in unchanged form throughout its near forty-year existence, with effects that were neither healing nor redeeming. The symbolically crucial dead here were those who had been extrajudicially murdered in Republican territory. Much more than the ones who had died on the battlefield, it was these others – largely, though not exclusively, civilian dead – who were the ones "named" for, and thus appropriated by, the Francoist state through a complex process of mass denunciation and military trials in the 1940s, as we have seen in chapter 6. These dead were in some regards the antithesis of the Republican disappeared in that their deaths were, from the start, supercharged with state symbolism and the disinterred bodies of many of them (such as those at Paracuellos, but there are many other examples) were made highly visible in the 1940s as part of a ceremonial process of state "sanctification".[34] Thus were these dead reproduced as "the martyrs of the cause", a process bolstered through a vast state-promoted, nationwide system of witness-bearing tribunals called the *Causa General* whose political objective was to prove the barbarity and iniquity of all things – and people – connected to the defeated Republic.

In doing so, the regime was taking these dead and reducing the meaning of both their lives and deaths to a binary and homogenizing narrative endlessly instrumentalized as the core political legitimation of itself. The fact that "ordinary Francoists" found tremendous emotional solace in the *Causa General* and in the regime's reinterpretation of their grief and their dead does not, of course, gainsay the argument. Borrowing from the anthropologist Michael Taussig, we could say that the Francoist dead lie under the spell of a malevolent state.[35] That state has gone, but its narrative enthralls those deaths still today. It is for this reason that the Francoist dead and the Republican dead are still not, nor ever were in the 1980s and 1990s, similar quantities to be "remembered and named". They cannot yet be precisely because of the still live meanings created by the Franco regime itself. The naming and releasing of the Republican dead which was gathering pace towards the end of the 1990s might have functioned as a staging post to release all the dead and to defuse the toxic myths of Francoism, in order that the Spanish population as a whole could recognize the complexities of the civil war for what they were, thereby disarming the war's still potent mythologies. What has occurred in Spain since the early years of the twenty-first century has not been this, but instead a gradual rehabilitation and reinforcement of civil war myth by a new populist conservatism inside the country which, while it clothes itself in neo-Francoist garb, increasingly draws its real and abiding force from parallel developments elsewhere across the continent that have seen the growing ascendancy of forms of highly intolerant populist ultra-nationalism. These currents are still, to some extent, constrained by a pre-existing broader European discourse of human rights, but not unduly – as we can see from the successful obstruction of Garzón.

It is not the purpose of the analysis that follows here to explore the wider empirical ramifications of these political shifts which, in Spain, as elsewhere, have to do with rapid social and economic change, including, most obviously, the impact of globalization, and especially of cyclical economic crisis, along with perceptions of a rarified and highly bureaucratized EU, and, particularly in Spain's case, inward economic migration which until the 1980s and 90s contemporary Spaniards had almost virtually no experience of – Spain having been, since the nineteenth century and throughout the Franco dictatorship, a country of outward migration. Nor will this analysis chart the burgeoning organizational links, both formal and informal, between the various European ultranationalisms; rather it will concentrate on exploring how this new continental climate has caused the still sociologically Francoist Spanish right to "lose its shame". Whereas at the time of the transition in the late 1970s and early 1980s a substantially different political climate in Europe required sociological and other unreconstructed Francoists to use a relatively more guarded language, especially to external audiences, the changes in that climate have meant a turnaround in what it feels able to say publicly. We should note too that, while Spain has its share of extreme right-wing organizations – many which can trace a genealogy of some sort back to Blas Piñar's *Fuerza Nueva*, the now defunct party which inherited the Falange's mantle during the transition – here we are really still referring to a set of political and social fundamentalisms *that inhabit the "mainstream" right* in the shape of the Partido Popular which consistently and to this day has sought to block – both nationally and internationally – all measures aimed at delegitimizing the Franco regime.[36]

Previous elisions around the Nazi past within conservative thinking and discourse in Spain also broke the surface in 1999 when, under the incumbency of the Popular Party, Spain's Ministry of Foreign Affairs was still denying historical researchers access to the personal files of Nazis who had taken refuge in Franco's Spain – on the grounds that such access would constitute an infringement of their right to safety and privacy.[37] Until well into the 1990s, when the social democratic PSOE was in power, it was still also perfectly legal – as well as far from socially unacceptable – for positive public portrayals of Nazism to be broadcast quite openly in the Spanish media.[38] By the end of the 1990s Spain had come more into Western line on the legal question of outright Holocaust denial – i.e. it became illegal in Spain too to justify it. But there remain some remarkable temporal and other unevennesses in evidence. There could be no clearer indication of this than the small, privately-placed commemorative death notice which was accepted for publication in *La Razón,* Spain's nationwide Catholic daily newspaper in December 2009, *and without any ensuing polemic in the political mainstream*: it was a fulsome commemorative death notice to SS-Aufseherin Irma Grese, sentenced at the Belsen trial and executed on that day in 1945, and which read – "your death was unjust and unnecessary and you deserve to be commemorated. I hope to see you one day in Heaven, with your sweet smile. *Hasta siempre.*"[39] Of course Spain would not be the only European country where one might adduce to the promulgation of Holocaust denial legislation other – pragmatic if not cynical – political motives or, at the very least, indicate that the existence of such legislation can so easily become reduced to a *bienpensant* discourse that in fact encourages not mindfulness but forgetfulness, while also having little effect on really existing intolerance or racist practices.[40]

In the new twenty-first century Europe of revivifying ultra-nationalism which is rehabilitating fascist and other nationalist collaborators of the Nazis, it is therefore unsurprising to find Franco being lionized as a strong and patriotic leader by Poland's Law and Justice party – whose leader caused a storm in 2001 by opposing a national apology for the Jedwabne pogrom when he implicitly denied the responsibility of "ordinary Poles" for the massacre of their Jewish neighbours in July 1941. (During the time of writing – late August 2011 – the local memorial at Jedwabne was vandalized.[41]) Indeed, Law and Justice, in government in March 2007, announced their intention to remove state pensions from the twenty-five still-living Polish citizens who had fought for the Spanish Republic as volunteers in the International Brigades, declaring, in a pure recycling of Francoist and cold war myth, that these individuals had fought for an anti-patriotic cause and also to install Stalinism in Spain. In the event, in May 2011 the incumbent PSOE government extracted from its Polish counterpart a promise that it would in fact honour these pensions. But the symbolic assault remains. The Polish brigaders have been airbrushed from the official history and on the tomb of the unknown soldier in Warsaw which carries a list of the principal battles in which Poles have participated, the names of those fought on behalf of the Spanish Republic – Jarama, Brunete and the Ebro – have been removed.[42] Whilst these populist nationalist currents have a higher profile currently in central and east Europe, they are also present in clearly identifiable forms in western Europe too: for example in Belgium where, as part of a long running crisis which has a strong ethnic charge, a proposal to accept draft legislation seeking to annul all sentences against Nazi collaborators, effectively amnestying them, was in May 2011 approved by a Senate majority that included social democrats.

> To articulate the past historically [. . .] means to seize hold of a memory
> as it flashes up in a moment of danger.[43]

Inside Spain it was the loss of national elections by the Partido Popular in March 2004 – itself triggered by a notorious bout of (atavistic?) Francoist behaviour in the wake of the Atocha train bombing – which would more or less inaugurate the new right's rapid moral offensive. It went into action against the PSOE government's social and educational reforms. In shades of the 1930s, mass mobilized Catholicism inveighed against "change coming from Madrid", and the many lay associations, including of Catholic parents and teachers – bussed thousands of provincial protestors to the capital to demonstrate on the streets.[44]

Meanwhile, in the conservative heartlands whence they came, the "time" of an unexorcized and unconquered sociological Francoism still ran on the clock. A perfect example of the phenomenon appeared in July 2004 in Zamora when the city's main newspaper published what can only be described as a broadside against the memory of Amparo Barayón in which she was described as an emotionally disturbed woman "in the last stages of syphilis".[45] The slander was delivered by the granddaughter of the medic who had served as prison doctor during the time of Amparo's incarceration in Zamora gaol in 1936. The occasion of the granddaughter's angry – and of course highly symbolic – outburst was an interview to mark the ceremonial presentation of her grandfather's portrait to the local authorities in Zamora.[46] The substance behind it, however, ran much longer and deeper – namely the annoyance of the doctor's family at the challenge to their "truth" of the past posed since the memoir of Amparo written by her son had been published in 1990.[47] Much like the sons of the ex-mayor of Almonte, the prison doctor's granddaughter sought to "put things right" – albeit in her case mainly within the limited ambit of a provincial newspaper.

It would take several months for the polemic to ignite because Amparo Barayón's family, unlike those of the doctor, had been scattered across different regions, countries and even continents by the effects of the Franco dictatorship. But once they had coordinated their efforts to demand of the granddaughter a retraction, then the turn of events would demonstrate to perfection how little had changed in Spain since the *Rocío* court case, indeed, in some ways, how little had changed in terms of the unspoken assumptions inhabiting parts of Zamora's public culture since the configuration of power which in October 1936 had taken Amparo's life. The ensuing polemic in the columns of the press did not involve the granddaughter of the doctor, for she never "spoke" again, not deigning to reply to the Barayón family, either publicly or privately. Instead, the retaining classes of Zamora were mobilized in defence of its local dignitary, the prison doctor and the good family to which he belonged, and against the upstart and "outsider" Barayóns. Leading the assault was the town's local chronicler – thus indicating too how not all practitioners of history had the uncovering of the difficult past as their aim, and indeed that some were aiming to keep the lid firmly on. The chronicler was astute enough to realize, however, that the reference to syphilis weakened the family's case and thus made an attempt to downplay it. But, just like the judges who had tried *Rocío* nearly a quarter of a century earlier, he also passed over the fact of extrajudicial murder which lay at the heart of the story, choosing instead, in the stream of articles he published in a clear attempt to drown out the Barayóns' core arguments, to concentrate on the minor details of the events and personages of summer and autumn 1936 in Zamora.[48]

In these newspaper articles the chronicler also displayed an insider's knowledge of this – albeit often peripheral – detail, thus displaying another tic inherited from high Francoism – namely that of "approved" historians appropriating public documents as if they were personal property and then excluding others from sight or use of them. Significant too in his account was an inclination to attribute the lethal violence of summer 1936 not to Zamora's rebel military authorities and their Falangist servants, but to this or that bad apple or itinerant psychopath who had just happened to "join up". By spinning this mythology, he was also disseminating a version of the post-coup killing in July 1936 which absolved the social establishment of Zamora of any responsibility for it.

As for Amparo Barayón, her fate was once again buried beneath the ornate, time-locked prose of the chronicler. For the object in play was none other than to ensure, through this rearguard action in the press, the re-establishing of the authority of members of Zamora's social elites which had descended through Francoism and across the transition without ever having their local power challenged within their *demesne*. In all this, moreover, the chronicler succeeded – albeit in a very small pool. For, in spite of a number of attempts, neither the doctor's granddaughter, nor her family nor the local newspaper has been successfully brought to account for what was said. Nor has anyone issued either an apology or a rectification in regard of Amparo Barayón, who, when she displayed signs of emotional distress during those days of her incarceration, did so not for reasons of physical illness, but because she had been imprisoned without trial, was sick with worry for her two young children, had been subject to sustained psychological abuse by a prison priest, and knew that she stood on the verge of being killed – as indeed was the outcome of her six-week imprisonment, on 11 October 1936.

Just as one unquiet ghost stalked the lines of the press in a provincial town in the north-west of Spain in April 2005 so, at the very same time in the south, that of *Rocío* would make its reappearance. This happened when a civic memory organization in Huelva announced its intention to screen the documentary at an event which would also be an homage to its director, Ruiz Vergara, who, ever since the court case, had resided in Portugal. But immediately the announcement was made, there arose intense local pressure from both the family of the plaintiffs of the 1981 court case and from other quarters within the local conservative establishment to halt the screening, and when the organizers stood firm, then to ensure, that, even in 2005, only the version censored in the early 1980s could be screened.[49]

These events in the north and south of Spain took place against an increasing number of court cases in which relatives of deceased perpetrators brought ideologically charged cases for defamation against historians and journalists who had examined instances of Francoist crime, in order to silence them and ensure that the history of this particular episode of state crime could never be written with real names.[50] The danger here was not that the plaintiffs always won in these later court cases – and certainly they did not win in the terms that some of them had clearly aspired to – but that the very mounting of such cases was effectively propagating a continued climate of fear which discouraged further similar investigations. That such plaintiffs were ever able to get beyond first base was of course entirely written into the tacit dispositions of the transitional process, which had thus led to a situation where justice had been turned on its head, and where those who were complicit in a murderous system were repeatedly able to sue the victims of that system, or those speaking in their name.

Nor is it hugely clear that the historical memory law of 2007 has tipped the balance much in favour of the victims. The law is without doubt a symbolic achievement, although, even as a symbolic measure, it only became possible through the change in political incumbency from the Popular Party to PSOE (the Spanish social democratic party) in March 2004. It also makes provision for a state census of the dead and disappeared – although it is less clear on the resources to be made available for achieving this. But given the longstanding preference across Spain's entire political class to close down a discussion of the past, then it is also not surprising that the tenor of the law seeks, as it were, *an end in symbolism*, but does not offer any means of allowing citizens to address what was actually done to whom, by whom and why. As such, the law has been criticized both by international jurists, and by various human rights bodies and other NGOs, including Amnesty International and Equipo Nizkor.[51]

The focus of their concern is that the law is one of *punto final* (full stop), very like the notorious law of 1986 in Argentina that put an end to the pros-ecution of state personnel for extrajudicial killing and torture committed during the dictatorship of 1976–83, but which was declared unconstitu-tional in 2005 in regard of those offences which were crimes against humanity. While these criticisms would be more accurately levelled at Spain's 1977 Amnesty Law, it is nevertheless true that the 2007 law, while it ostensibly addresses what is due to the victims of Francoism, also protects to a very high degree the right of perpetrators to "privacy" – effectively anonymity. So it is a law which identifies victims and abuse, but no abusers, and in terms of everyday practice offers no solution to an enduring state obstructionism: there are ageing victims who find themselves up against this wall if they try to find out who their denouncers were.[52] Nor has there been any response from either the executive or judiciary in Spain to the UN's formal call in 2008 for them to investigate human rights abuses committed by the Franco regime and also, crucially, to revoke the earlier amnesty law, since this covered crimes against humanity to which no statute of limitations applies and regarding which no individual sovereign state has the right to offer amnesty. This too was the assumption which underpinned Garzón's bid in 2008 to oblige the Spanish authorities to back a judicial investigation that could bring into political focus nationwide the opening of the mass graves and what they meant. The result was not this, however, but a judiciary in a western European constitutional democracy which indicted, in May 2010 suspended, and in due course is likely completely to cashier, a judge who sought to investigate the whereabouts of its extrajudicially murdered citizens.

The attempt by Garzón to bring state action to bear in Spain also extended to other areas of Francoist human rights abuse, most notably the case of children stolen from Republicans, often while their mothers were prisoners, and illegally adopted by pro-regime families (discussed in chapters 3 and 6 above). Not only did this too fall with the rest of Garzón's bid, but in the course of 2011 it has now also become apparent that the child trafficking which began in this way in the 1940s continued in Spain right into the 1990s.[53] There has inevitably been some mutation in the nature of this activity – from the overt political repression of the 1940s to the moral agendas of the 1950s and 60s (taking babies from the poorer – often urban migrant labouring – classes, including (but not exclusively) from un-married mothers) to the more overtly profit-motivated "business" of the 1980s onwards – although money became a major propelling factor long ago, once the whole enterprise became privatized in the 1950s. But for all the surface mutation, the underlying continuities are striking: not only are the victims drawn from the same social classes as the ones targeted politically by Francoism – and when one considers the "moral" criteria of the later trafficking, we need to keep in mind too the regime's hallmark definition of its political enemies as "moral degenerates". But the perpetrators too are drawn from the same sectors of politically conservative professionals – lawyers and doctors for obvious reasons – with family or other connections to the dictatorship's power networks or to its constitutive political clienteles which, as we have already seen, were not in any serious way disarticulated by the process of transition. Crucially too, this decades-long trafficking has depended on the involvement of Catholic Church personnel – whether those working in hospitals or children's homes – a fact that has redoubled the strength of the controversy currently exploding in Spain, as new civic pressure groups of victims are formed and the full extent of the scandal is revealed by the work of investigative journalists.

For a historian taking the longer view, one thing is clear: that the attitudes of powerful and socially conservative elites towards the poor and marginalized have remained in the mould of those expressed with such searing memorability in Carlos Giménez's cult cartoon, *Paracuellos*, first published at the start of the transition in the 1970s, but conjuring the world of powerlessness and "impunity" enshrined in the Francoist state orphanages of the 1940s. Notwithstanding the clear financial engine driving this subsequent form of human rights abuse in Spain, it is, nevertheless, still a Francoist paradigm that informs it – yet another re-appearance, then, of the dictatorship's afterlife of violence, as well as an indirect reminder of what it was that the Second Republic sought structurally to challenge in 1931.[54] Faced by today's scandal of stolen children, the Spanish state is keen to help – provided no one mentions the legacy of Francoist political and social values which still clothe the events. Perhaps this assistance is intended as compensation in the light of Garzón's failure. And the powerless too can make the calculation demanded by political realism: best to accept whatever institutional support is available on the state's terms, because the example of the judge who challenged the system, with all his insider power and political and cultural capital, is there for all to see.

Nor should it really take a historian to point out the links between the unspoken social assumptions underpinning the child trafficking and a state memory law that treats the perpetrators of state and social violence as equally deserving of consideration as their victims. It is an equation that can only give succour in those sectors of Spanish society where the whole of the memory movement and the opening up of the difficult past can still provoke the comment: "But what do they want? After all, we *forgave* them".[55] It is arguable too that the continuing failure to broadcast the documentary *Mari-Carmen España: the End of Silence* in Spain is related to its most notorious component (freely available however on YouTube for those who are motivated enough to look) where the Abbot of Franco's mausoleum in the Valley of the Fallen is recorded on film denying the regime's repression while simultaneously justifying it, and all in a language that, while it may still be common in certain Spanish drawing rooms, is simply too overt and unresconstructed to be assimilated to Spain's twenty-first-century conservative nationalism.

The social and political fossilization which speaks through commentaries such as these was arguably also greatly reinforced by another singular elision of the political transition – namely the decision to keep closed the files of those who had been the dictatorship's informers. The power of armed Francoism prevented it anyway. But to have opened the files would have obliged an acknowledgment by both state and society of the extent of Francoism's "everyday barbarism" in its most socially erosive form, the complicity of ordinary nationals in the repression of their compatriots. The price of not confronting this question, in "covering for Francoism", in not drawing a line between this kind of practice and the norms of a constitutional democracy, has perpetuated or indeed increased public disengagement, through a tendency uncritically to accept the prevailing "order", and to view the evidence of financial corruption and political clientelism as inalterable, and thus all political questions, indeed politics itself, cynically as part of a *Systemzeit*.[56] The current extra-parliamentary protest movement of the *indignados* in Spain may potentially make some healthy inroads into this. But the weakness of the movement is precisely at the level of policy, not protest – and it has an entire political machine against it, not just "the right", so what its lasting impact will be remains uncertain. What is certain is that to date attitudes of majority disengagement have eased the rapid rise in the new century of forms of ultra-nationalism which – in southern Europe just as in the centre and east – depend to a significant degree for their success on a historical vacuum, that is to say an absence of knowledge about the recent past; or, as has frequently occurred, the filling of the vacuum with highly selective versions of that past.[57]

Conclusion

The ascendancy of ultra-nationalist myths in Spain, even though their ideologically convinced believers are a minority, is being facilitated by the increasing blockage of the memory wave, in spite – or perhaps even because of the forms of – the 2007 Memory Law, and certainly after Garzón's stellar defeat. With the triumph of the Popular Party on 20 November 2011 in a general election dominated by the debt crisis and nearly five million unemployed, *desmemoria* is likely now to be in the ascendant. This in spite of the luminous work of citizenship and solidarity epitomized by Mari-Carmen España, the grandchild and her gaze at the heart of Martin Jönsson's film who, in seeking to uncover the remains of her extrajudicially murdered grandfather, did so in the full knowledge that this was not only a debt paid to the past, but also a restorative act revivifying democracy which, by definition, is never passively possessed nor secure unless we engage in "doing" it as an everyday, inclusive practice. In the meanwhile, and politically convenient for some, *desmemoria* is allowed its head by the *Systemzeit* disillusion of the majority. Once upon a time in Spain, *cuando la transición*, the population was told to abandon the past and "look forward" to a promise of economic growth and consumerist plenty, via entry to what was then called the EEC (European Economic Community). In other words, consumerism was being posited as an alternative to democratic memory itself – by which is meant a publicly-circulating understanding of the past that fully encompasses the human stories of the cost of historical change (an understanding to which this book seeks to contribute). But that "deal" is now undeliverable – even to those Spaniards whom the difficult past does not touch at a personal or family level. Moreover, in the current enveloping economic crisis, and where the national idea is still live and legitimate, there arises an alternative scenario in which fears about an uncertain economic future, in the face of an international banking crisis, and with very high youth unemployment, will arm, in Spain as elsewhere, an intransigent and socially intolerant ultra-nationalist politics far beyond its ideological core – and one whose consequences, however sleek and sanitized the public "spin", would be highly unpredictable and potentially lethal.

The hybrid components that have come together in the civic memory movement in Spain in many ways exemplify how the existence of difficult pasts right across the European continent can and has precipitated "communities of memory and civic-mindedness" which are not congruent with, nor delimited by, the nation states in which they arise: for these are communities existing transnationally just as they also exist transgenerationally, crossing many other cultural and material borders too, but always committed to uncovering the past, and, in the process, disarming the lethal myths of nationalism. Their power is that they constitute a permanent act of witness to the extrajudicially murdered as our *irreparable*, as the rip in modernity, the fatal flaw in the "national" idea. The challenge of our times, by no means an easy one, is to find a way to mobilize that power in a politically effective way. For the moment, these visible acts of witness represent the best holding action we have against resurgent fascism. They also function to remind us that one of the most urgent challenges of the twenty-first century is to find effective ways to prevent the mythologizing of our fears. That is an anti-utopian utopian goal. It is also very likely to be the price of our survival as something worthy of the name "humanity".

Glossary

An asterisk indicates that the term also appears in the glossary.

ARMH: Asociación para la Recuperación de la Memoria Histórica (Association for the Recuperation of Historical Memory) – the largest of Spain's civic memory associations.

Carlists/Carlism: Navarre-based brand of Catholic traditionalism that backed the military rising in July 1936, contributing paramilitaries known as the *requetés*.

Causa General: (General Cause) – a nationwide system of witness-bearing tribunals established by the Franco regime to enquire into crimes and alleged crimes committed in the wartime Republican zone.

CEDA: Confederación Española de Derechas Autónomas (Spanish Confederation of Right-wing Groups) – nationwide mass Catholic party established in 1933.

CICRC: Commission Internationale contre le régime concentrationnaire (International Commission against Concentration Camp Regimes) – established under UN auspices by former deportees of Nazi concentration camps.

Civil Guard: a militarized police force with a reputation for brutality, originally founded in the mid-nineteenth century to enforce a highly unequal social order in rural Spain. Demilitarized after the end of the Franco dictatorship.

CNT: Confederación Nacional del Trabajo (National Confederation of Labour) – anarcho-syndicalist labour union founded in 1910.

COPE: Cadena de Ondas Populares Españolas – radio station owned by the Catholic Church which broadcasts nationwide in Spain.

CPUSA: Communist Party of the USA.

DDR: German Democratic Republic (1949–1990).

Desmemoria: forgetfulness, absence of mind – but used particularly to refer to the "historical amnesia" underpinning the transitional process in Spain, and which has ever since haunted its public sphere in matters of the difficult and violent recent past.

ETA: Euskadi ta Askatasuna (Basque Homeland and Liberty) radical Basque nationalist organization established in 1959 and adopting a strategy of violent direct action from the 1960s.

FAI: Federación Anarquista Ibérica – Spanish anarchist federation founded in 1927 with the ostensible aim of defending core anarchist principles in the CNT*.

Falange: Spanish Fascist Party – founded in 1933 and later coopted by Franco (along with the Carlists*) as the basis of the single party of the regime.

Fuerza Nueva: neo-fascist party that inherited the mantle of the Falange* during Spain's democratic transition – dedicated to defending the core values of the Francoist state and the military coup of 17–18 July 1936 .

HUAC: House Un-American Activities Committee – US House of Representatives committee established in the late 1930s to investigate matters of internal security and which focused intensively on alleged communist subversion during the 1940s and 1950s.

Indignados: one of the names given to the grass roots movement of civic protest which crystallized on 15 May 2011 (15-M), calling for a more active and participatory form of politics in Spain to deliver real democracy, thus ending the domination of two 'machine-parties' – PP* and PSOE*.

JAP: Juventudes de Acción Popular – the CEDA's* rapidly fascistized youth movement which passed virtually *en masse* to the Falange* in the summer of 1936.

JSU: Juventudes Socialistas Unificadas (JSU) – the united socialist-communist youth organization initiated in April 1936, and by November 1936 (with the siege of Madrid) entirely in the political orbit of the Spanish Communist Party (PCE*).

KPD: Kommunistische Partei Deutschlands (German Communist Party) – founded December 1918.

MOI: *Main d'oeuvre immigrée* (Migrant labour front) – a French trade union organization for migrant workers which during the Nazi occupation became an important element of the armed urban resistance.

NKVD: Soviet intelligence service.

OSS: Office of Strategic Services – a force of irregular operatives (among whom many American International Brigade veterans figured) recruited by the US authorities for service in occupied Europe.

PCE: Partido Comunista de España – the Spanish Communist Party.

PP: Partido Popular (PP)*– the conservative Popular Party. Emerging from Alianza Popular, the ideological heir of Francoism, the PP is now, along with the PSOE*, one of the two mainstream parties of government in post-Franco Spain.

PSOE: Partido Socialista Obrero Español – Spain's social democratic party. It dominated the governments of the immediate post-transition period and has since alternated in power with the conservative PP* (Popular Party).

retirada: (retreat) describes the exodus to France of Spanish civilians and soldiers of the Republican army (including International Brigaders) in late January/early February 1939, as Catalonia fell to Franco's forces.

romería: a popular religious pilgrimage/festival.

SED: Sozialistische Einheitspartei Deutschlands (Socialist Unity Party of Germany) – the governing party of the German Democratic Republic (DDR)*.

Systemzeit: "time of the system" – originally a national socialist-coined criticism of the Weimar period of government as 'inorganic', impersonal and remote from the needs of ordinary people. More generally the term alludes to popular alienation from politics, perceived as remote, self-serving and clientelist, sometimes also corrupt (see *indignados** above).

UGT: Unión General de Trabajadores – socialist-led trade union founded in 1888. Historically the labour wing of the PSOE*, from which it in practice decoupled during the liberal market reforms of the 1980s.

UNPROFOR: United Nations Protection Force, operative during the Yugoslav wars of the 1990s.

VALB: Veterans of the Abraham Lincoln Brigade.

Volksgemeinschaft: ("community of the people") – a term now synonymous with Hitler's "organic" national community, the construction of which lay at the heart of the Nazi project. It was predicated upon the brutal and absolute exclusion of all racial and political "enemies" as well as those deemed socially "inadaptable". Originally the term was used across the German political spectrum to denote the ideal of a non-class based society.

Notes

Introduction

1 Jennifer Tucker with Tina Campt, "Entwined Practices: Engagements with Photography in Historical Inquiry", *History and Theory* Theme Issue 48 (December 2009): 3.

2 Noteworthy in most cases, however, is the presence of a colonial experience – whether within European space or beyond.

3 Winfried Georg Sebald, *Austerlitz* (London: Penguin, 2002), pp. 22–3 (first published in the original German and in English translation in 2001).

4 By the 1980s the constituent republics of Yugoslavia were locked in battles over the distribution of revenue and resources which would eventually become constitutional issues. The waning of the Cold War had meant the end of Western readiness to allow Yugoslavia easy (or, at any rate, easier) economic terms. In 1980 the IMF imposed – as the terms of continued loans to Yugoslavia – a set of harsh "recovery" measures (dinar devaluation, real interest rates and free movement of prices). By the end of the 1980s there was high inflation and an unemployment rate of nearly 20 percent and the gap between the richer and poorer republics had increased considerably. The ensuing rows over political forms (decentralization versus more centralization) were integrally linked to these economic issues, with Serbia (poorer than Slovenia and Croatia, though richer than Bosnia, Macedonia and Kosovo) seeking to prevent decentralizing political change which, if successful augured the end of access to federal resources (i.e. cross-subsidy). Ultimately war was the Serbian nationalist tool of choice in a bid to re-legitimize the idea of centralized power: Klejda Mulaj, *Politics of Ethnic Cleansing: Nation-State Building and Provision of In/Security in Twentieth-Century Balkans* (New York: Lexington Books, 2008), pp. 80–2. See also Nebojša Popov (ed.), *The Road to War in Serbia: Trauma and Catharsis* (Budapest: Central European University Press, 2000) and Cathie Carmichael, "Brothers, Strangers and Enemies: Ethno-Nationalism and the Demise of Communist Yugoslavia", in Dan Stone (ed.), *The Oxford Handbook of Postwar European History* (Oxford: Oxford University Press, 2012), pp. 546–59.

5 Not least because, for Europe, the killing fields of the earlier, mid-century wars were themselves part of a process that exorcized, or at least substantially reduced, the social fears associated with the idea of urban space/city inhabitants, as dangerously heterogeneous and uncontrollable. That there were some urban-rural tensions which contributed to the political crisis in Yugoslavia in

the 1980s seems, nevertheless, clear: John B. Allcock, "Rural-urban differences and the break-up of Yugoslavia", *Balkanologie. Revue d'études pluridisciplinaires* IV, 1–2 (December 2002): 101–22. In a different though related vein, on the discursive consequences of the war, see Xavier Bougarel, "Yugoslav Wars: The 'revenge of the countryside' between sociological reality and nationalist myth", *East European Quartery* XXXIII, 2 (June 1999): 157–75.

6 It has been estimated that some 74 percent of the total war dead in Bosnia during the Second World War were Serb: Tomislav Dulić, *Utopias of Nation: Local Mass Killings in Bosnia and Herzegovina, 1941–42* (Uppsala: Acta Universitatis Upsaliensis, 2005), p. 321. Part of the mythological mobilization of the 1980s involved inflating the figures for Serb losses further, for example with respect to the number of Serbs killed in the Utaša concentration camp at Jasenovac (Croatia). For exhumations of Second World War dead during the 1980s and how this influenced Serbian memory, see Robert M. Hayden, "Mass Killings and Images of Genocide in Bosnia, 1941–5 and 1992–5" in Dan Stone (ed.), *The Historiography of Genocide* (Basingstoke: Palgrave Macmillan, [2008] 2010), pp. 487–516 and "Recounting the Dead: The Rediscovery and Redefinition of Wartime Massacres in Late- and Post-Communist Yugoslavia", in Rubie S. Watson (ed.), *Memory, History and Opposition under State Socialism* (Santa Fe, NM: School of American Research Press, 1994), pp. 167–84.

7 Peter Anderson makes this point cogently, as well as its inevitable concomitant, regarding the already deeply divided nature of society in the towns and villages of the rural south. Peter Anderson, *The Francoist Military Trials: Terror and Complicity, 1939–1945* (London and New York: Routledge, 2010), pp. 6, 68, 100.

8 Nicolas Werth, "The Crimes of the Stalin Regime: Outline for an Inventory and Classification", in Dan Stone (ed.), *The Historiography of Genocide*, pp. 400–19; Donald Bloxham and A. Dirk Moses (eds), *The Oxford Handbook of Genocide Studies* (Oxford: Oxford University Press, 2010). The Stalinist system perpetrated extreme, and in practice lethal, violence against specific ethnic groups perceived to threaten state security, removing them to non border locations. Whether or not this constituted state-driven ethnic cleansing is a matter of scholarly debate (certainly at the local level inter-ethnic hatreds sometimes kicked in to fuel popular involvement in the coercion). Like other forms of state-led violence in the Soviet Union, violence against ethnic groups began with the justification that it was to protect the "purity", legitimacy, and infallibility of the revolution, but rapidly became killing for no apparently identifiable reason at all, as the work of fear took hold. This process is described by Alexander Etkind, "Post-Soviet Hauntology: Cultural Memory of the Soviet Terror", *Constellations* 16, 1 (2009): 182–200, esp. 184, 185. He comments acutely, if idiosyncratically: "If the Holocaust was the construction and extermination of the Other, the Great Terror was similar to a suicide" (184).

9 For a discussion of the need to historicize in order to make further intellectual

advances in the comparative study of genocides, see Donald Bloxham and A. Dirk Moses, "Editor's Introduction: Changing Themes in the Study of Genocide", in Bloxham and Moses (eds), *The Oxford Handbook of Genocide Studies*, pp. 1–15.

10 See Christian Gerlach, *Extremely Violent Societies: Mass Violence in the Twentieth-Century World* (Cambridge: Cambridge University Press, 2010), *passim*, for a strong argument along these same lines and extending to a refusal to use the term "genocide".

11 It remains of course to explain why violence is the outcome at some moments but not others – on this see Willem Schinkel, *Aspects of Violence: A Critical Theory* (Basingstoke: Palgrave Macmillan, 2010).

12 British Consular reports on the repression in Madrid in the early 1940s were regularly dispatched to London. Michael Richards, *A Time of Silence: Civil War and the Culture of Repression in Franco's Spain, 1936–1945* (Cambridge: Cambridge University Press, 1998), p. 43, n. 140; Peter Anderson, *The Francoist Military Trials*, pp. 1–2, 110. Cf. Mark Mazower, *Dark Continent. Europe's Twentieth Century* (London: Penguin, 1998), p. 100, for how only the outbreak of war itself in 1939 prevented the planned visit to Dachau concentration camp by the head of Scotland Yard, Sir Norman Kendal, in order to study "contemporary policing methods".

13 Aside from the vast flight/expulsion of ethnic Germans from numerous countries (between 12 and 13 million people), there were also other forms of ethnic cleansing, including 90,000 ethnic Hungarians from Czechoslovakia and 73,000 Slovaks from Hungary. 2 million Poles were expelled from Soviet-occupied Poland, and, in retaliation, 700,000 Ukrainians from South-East Poland. An overview in Mazower, *Dark Continent*, pp. 219–22 and Tony Judt, *Postwar: A History of Europe since 1945* (London: Heinemann, 2005), pp. 22–8.

14 Although the process of identification produces its own ethical dilemmas. See the anthropological study by Sarah E. Wagner, *To Know Where He Lies: DNA Technology and the Search for Srebrenica's Missing* (Berkeley: University of California Press, 2008).

15 As Mark Mazower has indicated, what post-1945 ethnic cleansing through "population transfer" ultimately delivered, notwithstanding a significant Soviet input, was a "Western" political vision in that it allowed the realization of Wilsonian ideals dating back to the Paris Peace Conference of 1919, turning "Versailles's dreams of national homogeneity into realities": *Dark Continent*, p. 222. The German expulsions from post-liberation regimes in Czechoslovakia, Poland, Romania, Yugoslavia and Hungary were also undertaken as deliberate nationalist policy as much as in retaliation for the depradations inflicted by the Third Reich.

I A War for Our Times

1 Extract from a broadcast made over Radio Jerez on 24 July 1936 by the monarchist intellectual, José María Pemán, and published in *Arengas y crónicas de*

guerra (Cádiz: Establecimientos Cerón, 1937), pp. 12–13. The reference to "political alternation" is to the monarchist system of "turno pacifico" whereby two establishment political parties managed the interests of elite groups and excluded the rest of the population from political representation. It was essentially this system (or, strictly speaking, a return to this system) that the Second Republic supplanted in April 1931.

2 Cited in Klaus Theweleit, *Male Fantasies* (vol. 1, *Women, Floods, Bodies, History*), (Minneapolis: University of Minnesota Press, 1987), p. x.

3 For a cogent current affairs analysis in English of this dimension of the Garzón controversy, see http://iberosphere.com/2011/04/spain-news-2550/2550 (accessed 30 June 2011). While the Garzón affair is densely layered, and with a strong admixture of personal enmity and many barbed strands which make is less easily reducible to a progressive/humanitarian versus authoritarian script, it is nevertheless true that the very fact that state authorities have felt able to suspend and seek the prosecution of a judge for attempting to uncover and record crimes against humanity, is indicative of the repeated failure in Spain to enact any process, legal or cultural, akin to what formal denazification, despite all its flaws and failings both qualitative and quantitative, constituted elsewhere in western Europe. The recent resurgence of ultra-nationalism in other areas of Europe – especially central Europe (where a reductionist denazification, flawed in a different way, and coupled with a fierce anti-communism, allowed the preservation of any number of unpalatable nationalist myths) – has played an important part in this "loss of shame" on the part of conservative, and sometimes still avowedly Francoist, sectors within Spain's state apparatus. This is discussed further in chapter 7.

4 Amongst the most recent work on this see especially Ángel Viñas's magisterial trilogy (*La soledad de la República*; *El escudo de la República*; *El honor de la República* (Barcelona: Crítica, 2006–9), based on an exhaustive use of Spanish, British, German, Italian and especially new Russian sources, but, sadly, like so much of the new Spanish historiography on the civil war, unavailable in English.

5 Comparative figures for Second World War deaths in Europe in Judt, *Postwar*, p. 18. In Europe 19 million non-combatant civilians were killed during the Second World War, which was more than half the total European war dead (figures exclude deaths from natural causes 1939–1945). The number of civilian war dead exceeded military losses in the USSR, Hungary, Poland, Yugoslavia, Greece, France, the Netherlands, Belgium and Norway. Only in the UK and Germany did military losses significantly outnumber civilian ones. UNICEF in 1995 estimated civilian deaths in the First World War at 14 percent, in the Second World War at 67 percent and by the wars of the 1990s worldwide at 90 percent. While the latter figure has been contested, arguments over statistical methodology cannot gainsay the stark truth that modern warfare is everywhere increasingly waged against civilians.

6 For an acute analysis which also resonates strongly with the Spanish experi-

ence, Omer Bartov, "Eastern Europe as the Site of Genocide", *Journal of Modern History* 80 (September 2008): 557–93, esp. 570–73. See also Jan T. Gross, *Neighbours: The Destruction of the Jewish Community of Jedwabne* (Princeton: Princeton University Press, 2000) which shows how, without any real involvement of the German occupying forces, the ordinary citizens of this small Polish town murdered their Jewish counterparts, face-to-face and in particularly cruel ways, often also spurred by the prospect of personal gain. In all of Europe's civil wars, including Spain's (see chapter 3), a mix of motives was frequently to be found, or more accurately, emerging ideological categories became fused with longstanding public prejudices and private desires of various kinds in a process of reciprocal legitimation. Much of what is, in many places, assimilated to brutal "new orders" remains differentiable from their ideological cores – while, for all this, never ceasing to be an integral part of the "really existing new order" – indeed the very reason why it could come to exist in the first place: cf. John Connolly, "The Uses of *Volksgemeinschaft*: Letters to the NSDAP Kreisleitung Eisenach, 1939–1940", *Journal of Modern History* 68, 4 (1996): 899–930.

7   Cf. here too Martin Conway and Peter Romijn (eds), *The War for Legitimacy in Politics and Culture 1936–1946* (Oxford: Berg, 2008), although the focus here is really on the Second World War years and immediate run up.

8   Anxieties such as these underlie a worried letter sent in 1925 to the Polish avant-garde poet Władyslaw Broniewski by his Catholic grandmother back in his hometown of Plock. Never happy with her grandson since he had left the army, and unimpressed by his poetic calls to build a new world, upon reading his latest poems she wrote, "I wept bitterly . . . I know that you have little faith, but that you would blaspheme against sanctities . . . that I never expected. It's true that people in Plock told me that you were 'very progressive', but I had understood that differently." Marci Shore, *Caviar and Ashes: A Warsaw Generation's Life and Death in Marxism 1918–1968* (New Haven/London: Yale University Press, 2006), p. 46. In a darker vein, such anxieties also form a deadly subtext in Michael Haneke's film about "order", repression, fear and loathing in a Protestant village in Northern Germany on the eve of the Great War, *The White Ribbon* (Austria/Germany, 2009).

9   Robert Gerwarth, "The Central European Counter-Revolution: Paramilitary Violence in Germany, Austria and Hungary after the Great War", *Past and Present* 200 (2008): 175–209.

10 Excerpt recalling a confrontation in Linz in 1918 from the memoirs of aristocratic officer and future Austrian Heimwehr leader Ernst Rüdiger Starhemberg, published 1937 and cited in translation in Gerwarth, "The Central European Counter-Revolution": 188–9.

11 A dimension evident in Margaret Yourcenar's 1939 novel *Coup de Grâce* and brought out to perfection in the 1976 Volker Schlöndorff/Margarethe von Trotta filmic version, *Der Fangschuss*. Set on the "lost borders of Europe", concretely in Latvia during the final stages of the civil wars of 1919–20

triggered by the Russian Revolution, it explores what the end of the old political order meant psychologically and erotically for those with a great
investment in it. Yourcenar's focus is on the character of a Prussian officer,
Erich von Lhomond, who has returned from Berlin to the region of Kratovice,
where he spent his childhood, to defend in border skirmishes there what he
implicitly acknowledges is already a lost cause – i.e. the old pre 1914 polit-
ical/imperial and social order. In the film he is a depiction of a man who is
losing all his certainties and whose psychological and gender order is crum-
bling too. Interestingly, though unsurprisingly, the 1970s film is much less
sympathetic to the character than is the original novel, and precisely because
he seems totally (congenitally) incapable of change. Ultimately a film about
border crossing, there are so many borders at issue in it – territorial, historical,
cultural, of ways of life and social class; of friendship/love, gender; the safe
psychological limits of identity. Both novel and film concur in that crossing
borders is vital, but that the human cost of social change is also immense.

12 On the *Somatén Nacional*, Alejandro Quiroga, *Making Spaniards. Primo de Rivera
and the Nationalization of the Masses, 1923–30* (Basingstoke: Palgrave
Macmillan, 2007), pp. 146–64; Eduardo González Calleja and Fernando Rey
Reguillo, *La defensa armada contra la revolución. Una historia de las "guardias
cívicas" en la España del siglo XX* (Madrid: CSIC, 1995); Eduardo González
Calleja, "La defensa armada del 'orden social' durante la Dictadura de Primo
de Rivera (1923–1930)", in J.L. García Delgado (ed.), *España entre dos siglos
(1875–1931). Continuidad y cambio* (Madrid: Siglo XXI, 1991), pp. 64–108.
See also Eduardo González Calleja, *El Máuser y el sufragio: Orden público, subversión y violencia política en la crisis de la Restauración (1917–1931)*, (Madrid: CSIC,
1999), *passim*.

13 Jane Durán, "Where did they go?", in *Silences from the Spanish Civil War*
(London: Enitharmon Press, 2002), p. 49. The poem is cited more fully in the
epigraph to chapter 5. On Robert Capa, see Richard Whelan, *Robert Capa: a
biography* (London: Faber, 1985) and Anne Makepeace's 2003 documentary
Robert Capa: In Love and War.

14 Vicki Caron, *Uneasy Asylum: France and the Jewish Refugee Crisis 1933–1942*
(Stanford, CA: Stanford University Press, 1999); Arthur Koestler, *Scum of the
Earth* (London: Eland, 2006), pp. 45–52 [first published 1941]); Rahma
Harouni, "Le débat autour du statut des étrangers dans les années 1930",
Mouvement Social 188 (1999): 61–71. A similar picture – of xenophobia and
antisemitism at odds with macro-economic need – could also be drawn for
Romania.

15 Koestler, *Scum of the Earth*, p. 93.

16 Robert Antelme, *The Human Race* (Northwestern Evanston, Illinois: The
Marlboro Press, 1998), pp. 14–15 (first published as *L'espèce humaine* [Paris:
Editions Gallimar, 1957]).

17 "What a find for Himmler's black-clothed men! Three hundred thousand
pounds of democratic flesh, all labelled, alive and only slightly damaged",

Koestler, *Scum of the Earth*, p. 140. As is well known, Le Vernet also became a holding camp of the Jewish deportation. In all, by the time the camp closed in 1944, some 40,000 people had been imprisoned there (mainly men, but also some women and children) – the final camp population being deported in June 1944 to Dachau and Mauthausen.

18 Carlos Jiménez Margalejo, *Memorias de un refugiado español en el Norte de África, 1939–1956* (Madrid, Fundación Largo Caballero/Ediciones Cinca, 2008); Cipriano Mera, *Guerra, exilio y cárcel de un anarcosindicalista* (Paris: Ruedo Ibérico, 1976).

19 Koestler, *Scum of the Earth*, p. 94.

20 The term "bare life" is Giorgio Agamben's (*Homo Sacer: Sovereign Power and Bare Life* (Stanford, CA: Stanford University Press, 1998 esp. pp. 126–35); and see chapter 6 (Franco's Prisons) below. The history of these French concentration camps (and also of beach internment camps such as Argelès, St Cyprien and le Barcarès) remains on the outer margins, especially in the historiography available in English, although see Francie Cate-Arries, *Spanish Culture behind Barbed Wire: Memory and Representation of the French Concentration Camps 1939–1945* (Lewisburg, PA: Bucknell University Press, 2004) and Scott Soo, *The Routes to Exile: Spanish Civil War Refugees and their Hosts in South-Western France* (University of Wales Press, 2011) and "Putting memory to work: A comparative study of three associations dedicated to the memory of the Spanish republican exile in France" in Henrice Altink and Sharif Gemie (eds), *At the Border: Margins and Peripheries in Modern France* (Cardiff: University of Wales Press, 2007). There is work in French on the beach internment camps, notably by Geneviève Dreyfus-Armand and also a doctoral thesis currently in train in Perpignan on the use of the French camps as an exercise in "social cleansing". See also Sharif Gemie, "The Ballad of Bourg-Madame: Memory, Exile and the Spanish Republican Refugees of the *Retirada* of 1939", *International Review of Social History* 51 (2006): 1–40; Assumpta Montellà, *La Maternitat d'Elne: Bressols dels exiliats* (Barcelona: Ara Llibres, 2005) and the short documentary on Rivesaltes made by Helena Michie, with Sylvia Ruth Gutman, who was interned there as a child, *Le dernier jour au camp du Rivesaltes* (France, 2008). In view of the fact that this history is a difficult one for French republican memory to absorb, it is not surprising that only in the twenty-first century, and partly as a result of cross-border Catalan initiatives, has there been any concerted or official effort to commemorate the sites of the *retirada*. In some cases too one notes the presence of a difficult memory in the elisions within the camp memorial texts which tend to brush over the fact of their having existed prior to May 1940. In the cemetery of Le Vernet – all that is left of the camp, and whose restoration began earlier, in the 1990s – are commemorated the more than fifty nationalities of refugee and political exile who were interned (and many buried) in the camp. There are two memorial plaques in the cemetery, one of which records the original uses of le Vernet and gives the foundational date of 1939. The mayor of Le Vernet in 2009 was brought as a small child from

Barcelona by female relatives after the fall of Catalonia in February 1939. His male family had died in the war in Spain, his grandmother died in Le Vernet camp (interview with author, 2 September 2009).

21 Koestler, *Scum of the Earth*, pp. 96, 100, 101, 102, 124–5. Spanish Republican memoirs of the French camps also strongly convey how the brutality of xeno-phobic officialdom, the harshness of the camp's physical routine and (in the case of the beach camps especially) the natural elements, all combined to strip away the identity of those incarcerated, while a normal life for others existed in very close proximity, just beyond the barbed wire and guards. See the (textual and pictorial) collective testimony in N. Molins i Fábrega and Josep Bartolí, *Campos de concentración, 1939–194 . . .* (Mexico City: Iberia, 1944), p. 117, and for relevant illustrations by Bartolí, Francie Cate-Arries, *Spanish Culture Behind Barbed Wire*, pp. 58, 59, 76, 110.

22 Dan Stone, "The 'Final Solution': A German or European Project?" in his *Histories of the Holocaust* (Oxford: Oxford University Press, 2010), pp. 13–63; Mark Mazower, *Inside Hitler's Greece: The Experience of Occupation 1941–1944* (Yale University Press, 2001) and Mark Mazower (ed.), *After the War was Over: Reconstructing the family, nation, and state in Greece, 1943–1960* (Princeton, NJ: Princeton University Press, 2000). Tomislav Dulić, *Utopias of Nation: Local Mass Killing in Bosnia and Herzegovina, 1941–42.*

23 This sculpting of new social and political order through the exercise of extreme violence is the central concern of Mark Mazower's pivotal study, *Dark Continent: Europe's Twentieth Century*, whose title indicates the connection he traces between the forms of earlier colonial violence visited by Europeans upon the subject peoples of their empires, and the "violence come home" which they then, in the 1930s and 40s, visit upon each other. See also Amir Weiner, *Landscaping the Human Garden* (Stanford, CA: Stanford University Press, 2003).

24 William A. Christian Jr., *Moving Crucifixes in Modern Spain* (Princeton, NJ: Princeton University Press, 1992) is a social historical and anthropological study of a number of such occurrences from 1919. Also on Catholic popular movements in northern Spain in times of social and political change, Julio de la Cueva, "The Stick and the Candle: Clericals and Anticlericals in Northern Spain, 1898–1913", *European History Quarterly* 26, 2 (1996): 241–65.

25 See chapter 2 below (photograph and caption) for the destruction of the statue by Republican militia in August 1936.

26 Ian Gibson, *La represión nacionalista de Granada en 1936 y la muerte de Federico García Lorca* (Paris: Ruedo Ibérico, 1971), p. 103; Antonio Bahamonde, *Un año con Queipo: Memorias de un nacionalista* (Barcelona: Ediciones Españolas, 1938), p. 113.

27 The larger historical picture is elucidated in chapter 2 and chapter 3 tells one story of a "new woman" and the human cost of this bid to halt change.

28 Paul Preston, *The Spanish Holocaust. Inquisition and Extermination in Twentieth-Century Spain* (London: HarperCollins, 2012), p. 281.

29 Julián Casanova, *The Spanish Republic and the Civil War* (Cambridge:

Cambridge University Press, 2010). For more on the question of the Church, Catholicism and anticlerical violence, see chapter 2.

30 Preston, *The Spanish Holocaust*, pp. xi, xviii.

31 For Greece, which in some important respects was comparable, see Mazower, *After the War was Over*.

32 István Deák, Jan T. Gross and Tony Judt (eds), *The Politics of Retribution in Europe: World War II and Its Aftermath* (Princeton: Princeton University Press, 2000).

2 The Memory of Murder

1 A gloss on Michael Taussig's analysis in *Law in a Lawless Land. Diary of a Limpieza in Columbia* (University of Chicago Press, 2003).

2 Maria Thomas, "Disputing the Public Sphere: Anticlerical Violence, Conflict and the Sacred Heart of Jesus", *Cuadernos de Historia Contemporánea* 33 (2011): 50–69, http://revistas.ucm.es/index.php/CHCO/issue/current (accessed 16 January 2012).

3 On this see Mary Vincent, "The Martyrs and the Saints: Masculinity and the Construction of the Francoist Crusade", *History Workshop Journal* 47 (1999): 68–98, esp. 70, 72.

4 The secret instructions to this effect, as given by General Mola, the director of the coup, to his fellow conspirators in April 1936 in Felipe Bertrán Güell, *Preparación y desarrollo del alzamiento nacional* (Valladolid: Librería Santarén, 1939), p. 123.

5 For the colonial officer corps perceiving Spanish workers in this way, see Preston, *The Spanish Holocaust*, pp. 21–3, 164–5.

6 Carolyn P. Boyd, "'Responsibilities' and the Second Spanish Republic 1931–1936", *European History Quarterly* 14 (1984): 151–82 and *Historia Patria. Politics, History and National Identity in Spain 1875–1975* (Princeton: Princeton University Press, 1997); Geoffrey Jensen, *Irrational Triumph: Cultural Despair, Military Nationalism, and the Ideological Origins of Franco's Spain* (Reno & Las Vegas: University of Nevada Press, 2002); Francisco Romero Salvadó and Ángel Smith (eds), *The Agony of Spanish Liberalism: From Revolution to Dictatorship, 1913–1923* (Basingstoke: Palgrave Macmillan, 2010), esp. chapters 1, 9 and 10.

7 Vincent, "The Martyrs and the Saints"; William Christian, *Visionaries. The Spanish Republic and the Reign of Christ* (Berkeley/Los Angeles, CA: University of California Press, 1996), *passim*; Javier Ugarte Tellería, *La nueva Covadonga insurgente. Orígenes sociales y culturales de la sublevación de 1936 en Navarra y el País Vasco* (Madrid: Biblioteca Nueva, 1998), pp. 9–101; Rafael Cruz, *En el nombre del pueblo: República, rebelión y guerra en la España de 1936* (Madrid: Siglo XXI, 2006), pp. 50–67; Julio de la Cueva, "Clericalismo y movilización católica durante la restauración" and Isidro Sánchez Sánchez, "El pan de los Fuertes. La 'buena prensa' en España", both in Julio de la Cueva and Ángel Luis López Villaverde (eds), *Clericalismo y asociacionismo católico en España: de la restauración*

a la transición (Cuenca: Universidad Castilla-La Mancha, 2005), pp. 27–52.

8 "In many places, town councils attempted to reduce the public presence of the Church during funerals to a bare minimum. In Pechina (Almería), burials officiated by priests were officially prohibited by the local authorities from 1932 onwards. Funeral corteges could, however, pass hurriedly in front of the church, whereupon the minister emerged to bless the mortal remains 'for the amount of time strictly necessary.'" Thomas, "Disputing the Public Sphere", 63. For more on clashes and tensions in public space, Cruz, *En el nombre del pueblo*, and Jesús Casquete and Rafael Cruz (eds), *Políticas de la muerte: Usos y abusos del ritual fúnebre en la Europa del siglo XX* (Madrid: Catarata, 2009).

9 For a nuanced cinematic depiction of the cultural and political clashes *within* Spanish Catholicism/the Catholic Church in 1930s Spain, and also of religious versus secular visions of redemption, see *La Buena Nueva* (*The Good News*), (Spain, 2008).

10 Angela Jackson, '*For us it was Heaven': The Passion, Grief and Fortitude of Patience Darton – From the Spanish Civil War to Mao's China* (Brighton, Portland, Toronto: Sussex Academic Press, 2011), p. 112. The interview with Patience Darton, parts of which are transcribed in Jackson, is on record in the collection of International Brigader interviews held at the Imperial War Museum (interview no. 8398). It gives Patience's account of the Aragonese villager who came to the field "cave" hospital near the Ebro front in summer 1938 in the run up to the Republic's gargantuan offensive to push across the river, relieve the pressure on Valencia and send a message to the international powers that it would not surrender. Patience, stretched to her limits by what she has had to treat with incendiary-bomb casualties, and seeing a group of fresh-faced teenage recruits pass by singing on their way to the frontline (see photoessay, chapter 5), questioned the man about the war: "And the chap was very serious, very nice man, a marvellous man, and he said he was just a Spaniard from the locality and he'd brought up fruit for us, he'd been taking it to the front but he heard about the hospital and he'd brought [it] up . . . and I said, 'Well, is it worth it, all this? Can you not hear those children singing?' And he said he was an analphabetic *(sic)* peasant in the locality there, they hadn't even got a road only a track to their village. They were terribly poor and they didn't know much that was going on, they were used to being voted for, they were voted as so many souls belonging to the owner of the land – he just put in their votes, so many numbered. But they'd heard, a couple of years before, that there was going to be an election in which they could vote. And they went and voted, it was the first time they'd known they'd voted . . . He learnt to read and write . . . he was elected the local Mayor . . . Every village had a Mayor . . . They organised everything, and then he, oh, five or six weeks before this battle, the Ebro, he was sent for to Barcelona, he had a letter, it was the first letter he'd ever had – and of course, he could read it . . . And he went to Barcelona where they were told that there was going to be this battle and the roads were going to be built and that the local authorities had got to be able to provide for both

the refugees coming our way . . . and for the army [. . .] And he did all those things, and they did very well at them, they managed an awful lot of food, they were ready to pass the refugees back but they didn't get any there. But he said, 'I became a man, and that's what we're fighting for.'"

11 In October 1932, in Tembleque (Toledo), the town council decided to prohibit the presence of priests dressed in religious clothes and carrying religious ornaments in public ceremonies. The mayor explained that the decision was taken to avoid social disturbances because "the people don't want to see them". AHN, Ministerio de la Gobernación. Interior A, legajo 53ª/7 (Toledo). (These are the reports sent from mayors to civil governors and thence to the Interior Ministry during the years of the Republic.) I would like to thank Maria Thomas for this data.

12 Christian, *Visionaries*, p. 7.

13 On the especially violent atmosphere in Valladolid after the coup and the role of old-guard fascist leader Onésimo Redondo in fomenting this, see Preston, *The Spanish Holocaust*, pp. 44–7, 91–2, 188–9.

14 For a reading of the Army of Africa's enterprise as "colonialism come home" (Aimé Césaire) and a form of fascism, see Helen Graham, *The Spanish Republic at War* (Cambridge: Cambridge University Press, 2002), pp. 123–4. See also note 5 above.

15 See here the seminal study of the JAP in Sid Lowe, *Catholicism, War and the Foundation of Francoism: The Juventud de Acción Popular in Spain* (Brighton & Portland: Sussex Academic Press, 2010). The importance and the originality of Lowe's study lies in its pinpointing of the moment and demonstrating of the mechanism by which radical Catholics in Spain became fascists. Lowe thus cuts the gordian knot that inhibits much of the conventional historiography on the Spanish Catholic right during the 1930s – i.e. in that it insists that Spanish fascism was limited to a failed, marginal and later subordinate party, the Falange; and argues that Francoism as a coalition cannot really be termed "fascist" because of the pivotal role played by the Church and institutional Catholic politics – when it is precisely the role played by the latter which needs to be re-appraised root and branch for the period of early Francoism (1936 through to the end of the 1940s). See here also Julián Casanova, *La Iglesia de Franco* (Barcelona: Crítica, 2009) and chapters 3 and 6 below.

16 Cf. Ángela Cenarro, "Matar, vigilar y delatar: la quiebra de la sociedad civil durante la guerra y la posguerra en España (1936–1948)", *Historia Social* 44 (2002): 65–86.

17 Pilar Espinosa was one of the "disappeared" named and commemorated by Spain's civil Asociación para la Recuperación de la Memoria Histórica (ARMH), (www.memoriahistorica.org). Amparo Barayón's story was first told by her son in Ramón Sender Barayón, *A Death in Zamora* (Albuquerque: University of New Mexico Press, 1989; 2nd edn, Calm Unity Press, 2003).

18 Julián Zugazagoitia, *Guerra y vicisitudes de los españoles* (Paris: Librería Española, 1968), p. 84; Francisco Moreno Gómez, "La represión en la España campesina",

in J.L. García Delgado (ed.), *El primer franquismo: España durante la segunda guerra mundial* (Madrid, 1989), p. 192.

19 A firsthand account of this process is to be found in the reports of the American journalist, John T. Whitaker, who was one of a number of foreign reporters accompanying the southern army columns. But those from the democratic countries were usually closely "chaperoned" and only allowed limited access to scenes of fighting, and, even then, after the event. Whitaker was virtually unique in escaping this embeddedness, as a result of having gained the confidence of some of Franco's senior military commanders, John T. Whitaker, *We Cannot Escape History* (New York: Macmillan, 1943), pp. 111–12; Whitaker, "Prelude to World War: A Witness from Spain", *Foreign Affairs* 21, 1 (October 1942), pp. 105–6. For more on what Whitaker saw, Preston, *The Spanish Holocaust*, pp. 312–13, 331–6. An analytical survey of the killings in the wake of the southern army's rampage, in Graham, *Spanish Republic at War*, pp. 105–17 and both an analysis and a detailed empirical account in chapters 5 and, especially, 9 of Preston, *The Spanish Holocaust*, pp. 131–78 and 303–40 respectively.

20 Francisco Espinosa Maestre, *La columna de la muerte. El avance del ejército franquista de Sevilla a Badajoz* (Barcelona: Crítica, 2003), for example, p. 30 – and see also plates 16/1; 16/2; 16/3 (pages unnumbered) for contemporary photographs of the "policía montada" ("mounted police") – the name given to a civilian vigilante force (including landowners) who first supplemented and then continued the work of the *Africanista* military columns.

21 War rape, internationally recognized as a crime against humanity in the context of the Bosnian war in 1992, is a complex issue for which a substantial theoretical and comparative bibliography exists, see Adam Jones, "Gender and Genocide", in Dan Stone (ed.), *The Historiography of Genocide*, pp. 228–52; Rose Lindsey, "From atrocity to data: historiographies of rape in Former Yugoslavia and the gendering of genocide", *Patterns of Prejudice* 36, 4 (2002): 59–78; Lynda E. Boose, "Crossing the River Drina: Bosnian Rape Camps, Turkish Impalement and Serb Cultural Memory", *Signs*, 28, 1 (2002): 71–96; Wendy Bracewell, "Rape in Kosovo: masculinity and Serbian nationalism", *Nations and Nationalism* 6, 4 (2000): 563–90; Todd A. Salzman, "Rape camps as a means of ethnic cleansing", *Human Rights Quarterly* 20, 2 (1998): 348–78. The Spanish civil war has not yet been subject to a sustained theoretical analysis in this regard (some preliminary observations in Alberto Reig Tapia, *Ideología e Historia (sobre la represión franquista y la guerra civil)*, (Torrejón de Ardoz, Madrid: Akal, 1986), p. 145 and Francisco Espinosa Maestre, *La justicia de Queipo (violencia selectiva y terror fascista en la II División en 1936): Sevilla, Huelva, Cádiz, Córdoba, Málaga y Badajoz* (Córdoba: Bibliofilia Montillana, Cofradía de la Viña y el Vino, 2000), pp. 249–55. On the difficulties facing historians researching the topic – both generic and particular to the Spanish case, Queralt Solé, *O Xornal*, 16 November 2009 at www.kaosenlared.net/noticia/queralt-sole-tabu-hablar-violaciones-tropas-franquistas. My object here is purely to

locate the subject in the broad context of rebel pathologies. For an analysis of gender-specific violence (including rape) perpetrated against women prisoners in the Francoist prison universe, see chapter 6 below. Although there were instances of the sexual abuse of women (including some religious personnel) in wartime Republican territory, there was no comparable phenomenon of the consistent, mass sexual abuse of women there – the reasons for which are discussed below in this chapter.

22 That the south was awash with rape as well as indiscriminate killing is clear from the consistent references in the contemporary accounts of Anglo-American war correspondents accompanying the Army of Africa – the most direct record, for the reasons already explained, in Whitaker, "Prelude to World War" and *We Cannot Escape History*, pp. 113–14. Whitaker describes an incident of gang rape and murder by the regulares and makes the point explicitly that no Francoist officer ever denied that rape was being used as an instrument of war. For numerous references to systematic rape from other contemporary press accounts, see Preston, *The Spanish Holocaust*, pp. 303–40.

23 In late September 1936 in Toledo, Falangists came to the prison with the intention of killing all the female detainees to "celebrate" the rebel capture of the town, but in the event were only able to extract from the prison governor a smaller number of women for extrajudicial execution (Preston, *The Spanish Holocaust*, pp. 133–4); in Zamora (which had been held by the rebels from the moment of the coup itself), for instances of rape, see Pilar Fidalgo, *A Young Mother in Franco's Prisons* (London: United Editorial Ltd, 1939), pp. 21–2; Pilar Sanjuan Misis' testimony in Sender Barayón, *A Death in Zamora*, pp. 145–6. All these "varieties" of rape – whether perpetrated by Africanista troops, Falangists or other elements – continued throughout the period of Franco's military conquest. For rapes during the conquest of Catalonia from December 1938, Josep Solé i Sabaté and Joan Villarroya i Font, *L'ocupació militar de Catalunya, març 1938–febrer 1939* (Barcelona: L'Avenç, 1987); Francisco Sánchez Ruano, *Islam y guerra civil española: Moros con Franco y con la República* (Madrid: La Esfera de los Libros, 2004), pp. 357–63; Núria Bonet Baqué, Amanda Cardona Alcaide and Gerard Corbella López, *Tàrrega 1936–61: Aproximació a la repressió, l'exili i la vida quotidiana* (Tàrrega: Ajuntament de Tàrrega, 2008), pp. 14, 76–7.

24 Nor did the practice end with the conclusion of military hostilities. Sexual assault remained a constant form of punishment and humiliation inflicted on female detainees/prisoners during Franco's uncivil peace, especially in the 1940s, see chapter 6 below.

25 Hate-filled commentaries accompanying pictures of *milicianas* were not infrequently published in the post-war Francoist press, including in Sección Femenina women's magazines.

26 On war, sexuality and loss of control, see also the thought-provoking analysis in Jo Labanyi, "Women, Asian Hordes and the Threat to the Self in Giménez Caballero's *Genio de España*", *Bulletin of Hispanic Studies* LXXIII (1996):

377–87, esp. 382 (for Falangist ideologue Giménez Caballero's hysterical denunciation of Madrid as a whore and medusa from the pulpit of Salamanca cathedral), and 385 (for Labanyi's fruitful incorporation of Theweleit's concept of war as the "ultimate permissible 'controlled explosion' of the self"). See the extraordinary case of General Queipo de Llano's sexual psychopathology – as manifest in his Seville radio broadcasts – in Gerald Brenan, *Personal Record 1920–1972* (London: Jonathan Cape, 1974), p. 297; Gamel Woolsey, *Death's Other Kingdom* (London: Longmans, Green, 1939), pp. 34–5. The versions of his radio speeches published afterwards in the press were significantly censored, Preston, *The Spanish Holocaust*, pp. 149–50 and cf. pp. 330–1.

27 Julián Casanova, Francisco Espinosa, Conxita Mir and Francisco Moreno Gómez, *Morir, matar, sobrevivir: la violencia en la dictadura de Franco* (Barcelona: Crítica, 2001), pp. 131–7, 159–72; Conxita Mir, *Vivir es sobrevivir: Justicia, orden y marginación en la Cataluña rural de posguerra* (Lleida: Editorial Milenio, 2000), pp. 37–58, 128–50, 164–87, 195–202. For rapes covered up in the south of Spain because the perpetrators were "of good family" and well connected to the rebels, Preston, *The Spanish Holocaust*, pp. 328–9.

28 Ángela Cenarro, "La lógica de la guerra, la lógica de la venganza: violencia y fractura social en una comunidad bajoaragonesa, 1939–1940", in Conxita Mir, Jordi Catalán and David Ginard (coords.), *Enfrontaments civils: Postguerres i reconstruccions. II Guerra civil de 1936 i franquisme* (Lleida: Associació Recerques i Pagès Editors, 2002), pp. 703–15.

29 The political and social consequences of this complicity are dealt with in chapter 6 below.

30 The standard work on anticlerical killings during the civil war is Fr. Antonio Montero Moreno, *Historia de la persecución religiosa en España 1936–1939* (Madrid: Biblioteca de los Autores Cristianos, 1961), pp. 430, 762. He calculated that 6,832 members of the clergy and religious orders were murdered or executed. His figures have not been substantially modified by more recent empirical academic work, although some slight modifications in Gregorio Rodríguez Sánchez, *El habito y la cruz: religiosas asesinadas en la guerra civil española* (Madrid: Edibesa, 2006), pp. 594–6. In 1936, Spain had something over 115,000 clergy, which included c. 45,000 nuns, 15,000 monks and the remainder were lay priests; 2,365 monks and 4,184 secular priests were killed, constituting over 30 percent of the monks and 18 percent of the lay clergy in Republican territory.

31 Aurora Bosch, *Ugetistas y libertarios: guerra civil y revolución en el País Valenciano, 1936–1939* (Valencia: Institución Alfonso El Magnánimo, 1983), p. 32; José Daniel Simeón Riera, *Entre la rebelió y la tradició (Llíria durante La República y la Guerra Civil, 1931–1939)*, (Valencia: Diputació de València, 1993), pp. 205, 273 (n. 72).

32 During the 1930s Chambers of Commerce called upon local government authorities in urban areas to deploy police to "resolve" disputes between shop owners and those engaged in alternative food procurement and sale for poor

and marginal sectors of the population. Graham, *Spanish Republic at War*, pp. 260–1.

33 Gabriel García de Consuegra Muñoz, Ángel López López and Fernando López López, *La represión en Pozoblanco* (Córdoba: Francisco Baena,1989), pp. 55, 60; Geoffrey Cox, *Defence of Madrid* (London: Victor Gollancz, 1937), p. 183; Manuel Ortiz Heras, *Violencia política en la II República y el primer franquismo* (Madrid: Siglo XXI, 2006), pp. 106–8; Gabriel Jackson, *The Spanish Republic and the Civil War* (Princeton, NJ: Princeton University Press, 1965), p. 343; Ian Gibson, *Paracuellos cómo fue* (Barcelona: Argos Vergara, 1983), pp. 178–9.

34 Hence the allusion in the title of Jaime Camino's classic film, *Las Largas Vacaciones del 36 (The Long Holidays of 1936)*, (Spain, 1976) – indeed these were holidays from which some never returned.

35 A detailed survey in Preston, *The Spanish Holocaust*, chapter 7, for example pp. 226–233, on the CNT-FAI "penumbra" in Barcelona, but also generally throughout the chapter. The fact that the anarcho-syndicalists had, wherever they were in control (mainly in Catalonia and parts of Valencia), emptied the gaols on the morrow of the coup was an exacerbating factor. As too was the general "porousness" of the anarcho-syndicalist movement after the military coup which facilitated infiltration by agent-provocateurs.

36 José Luis Ledesma, *Los días de llamas, de la revolución: Violencia y política en la retaguardia republicana de Zaragoza durante la guerra civil* (Institución Fernando el Católico, Zaragoza, 2003), pp. 235–68; Preston, *The Spanish Holocaust*, pp. 257–8.

37 For the remarkable frequency with which governments of the monarchy suspended constitutional guarantees and declared "states of alarm" of various levels, see Eduardo González Calleja, *La Razón de la fuerza. Orden público, subversión y violencia política en la España de la Restauración (1875–1917)*, (Madrid: CSIC, 1998), pp. 57, 65–73.

38 Chris Ealham, *Class, Culture and Conflict in Barcelona, 1898–1937* (Routledge/Cañada Blanch: London, 2005), pp. 16–22, 39.

39 Maria Thomas, "'We have come to place you at liberty and to burn the convent': Masculinity, Sexuality and Anticlerical Violence during the Spanish Civil War", Abraham Lincoln Brigade Archive George Watt Memorial Essay Prize 2011, http://www.albavolunteer.org/2011/12/masculinity-sexuality-and-anticlerical-violence-during-the-scw/ (accessed 16 January 2012) and "The Faith and the Fury: The Construction of Anticlerical Collective Identities in Early Twentieth-Century Spain", article forthcoming, *European History Quarterly*. My understanding of the empirical base of the process of emotional alienation explored in these paragraphs owes a great deal to my discussions with Maria Thomas whose book on anticlericalism during the Spanish civil war will be published in 2012.

40 Emil Salut, *Vivers de revolucionaris: apunts històrics del districte cinquè* (Barcelona, 1938), pp. 9–20.

41 Cultural powerlessness came too in many other shapes and forms, and partic-

ularly around issues of death and burial where the ecclesiastical authorities had the right to intervene (and frequently did) in ways that went against family wishes – whether this meant insisting on Catholic rites of burial or, conversely, denying access to consecrated cemetery ground and insisting on burial in the (inevitably overgrown and untended) parts reserved for non-Catholics, Rafael Cruz, "El sabor fúnebre de la política española entre 1876 y 1940", in Jesús Casquete and Rafael Cruz (eds), *Políticas de la Muerte*, pp. 80–3. The teaching provided by the religious orders in the many poor schools they ran was, inevitably, schooling in submission and in knowing one's place.

42 Peadar O' Donnell, *Salud!: An Irishman in Spain* (London: Methuen and Co., 1937), p. 94. I would like to thank Maria Thomas for bringing this memoir to my attention.

43 Letters from Joan Miró to Enric Ricart, 19 August 1917 in Joan Miró, *Epistolari català* (Barcelona: Fundació Joan Miró, 2009), vol. 1, 1911–1945, pp. 63, 65. See especially Miró's triptych made in early February 1974, "The Hope of a Condemned Man" which Miró linked explicitly to Salvador Puig Antich, one of the last prisoners to be executed by the Franco regime, in March 1974, and the final execution in which prisoners were killed by garrotte vil.

44 This in the *Causa General*, a nationwide investigation of Republican "crimes" that was highly unsafe, in judicial terms, and which constituted the Franco regime's institutionalization of its victory through the social and political exclusion of the defeated. *Causa General, La dominación roja en España* (Madrid: Ministerio de Justicia, 1945); Isidro Sánchez Sánchez, Manuel Ortiz Heras and David Ruiz, *Espana franquista: causa general y actitudes sociales ante la dictadura* (Albacete: Universidad De Castilla-La Mancha, 1993).

45 A file on the destruction of the statue, including a report dated 7 August 1936, from the mayor of Getafe (the nearest town) is to be found in the documentation of Franco's *Causa General*: AHN, *Causa General* legajo 1557-2: Madrid, pieza No. 10, exp. 5/95 and AHN, CG legajo 1557-2: Madrid, pieza No. 10, exp. 9/29.

46 Mary Vincent, "The Keys to the Kingdom: Religious Violence in the Spanish Civil War", in Chris Ealham and Michael Richards (eds), *The Splintering of Spain: Cultural History and the Spanish Civil War* (Cambridge: Cambridge University Press, 2005), pp. 68–92.

47 Preston, *The Spanish Holocaust*, pp. 235–6 gives the latest figure of 296 female religious personnel killed during the war, just over 1.3% of the total present in Republican territory; also pp. 249–50 for other cases of sexual abuse in Huesca (Aragón) in the north east, a region that experienced an especially high incidence of anticlerical violence after the coup.

48 Manuel Sánchez del Arco, *El sur de España en la reconquista de Madrid* (Seville: Editorial Sevillana, 1937), p. 55 and Hubert Renfro Knickerbocker, *The Siege of the Alcazar: A war-log of the Spanish revolution* (London: Hutchinson, 1937), p. 86.

49 "People were killed for pointless things – for example, because someone sang

in church or was a bellringer." An oral testimony collected by a local historian who then comments, "the motives might seem pointless to our way of thinking now, but for those who did the killing, the Church singer and the bellringer were part of a world that had to be annihilated." Riera, *Entre la rebelió y la tradició*, p. 273, n. 73.

50 Durruti said this in a newspaper interview in July 1936. The location and timing of the interview in Abel Paz, *Durruti en la revolución española* (Madrid: Fundación Anselmo Lorenzo, 1996), pp. 529–31.

51 Graham, *Spanish Republic at War*, p. 91.

52 José Luis Ledesma calls them the "new leading minority", *Los días de llamas*, pp. 238–40. Afterwards there would be attempts to cover up this breaking of a taboo (in the commission of intra-communal killing) by blaming it entirely on incoming groups. It was sometimes true that the committees of different localities agreed reciprocally, each appointing squads to "clear up" in the territory of the other. Preston, on the "ghost cars" arriving from neighbouring districts or towns, in *The Spanish Holocaust*, pp. 249, 266. But however it happened, then local inside knowledge was crucial to the identification of those to be killed or otherwise punished.

53 Graham, *Spanish Republic at War, passim*. A minutely forensic account of the post-coup repression and extrajudicial killing in Madrid, including with its fair share of the sociopathic, in Preston, *The Spanish Holocaust*, pp. 259–302.

54 For the acutely claustrophobic atmosphere inside Madrid, and the sense of zero-hour among its defenders, Graham, *Spanish Republic at War*, pp. 189, 193 (esp. n. 239*)*. The most recent analysis of Paracuellos specifically in Preston, *The Spanish Holocaust*, pp. 341–82.

55 Preston*, ibid.*, pp. 347–50, 360–3.

56 There is an extensive discussion of this in Graham, *Spanish Republic at War*. For the consolidation of a constitutional framework, see especially pp. 338–41; 346–51; 378–9; 383–87.

57 British National Archives, Foreign Office General Correspondence: Spain (NA, FO371) W13853/29/41. See also Maria Thomas, "The front line of Albion's perfidy. Inputs into the making of British policy towards Spain: the racism and snobbery of Norman King", *International Journal of Iberian Studies* 20, 2 (July 2007): 103–23.

58 Sir Robert Vansittart, the chief diplomatic adviser to the Foreign Office, reacted thus to the news of Paracuellos: "This is a ghastly tale of ghastly gangsters in whose hands the so-called 'government' . . . is a bad joke.", but he was silent on the dynamic of the violence. Vansittart quoted by Tom Buchanan, "Edge of Darkness: British 'Front-line' Diplomacy in the Spanish Civil War, 1936–1937", *Contemporary European History* 12, 3 (2003): 300.

59 This episode, recalled by Mark Mazower in *Dark Continent,* is endnoted (12) in the Introduction.

60 Preston, *The Spanish Holocaust*, p. 337, based on the accounts of North American journalists John T. Whitaker and Webb Miller, who arrived on the

scene three days later (29 September 1936). The rebels had learned the lessons of the southern campaign, of Badajoz especially. No journalists were allowed into Toledo until after it had been "pacified" by the African Army. In the words of one of its senior commanders, Yagüe, "we made Toledo the whitest town in Spain", Preston, *ibid.*, pp. 336–7.

61 Natalie Zemon Davis, "The Rites of Violence: Religious Riot in Sixteenth-Century France", *Past and Present* 59, 1 (1973): 51–91, esp. 57.

62 To date most of the information we have on this appertains to the south or to Carlist Navarre in the north (for a southern priest who enlisted in the Carlist militia and left a memoir, P. Bernabé Copado S.J., *Con la columna Redondo. Combates y conquistas. Crónica de guerra* (Sevilla: Imprenta de la Gavidia, 1937). But it occurred elsewhere too in northern Spain, for example, the case of Capuchin monk, Father Hermenegildo de Fustiñana, who shot men and women in Jaca, P. Preston, *The Spanish Holocaust*, p. 455; and for the case of a priest in Zamora, see chapter 3 below. Examples from the south include Juan Galán Bermejo, a priest from Zafra (Badajoz) took part in the massacres which occurred in August 1936 in the provincial capital there, P. Preston, *The Spanish Holocaust*, pp. 308–9. There was also a priest (*Don Litro*) in Huelva who participated directly in the killing of the local miners and who then also killed someone who had happened to witness the execution of the miners, Francisco Espinosa, *La guerra civil en Huelva*, 4th edn (Diputación Provincial de Huelva, 2005), p. 710. Many priests also used extreme physical force against detainees before they were killed by others: for example the priest of Salvochea (El Campillo, Huelva) kicked one young man in the face as he appealed to him to intervene as he was being detained, F. Espinosa Maestre, "Guerra y represión en el sur de España", unpublished essay, courtesy of the author. The priest in Llerena (Badajoz) kicked and verbally abused a woman who refused to make her confession and then hit her in the mouth with his crucifix before she was taken away to be executed, Ángel Olmedo Alonso, *Llerena 1936: Fuentes orales para la recuperación de la memoria histórica* (Badajoz: Diputación de Badajoz, 2010), pp. 149–51.

63 Francisco Moreno Gómez, *La guerra civil en Córdoba* (Madrid: Alpuerto,1985), pp. 463–4.

64 On "terror and fiesta" see Ángela Cenarro's resonant account of events in Teruel in *El fin de la esperanza: fascismo y guerra civil en la provincia de Teruel (1936–1939)*, (Teruel: Diputación Provincial de Teruel, 1996), p. 75; on Valladolid, Preston, *The Spanish Holocaust*, p. 192; and for the possible consequences of this years later for some perpetrators, *ibid.*, p. 525.

65 Cf. a similar process in 1990s Bosnia where ritual/religious violence was deployed with the goal of producing ethnic homogenization, Cathie Carmichael, "Violence and Ethnic Boundary Maintenance in Bosnia in the 1990s", *Journal of Genocide Research* 8, 3 (2006): 283–93.

3 Ghosts of Change

1   This family story is also referred to in chapters 6 and 7.

2   Sender Barayón, *A Death in Zamora*, p. 163. There is also a Spanish edition, *Muerte en Zamora* (Barcelona: Plaza & Janés, 1990) translated by Mercedes Esteban-Maes Kemp, the daughter of Magdalena Maes, and also a second edition in English published in 2003 by Calm Unity Press. In the late 1990s the Spanish film director Carlos Saura wrote a book and a screenplay, *¡Esa Luz!*, which incorporated, somewhat loosely, elements of Amparo's story.

3   In the same way, the necessity of recognizing and conveying these qualities as dominant in the 1940s impels the allusive and fragmented structures deployed by Juan Marsé in his seminal novels of the Spanish post-civil war period, for example, *Si te dicen que caí* (Mexico: Novaro, 1973; Spain: Seix Barral, 1976), (trans. *The Fallen*, London: Quartet Books, 1994) or the quite brilliant *Un día volveré* (Barcelona: Plaza y Janés, 1982), ("One day I will return") sadly still unavailable in English translation.

4   As an example of this, see the discussion in chapter 7 of the polemic over Amparo which played out in the local press in Zamora in 2005.

5   The Spanish case, in Ángela Cenarro, *Los niños de Auxilio Social* (Madrid: Espasa Calpe, 2009) and her article, "Memories of Repression and Resistance. Narratives of Children Institutionalized by Auxilio Social in Postwar Spain", *History & Memory* 20, 2 (2008): 39–59. Campaigning journalists have played a crucial role in uncovering the story of the institutionalized abuse of children, as is discussed later in this chapter.

6   *A Death in Zamora* contains other stories of loss and memory which run in parallel to the ones considered here, but which, for reasons of space and thematic exigency, are not directly part of my analysis in this chapter.

7   Michael Ondaatje, *Anil's Ghost* (London: Bloomsbury, 2000), p. 56. Still largely unrecognized by the Western mainstream is the genocide that occurred in April-May 2009 at the "end" of Sri-Lanka's thirty-year civil war when government forces were responsible for the massacre of at least 40,000 Tamil civilian non-combatants, many thousands of whom were killed by shelling, having been corralled into a supposed "safe haven", a sand spit in the island's remote north east, deemed by the government a "no-fire zone". Gordon Weiss, a veteran journalist and long-serving UN official in wartime Sri Lanka, who broke with the organization to publish a book length study of the war, *The Cage. The Fight for Sri Lanka and the Last Days of the Tamil Tigers* (London: The Bodley Head, 2011), calls it "Sri Lanka's Srebrenica". Not only did the UN acquiesce in the Sri Lankan military's perpetrating of atrocities against Tamil civilians (systematic murder, rape and torture), but the Red Cross provided the government with the coordinates that allowed it to bomb clinics and hospitals in supposed "no-fire" zones. For a review of *The Cage* that is symptomatic in its obliviousness of the afterlife of violence, Jason Bourke (*Guardian* South Asia correspondent), "The End of Violence", *Literary Review* (June 2011). On the events, see also the Channel 4 documentary *Sri Lanka's Killing Fields,* first

broadcast 14 June 2011, and on the aftermath, the International State Crime Initiative website (Kings College London, Universities of Harvard, Hull and Ulster) at http://statecrime.org/state-studies/gg-sri-lanka/237.

8   As the coup's leader, General Emilio Mola commented: "Re-establishing the principle of authority demands unavoidably that punishments be exemplary both in terms of their severity and the speed with which they will be carried out, without doubt or hesitation". Emilio Mola Vidal, *Obras completas* (Valladolid: Librería Santarén, 1940), p. 1173.

9   Juan de Iturralde, *La guerra de Franco, los vascos y la Iglesia*, 2 vols (San Sebastián: Publicaciones del Clero Vasco, 1978) I, p. 433. See also Hugh Thomas, *The Spanish Civil War*, 3rd edn (London: Hamish Hamilton, 1977), p. 260.

10 In Navarre, Álava, the eight provinces of Old Castile, the three of León, the four of Galicia, two thirds of Zaragoza and virtually all of Cáceres, the coup was successful within hours or days. For a detailed analysis, see chapter 6 ("Mola's Terror: The Purging of Navarre, Galicia, Castille and León") in Preston, *The Spanish Holocaust*, pp. 179–220.

11 Cf. Cenarro, "Matar, vigilar, delatar."

12 "La violencia no se hace en servicio del anarquismo, sino lícitamente en bene-ficio del orden, la Patria y la religión". ("The violence does not stem from anarchism *(sic),* but arises legitimately as a means of defending social order, country and religion.") Arce Ochotorena, who was originally from Navarre, also spoke of "la guerra sin cuartel contra las hordas criminales" ("war without quarter against the criminal hordes"), Alfonso Álvarez Bolado, *Para ganar la guerra, para ganar la paz: Iglesia y guerra civil 1936–1939* (Madrid: Universidad Pontificia de Comillas, 1995), p. 44. A long pastoral in defence of the war, *ibid.*, pp. 74, 118. (Alvarez Bolado's is a crucial text, deploying as it does the ecclesiastical bulletins in which these statements originally appeared.) On Arce Ochotorena's commitment to the coup see also Marino Ayerra Redín, *No me avergoncé del evangelio (desde mi parroquia)*, 2nd edn (Buenos Aires: Editorial Periplo, 1959), p. 30. Cf. the verdict on him as Bishop of Zamora, given by Palmira Sanjuan Misis who, as a girl, was imprisoned with her mother in the same cell as Amparo. Testimony cited in Sender Barayón, *A Death in Zamora*, p. 144.

13 José Alvarez Miranda, Bishop of León, cited in Álvarez Bolado, *Para ganar la guerra, para ganar la paz*, p. 52.

14 Miguel Franco Olivares appears in the *Boletín del Movimiento de Falange Española Tradicionalista y de las J.O.N.S.* Año VII, n° 193, 10 Sept. 1943, pp. 2212–13, as a recipient of regime preferment, specifically the "Medalla de La Vieja Guardia", which indicates that he was a priest who was already sympathetic to the Falange in the period before the military rising of July 1936. The refer-ences to him being involved in the killing of prisoners and administering the *coup de grâce*, in Laura de Dios Vicente, "Control y represión en Zamora (1936–1939). La violencia vengadora ejecutada sobre el terreno", *Historia y Comunicación Social* 7 (2002): 47–74, esp. 61. The document on which the

author bases her assertion is undeclared but likely comes from documentation held in the private archive of Zamora's chronicler, Miguel Ángel Mateos Rodríguez whom she cites. Access to this material is on a grace and favour basis, in the best manner of high Francoism. See chapter 7 for more on Mateos Rodríguez and his questionable role in the polemic over Amparo Barayón which erupted in Zamora's local press in 2005. In an oral history project undertaken in Zamora by ARMH, the largest of the civic memory associations, interviewees also recalled Franco Olivares as a source of terror on the streets and as a priest who used his crucifix as a weapon against prisoners. One interviewee, whose own father was a victim of extrajudicial execution in the town in 1936, referred to her mother's frustration and disgust when, after her husband's death, Franco Olivares came into the small jewellery, watch and clock shop the family ran. She would not serve him or let her daughter do so, but through another assistant, who was not a family member, communicated to him that the shop no longer offered a repair service. The interviewee's mother was a practising Catholic but, from that moment on, she never went to confession nor took communion again. ARMH, Zamora, transcript of interview with P.M.B. and A.G.D., 19 May 2005. Franco Olivares also pursued (as did many priests) a relentless campaign to have those liberal professionals who survived the coup fined and excluded from their posts, providing reports to the regime's Political Responsibilities Tribunal for the purpose. Franco Olivares' report on José Datas Gutiérrez, former Director of the Teacher Training College, 21 December 1939 (to the Juzgado Provincial de Responsabilidades Políticas) in Archivo Histórico Provincial de Zamora (AHPZA), AP/RP Caja 10 Exp. 5.

15   Indeed the cover of the Spanish translation (both its visual design and wording) is packaged to suggest that the key to Amparo's death was her husband, Ramón Sender. Certainly it is true that some women were executed in the rebel zone in lieu of their husbands who could not be found – what was termed 'right of representation' (*por derecho de representación*), Paul Preston, *The Spanish Holocaust*, p. 205. But this does not fit with Amparo's story. The rumour that Franco himself signed her death warrant seems, on the basis of what we currently know, to be just that. It is true that from some point in the autumn of 1936 (and certainly from 1 October) Franco liked to have a sight of official death sentences (as opposed to extra-judicial ones – for which there was obviously no paperwork). But at the time of Amparo's death, Franco was heavily involved in the opening stages of his attack on Madrid (announced to the press on 6 October), so even if there was any paperwork attached to the decision to kill Amparo, it is plausible that he did not even see the file. This does not preclude a verbal order, but, again, the timing makes that seem unlikely.

16   Unless otherwise referenced, all the biographical information for Amparo and her family comes from interviews and correspondence I have had with family members, or from primary historical documentation now in the family's possession/archive, some of which has only been successfully retrieved from

state and municipal archives in the last ten years. A few of these items are also reproduced in Ramón Sender's *A Death in Zamora*.

17 See plate of Barayón family tree. Please note that in the chapter text I have not generally distinguished Amparo's half-siblings from her full ones, as this does not bear meaningfully on the events described.

18 Although Lorca himself had been well advised to the contrary. Ian Gibson, *Federico García Lorca. A Life* (London: Faber & Faber, 1989), pp. 442–3. "Going home" was a widespread phenomenon, sometimes in the months after the coup, or even much later. One such case was the man who had been mayor of Zafra (Badajoz) under the pre-war Republic, José González Barrero. In spite of the fact that forty people were shot on the first day of the military occupation of Zafra, and two hundred in total over the next months, at the end of the war, he returned home from Madrid, apparently believing Franco's public promise that those without blood on their hands had nothing to fear. He was immediately arrested and interned in the concentration camp of Castuera and executed at the end of April 1939, José María Lama, *Una biografía frente al olvido: José González Barrero, Alcalde de Zafra en la segunda República* (Badajoz: Diputación de Badajoz, 2000), pp. 83–126, 136–8; this misplaced sense of safety in one's place of origin sometimes worked also to prevent people fleeing before the arrival of rebel forces, only then to be murdered by them and collaborating vigilantes. Preston, *The Spanish Holocaust*, pp. 139–40.

19 Sender Barayón, *Death in Zamora*, p. 99.

20 Her name was recorded as such ("conceptuada como espía") in a list of political suspects compiled by Colonel Raimundo Hernández Comes, civil governor of Zamora (and one of the original military conspirators there) and dated for the period 19 July 1936 to 11 February 1937.

21 Saturnino's prison entry record is dated 26 July 1936. Expediente procesal, Prisión de Partido de Toro. I am grateful for the help of John Palmer, a historical researcher and volunteer with the civic memory association, ARMH in Zamora, for locating this document.

22 She was detained on 4 August 1936 according to a Zamora Falange report dated 17 September 1941. Copy in family archive.

23 Interviews with his niece, Magdalena Maes Barayón, July 2003 and July 2011.

24 Cf. these sentiments as expressed in 1927, "Russia, together with other expressions of modernity such as aviation, the radio, telephone, gave life great interest", cited by Enrique Montero, 'Reform Idealized: The Intellectual and Ideological Origins of the Second Republic', in Helen Graham and Jo Labanyi (eds), *Spanish Cultural Studies: An introduction: the struggle for modernity* (Oxford and New York: Oxford University Press, 1995), pp. 124–33, quote p. 131. See also in a similar vein, the 1934 diary correspondence of one Cipriano López Crespo, an enterprising individual of the middling sort, who envisaged the utopic transformation of his Cuenca village (Villaconejos), published in Ángel Luis López Villaverde and Isidro Sánchez Sánchez, *Honra, agua y pan: Un sueño comunista de Cipriano López Crespo (1934–1938)*, (Cuenca: Universidad Castilla-

La Mancha, 2004) and also Helen Graham, *The Spanish Civil War. A Very Short Introduction* (Oxford: Oxford University Press, 2005), pp. 61–3. The memoirs of two young women activists also draw attention to this "breath of fresh air" in which the PCE is seen as an extension of the Republic's, and more as a medium for change than as a doctrinal instrument, Carmen Parga, *Antes que sea tarde* (Madrid: Compañía Literaria, 1996), p. 50, and Aurora Arnaíz, *Retrato hablado de Luisa Julián* (Madrid: Compañía Literaria, 1996), p. 26. This social history of communism in 1920s and 30s Spain is yet to be seriously tackled, but see Rafael Cruz, "¡Luzbel vuelve al mundo! Las imágenes de la Rusia Soviética y la acción colectiva en España", in Rafael Cruz and Manuel Pérez Ledesma (eds), *Cultura y movilización en la España contemporánea* (Madrid: Alianza, 1997). For complaints from the Almería branch of the PSOE during the war regarding the PCE's populist talents and ability to attract the politically "unschooled" to itself, see Helen Graham, *Socialism and War: The Spanish Socialist Party in Power and Crisis 1936–1939* (Cambridge: Cambridge University Press, 1991), p. 119. For the appeal of the wartime PCE to a mass audience, especially within the socialist and communist youth movement, newly unified in March 1936 and which rapidly became massified in the early months of the war. Fernando Claudín, *The Communist Movement. From Comintern to Cominform* (Harmondsworth: Penguin, 1975), pp. 230–1.

25   For the the Zamora city returns from April 1931, M. A. Mateos, *La República en Zamora (1931–1936). Comportamiento político electoral en una sociedad tradicional* (Zamora: IEZ Florián de Ocampo, 1995), vol. I, p. 283. In the municipal elections of 12 April 1931 in Zamora city, the republicans and socialists together polled 46.2% of the vote. Some contextualizing detail for Saturnino's role in Zamora's municipal politics after 1931 can be gleaned from the minutes of town council meetings (Libros de Actas de Sesiones) in the Archivo Municipal de Zamora (AMZ) which is at present kept in the Archivo Histórico. Provincial de Zamora (AHPZA): for example in AHPZA, AMZ, L-1832 for the first constituting session of the new Council after the establishment of the Second Republic; AHPZA, AMZ, L-1838 for the suspension of the Council in October 1934 and AHPZA, AMZ, L-1840 for the incoming Popular Front in February 1936.

26   Manuel Ballbé, *Orden público y militarismo en la España constitucional (1812–1983)*, (Madrid: Alianza Editorial, 1983), pp. 402–9. For the Second Republic's failure to demilitarize public order, thus facilitating the legal fiction used by the rebels to legitimize their actions, see Ballbé, pp. 391, 393–5. From initial investigations in Zamora, we know that the imprisoned Saturnino Barayón was the subject of a preliminary "judicial" investigation (*"diligencias previas"*), on the basis of the accusation levelled against him in August 1936 of "reunion clandestina y campaña contra el movimiento nacional" ("taking part in a conspiracy and campaign against the national movement" – the name given to the military coup). This suggests that the original intention was to submit him to summary justice via a military trial

(*consejo de guerra*), many of which also ended in execution. But at the time of writing it has not been possible to access Saturnino's file – as, along with many other similar files (namely all the *consejos de guerra* in Zamora province), it is awaiting state-funded digitization. This has been agreed, but is currently delayed because of what is apparently institutional obstruction within the Ministry of Defence (which controls the military archive in El Ferrol (Galicia) where these *consejo de guerra* files are currently located).

27 The overall repression in Zamora of course went far beyond the "hot" terror of the *sacas* in which hundreds lost their lives. Across the whole province some 1,331 died in the "cleansing" administered by the rebels, with 396 victims in the provincial capital. For an overview see Cándido Ruiz González and Juan Andrés Blanco Rodríguez, "La represión en la provincia de Zamora durante la guerra civil y el franquismo", in Enrique Berzal de la Rosa (coord.), *Testimonio de voces olvidadas* (Valderas, León: Fundación 27 de Marzo, 2007) II, pp. 237–307. The figures appear on p. 259. Also Cándido Ruiz González, Pilar de la Granja Fernández, Eduardo Martín González, "Un largo período de represión", in Juan Andrés Blanco Rodríguez (ed.), *A los 70 años de la Guerra Civil española: actas del Encuentro celebrado en Zamora, 21 y 22 de diciembre de 2006* (Zamora: Centro de la UNED de Zamora, 2010), pp. 157–210; and Pilar de la Granja Fernández, *Represión durante la guerra civil y la posguerra en la provincia de Zamora* (Zamora: Instituto de Estudios Zamoranos Florián de Ocampo, 2002). Also Adoración Martín Barrio, María de los Ángeles Sampedro Talabán and María Jesús Velasco Marcos, "Dos formas de violencia durante la guerra civil. La represión en Salamanca y la resistencia armada en Zamora", in Julio Aróstegui (coord.), *Historia y memoria de la guerra civil,* 3 vols (Valladolid: Junta de Castilla y León, 1988) II, pp. 413–37 and Ángel Espías Bermúdez, "Memorias, Año 1936. Hechos acaecidos en Zamora y provincia", *Ebre 38. Revista Internacional de la guerra civil* 2 (2003): 62–84.

28 The authorization letter of 27 August 1936 from Zamora's civil governor, Lt Colonel Hernández Comes, to the head of the Toro prison indicates that Antonio was handed over to Juan Luis Rodríguez, the head of the local Falange.

29 It has been noted by researchers examining the Zamora documentation on the prison transfers that in the case of those prisoners designated for extrajudicial execution, the letters from the civil governor's office authorizing their transfer lacked the usual system of numerical tags for administrative reference which were instead left blank.

30 Saturnino's death certificate, logged on 6 October 1936 in Toro's Registro Civil (Section 3a, vol. 54, no. 150, page (folio) 197v), gives the date of his death as 18 September 1936 (23.00 hours), "as a result of fire sustained from a police weapon as the prisoner fled, and during a period in which the state of war is in force" ("a consecuencia de disparo por la fuerza pública cuando huía yendo conducido por ésta en estado de guerra"). Antonio's death certificate, giving the date of death as 28 August, and was logged on 13 October 1936 (Section 3a, vol. 55, no. 172, page (folio) 8v. It lists the same manner of death.

31 As a result of further researches undertaken on the basis of information contained in Antonio's death certificate.

32 Interview with Magdalena Maes Barayón, Málaga, July 2003. All that remained to them of Antonio was a radio he had owned, the latest (American) model of its day, which her mother had spirited away in the face of the impending seizure of the family's assets. It haunts the Barayón story: it condemned Amparo, and also, in a sense, her uncle Antonio. But it also signals his belief in the new. Saved from the seizure of family assets by Magdalena senior, the radio will also stand for Magdalena Maes' lifeline to the world outside. In a letter to Ramón Sender of 5 July 1945 letter, she explains how, gathered around Antonio's old radio, they heard him broadcasting from New York on *Voice of America*, thus confirming what they had gleaned from a family member in Madrid, that Sender was alive, even though the Franco regime had announced his death.

33 There is a confusion here in *A Death in Zamora* where the military governor is referred to as Claomarchirán (*sic*). Claumarchirán was the surname of Hernández Comes' wife. The error arises because the son of the governor, Venancio Hernández Claumarchirán, was interviewed by Ramón Sender Barayón. He then assumed that the father's surname would be the same as the son's – whereas the Spanish rules here are different, dictating that a child takes one surname each from both his father and mother.

34 The civil and military governors were usually separate roles, but when Hernández Comes assumed military control of urban Zamora after the coup (*comandante militar de la plaza*) he also absorbed the civil governor's functions.

35 Sender Barayón, *A Death in Zamora*, pp. 146–7 (relaying the testimony of Amparo's prison companions, Pilar Fidalgo and Palmira Sanjuan Misis).

36 The later (nominal) return of family monies booted them little, however. The couple would be involved – as interlocutors with the rebel authorities – in the Red Cross negotiations to have Amparo's children sent out of the rebel zone and back to their father. From that point on, however, Casimira and Sevilla were ostracized by the Barayón family and would leave Zamora after the war, more or less in disgrace, Magdalena Maes, letter to Ramón Sender sr, 5 July 1945.

37 For the same reason, Magdalena had also been forbidden to see Saturnino in the mourning black she was wearing for Antonio, and had thus been obliged to change her clothes at the gaol. Sender Barayón, *A Death in Zamora*, p. 162. On the common practice of the military authorities banning all public manifestations of grief and mourning for the victims of extrajudicial killing, Preston, *The Spanish Holocaust*, pp. 141–2 cites numerous testimonies and examples.

38 Fidalgo, *A Young Mother in Franco's Prisons*, p. 32. A French edition also exists. Fidalgo's testimony originally appeared in the Republican press, in *El Socialista* 20–22, 24 May 1937. Fidalgo refers to the psychological assault upon the

imprisoned Amparo on p. 15, and to her execution (and blaming of Miguel Sevilla) on p. 28.

39   Fidalgo, *A Young Mother in Franco's Prisons*, p. 28.

40   Zamora police report of 21 March 1937 refers to an investigation about Amparo being instigated on 3 December 1936 in response to a judge's order. It seems likely that this too was triggered by the Red Cross intervention. The children's final departure was documented and signed in Burgos on 21 January 1937 by the international delegate of the Red Cross in the rebel zone, Horace de Pourtales. The document refers to two year old Ramón and ten-month-old Andrea, "dont la mère avait été fusillée á Zamora ont été repatriés par ma Délégation de cette ville et remis á leur père á Bayonne en date des 12 et 18 Janvier" (whose mother had been shot in Zamora, have been repatriated (*sic*) by my local delegation and returned to their father in Bayonne on the 12 and 18 January). Document from the Barayón family archive.

41   Fidalgo, *A Young Mother in Franco's Prisons*, p. 31.

42   Preston, *The Spanish Holocaust*, pp. 187–8. This expands our picture of the ways in which the clergy too became victims of Francoism – although of course it has long been known that the rebels executed a number of Basque priests as separatists.

43   For example, the intelligence officer in Burgos who in 1937 in response to his Quaker interlocutors' concerns about how there was significantly greater material deprivation being endured by the Republican population commented that "just as soon as we can get things cleaned up in the North then there'll be more suffering there too . . . ", Dan West, "Needy Spain", Reports from the field, vol II (report authored Feb. 1938), Friends Service Council /R/Sp/4, Quaker archive, Friends House, London. For an analysis of the political functions of "suffering" and "penitence", see Richards, *A Time of Silence*. Also Carlos Barral's memoir, *Años de Penitencia* (Barcelona: Plaza & Janés, 1994). There is also some interesting anthropological work in train in Aranda del Duero (Burgos, Castile and León) which explores the ways in which the impact of violent repression was experienced differently in the "believing north/centre". For example, the lack of a body to bury, while grievous in its impact on survivors everywhere, obviously had significantly different meanings for an anticlerical or non-believer than it did for a pious villager who believed that an unburied body entailed purgatory and the spiritual, as well as physical, loss of their loved ones.

44   *Patronato central para la redención de penas por el trabajo.* For more on the uses and meaning of work within the Francoist prison universe, see chapter 6.

45   Michael Richards, "Biology and Morality in the Spanish Civil War: Psychiatrists, Revolution and Women Prisoners in Málaga", *Contemporary European History* 10 (2001): 395–421 (special issue on Gender and War). See also chapter 6 in this volume.

46   "En busca del gen rojo", *El País*, 7 January 1996. http://www.elpais.com/ articulo/espana/ESPANA/SOCIALISMO/GUERRA_CIVIL_ESPANOLA/C OMUNISMO/FRANQUISMO/busca/gen/rojo/elpepiesp/19960107elpepina

c_22/Tes. "Marxists are retards", Giles Tremlett reporting on the experiments of Franco's psychiatrists in *The Guardian*, 1 November 2002. http://www. guardian.co.uk/world/2002/nov/01/spain.gilestremlett (sites accessed 15 January 2012).

47 Miguel Ángel Mateos, "Muerte en Zamora, la tragedia de Amparo Barayón", serialized in *La Opinión El Correo de Zamora*, 3, 4, 5, 6, 7, 8, 24 April 2005; Fidalgo, *A Young Mother in Franco's Prisons,* p. 22; Sender Barayón, *A Death in Zamora*, pp. 110, 145, 164–5.

48 The law was a major instrument of war: especially the (retroactive) Law of Political Responsibilities (February 1939) which, as we can see here, directly affected the Barayón family, and also the Law against Communism and Freemasonry (March 1940). There was also a (February1939) law to purge the civil service/state employees. For the Law of Political Responsibilities, *ABC,* 12 February 1939: "La justicia de la España Imperial. Una Ley plena de serenidad. Ha sido firmada la ley de Responsabilidades políticas." The full text in *ABC*, 17, 19 February 1939; Manuel Álvaro Dueñas, *'Por ministerio de la ley y voluntad del Caudillo'. La Jurisdicción Especial de Responsabilidades Políticas (1939–1945)* (Madrid: Centro de Estudios Políticos y Constitucionales, 2006), pp. 68–80, 97–110. For instances of the political responsibilities law's application, and which give a clear sense of its vindictive origins, Preston, *The Spanish Holocaust*, pp. 504–5.

49 "Me partió la vida" (it destroyed my life), interview with Magdalena Maes Barayón, July 2003.

50 Magdalena Barayón Hernández's formal renunciation of the Barayón fortune was made to the courts in Zamora (Juzagado de Primera Instancia) on 17 December 1942. Copy of document in Barayón family archive.

51 Unlike many families, the Barayons, including Ramón and Andrea, did eventually get some funds returned to them from the seized family assets, but it was a purely nominal amount (Ramón Sender senior exclaimed down the phone to Magdalena that he'd spent more on the children's Christmas gifts than was being returned to them by the Francoist state). It was generally the case that, as time went on, the political responsibilities tribunals did make some token efforts at "fairness", albeit very much after the event. Cf. Francesc Vilanova i Vila-Abadal, *Repressió política i coacció econòmica. Les responsabilitats polítiques de republicans i conservadors catalans a la postguerra (1939–1942)* (Barcelona: Publicacions de l'Abadia de Montserrat, 1999), pp. 44–51.

52 This was the same person whose presence in the Maes Barayón household had made it very difficult for Ramón and Andrea to come to stay after Amparo's execution, thus necessitating their departure to an orphanage. It is ironic, then, that it was his death, and the subsequent opening of the family tomb which provided the young Magdalena with the opportunity to re-inter Amparo's remains, described at the beginning of the chapter.

53 Magdalena Maes to Ramón Sender sr., 5 July 1945 (this letter avoided the censorship apparatus because Magdalena sent it to the US with some returning

relatives of friends in Zamora). Thereafter Magdalena avoided similar problems by addressing her letters to Ramón Sender to his third wife, Florence. Magdalena Maes, communication to the author, 31 July 2011. Magdalena was involved with the PCE because, by way of anti-Franco resistance at the time, "that's what there was" (correspondence with the author, July 2011). But it seems likely that the memory of her favourite uncle Antonio also lent itself to her course of action.

54 At which point she was released under one of the regime's periodic pardons which served the purpose of freeing up the prisons which were under continual new influx, see chapter 6 below.

55 An example of this in the dictated "set piece" letter in which Magdalena expresses her "gratitude" to the authorities for the "cultural education" of prison, and which she was obliged to sign at the end of her incarceration. It was published on 12 March 1949, in *Redención* ("Redemption"), the prison newspaper which inmates were coerced into buying with their exiguous resources. It cost as much as a commercial newspaper, the profits going to the state. On *Redención* see Ángela Cenarro, "La institucionalización, del universo penitenciario" in Carme Molinero *et al.* (eds), *Una inmensa prisión. Los campos de concentración y las prisiones durante la guerra civil y el franquismo* (Barcelona: Crítica, 2003), pp. 143–5 and Preston, *The Spanish Holocaust*, p. 510. Cf. Herta Müller's autobiographical novel, *The Land of Green Plums* (London: Granta, 1996) – original German version *Herztier* (Hamburg: Rowohlt Verlag, 1993) – for a powerful poetic evocation of very similar processes of "making ugly" in Ceauşescu's Romania.

56 Ramón Sender Barayón, *A Death in Zamora*, p. 149.

57 Magdalena Maes, letter to Ramón Sender sr, 5 July 1945 (family archive).

58 While this phenomenon is far from unique to Francoism, the very longevity of the regime intensified it to the point that it has acquired a very idiosyncratic social force in Spain, and one which endures to this day – yet another after effect of the dictatorship. Many of the works on the repression refer to its negative impact upon the recovery of the history of those traduced by the regime: so-and-so was taken away because he "spoke out of turn" or because "she had fancy ideas" or because "he had got mixed up in politics" all of which transform a victim into the guilty party, responsible for his/her own demise, Cándido Ruiz González, Pilar de la Granja Fernández, Eduardo Martín González, "Un largo período de represión", p. 173.

59 Cemetery lists frequently offer fuller and more accurate records because many people were too frightened to register deaths officially lest they too became the object of police/state attention. In this regard Amparo and her brothers were in a minority in having death certificates issued by the authorities – albeit ones that falsified or omitted the crucial detail of how they had died. (A "résumé" of Amparo's is published in Sender Barayón, *A Death in Zamora*, p. 138.) Death certificates also tended to be issued more in the north of Spain than in the south, where the bulk of the extrajudicial killing perpetrated by the rebels

occurred. Whether or not they were issued depended to some extent on local circumstance, but if the victims were well known, or of a certain social standing, then their killings were more likely to produce some form of documentation.

60   The totalitarian nature of the original Francoist project is clear: whether it can also be described as fascist is still a matter of scholarly debate. It is a debate that needs to be less concerned with the Franco regime's Axis "mimicry" or the role of the Falange, than with what the regime did to the defeated. In the light of the evidence, if Francoism was not "fascist", then it was not fascist in the same way as Nazism has been argued as being not fascist – i.e. that Francoism and Nazism were less concerned to discipline and control 'enemy' groups than to kill them.

61   For more on this see chapters 6 and 7.

62   Cf. the retrospectively optimistic (and surprisingly political) voice-over at the end of Pedro Almodóvar's 1997 film, *Live Flesh* (*Carne Trémula*): "Luckily for you my son, we stopped being afraid a long time ago in Spain".

63   Notably, the Association for the Recuperation of Historical Memory: http://www.memoriahistorica.org.es/ founded by Emilio Silva in the search to identify the remains of his own grandfather, see Santiago Macías and Emilio Silva, *Las fosas de Franco: los republicanos que el dictador dejó en la cuneta* (Madrid: Temas de Hoy, 2006). These questions are taken up again in chapter 7 in the discussion on Spain's present day memory wars.

64   Televisió de Catalunya screened a documentary of the same name (*Els nens perduts del franquisme*) in March 2002 which was subsequently shown in the Basque Country and abroad. But it would take another three years before it achieved a nationwide screening in Spain. There is an accompanying book, Ricard Vinyes, Montserrat Armengou and Ricard Belis, *Los niños perdidos del franquismo* (Barcelona: Plaza & Janés, 2002). See also Ricard Vinyes, *Irredentas: Las presas políticas y sus hijos en las cárceles franquistas* (Madrid: Temas de Hoy, 2002).

65   By the decree of 30 March 1940, women prisoners had the right to nurse their children until they were three years old. This measure made it possible for the authorities legally to remove 3 year olds from prison. But it did not of course legalise the subsequent "disappearance" of those children. Children were not usually passed to prisoners' families but to state tutelage. Under the terms of the law of 4 December 1941 "red" children who couldn't remember their names – for whatever reasons (i.e. repatriated refugees, orphans, children whose parents couldn't be located etc.) could be given new names. It was this law that facilitated the "disappearances"/illegal adoptions. The Servicio Exterior de Falange frequently "retrieved" children from abroad against the wishes of their parents resident in Spain. An estimated 11,000 children were still listed as refugees in the 1940s (i.e. excluding those who were part of exiled families). By 1943, 12,042 children were under state tutelage. But there were many more thousands in state institutions. For further context see chapter 6.

66 As will be discussed in chapter 7, however, the recuperation of these voices and memories has not gone unchallenged. The same democratic space which has permitted their slow recuperation since the 1980s is also now witnessing the resurgence of pro-Franco voices, these with a newfound confidence deriving from the populist conservative nationalism emergent across much of Europe since the late twentieth century.

67 Cf. editor's introduction to *Muerte en Zamora*, p. 8. This introduction was written by Magdalena Maes' daughter, Mercedes Esteban-Maes Kemp. No doubt the family's particular circumstances have played a part here in this lack of silence. Unlike many others who had suffered repression, but whose subsequent lives were less secure, both materially and in other ways, Magdalena did not feel by the 1960s that she was actively putting her children at direct risk with the knowledge she imparted. That said, the ringing and ongoing silence inside many families in Spain went far wider than those who felt themselves to be personally at risk – that too was a Franco effect. That Magdalena always spoke of these things was also a reflection of her personality and strength of mind, and most of all of the driving need she felt to cut through what the past and historical circumstance had imposed upon her, in order to create some space which might be free of the necessary elisions and conformity demanded of everyone in the Francoist public sphere.

4 Border Crossings

1 These lines of Machado's are some of the most famous in Spanish poetry, and Machado himself, one of Spain's greatest poets, is still hugely and popularly read today. He was also a poet of the exile, crossing the border into France as part of the vast tide of refugees – some half a million civilians, Republican soldiers and International Brigaders – who fled Franco's advancing armies after the fall of Catalonia in February 1939. He died a few days after the crossing and was buried by the sea at Collioure.

2 This chapter is thus not intended as a systematic, macro-historical survey of the Brigades, but an interpretative essay on what the brigaders meant as a phenomenon in inter-war Europe. There is, as yet, no transnational or comparative study of the International Brigades available in English. One such preliminary analysis in Rémi Skoutelsky, *Novedad en el frente: Las brigadas internacionales en la guerra civil* (Madrid: Temas de Hoy, 2006).

3 Victor Serge, *The Long Dusk* (New York: The Dial Press, 1946), p. 87. This is a novelized account of European antifascist exiles living through the arrival of the Nazis in Paris in June 1940 and these are the words of Serge's patient (and somewhat infuriating) revolutionary, Ardatov. For an historically acute review of the novel, Lorna Scott Fox, *London Review of Books* 25, 10 (22 May 2003), pp. 25–7.

4 "My own taste has always been for unwritten history and my present business is with the reverse of the picture." Henry James, "The Story of a Year", first

published in *The Atlantic Monthly. A Magazine of Literature, Art and Politics* XV, LXXXIX (March 1865).

5 Arjun Appadurai, "Disjuncture and Difference in the Global Cultural Economy", in Simon During (ed.), *The Cultural Studies Reader*, 3rd edn (London: Routledge, 2007), pp. 216–26, esp. 221.

6 Peter Carroll, *The Odyssey of the Abraham Lincoln Brigade. Americans in the Spanish Civil War* (Stanford, CA: Stanford University Press, 1994), p. 16. On the Canadians, see Michael Petrou, *Renegades. Canadians in the Spanish Civil War* (Vancouver: UBC Press, 2008), pp. 13–25. Canadian volunteers were mainly themselves migrants, while among the US contingent approximately one third were, with some 80 percent being children of migrants (with at least one European parent). This also explains the sociological differences – the Canadians tended to be poorer, older (in their 30s) and more socially marginal – having come from rural areas and also work camps. They had less education too as a rule. This contrasts with the urban, better educated and slightly younger US volunteers. Nevertheless, as Carroll indicates, the median age of the US volunteers was 27 and the average age, slightly older again – so neither branch of the North American volunteers represented "callow" or "impetuous" youth.

7 Petrou, *Renegades*, p. 37.

8 Koestler, *Scum of the Earth*, pp. 76–7 for the story of nineteen-year-old Yankel from Poland, who had "travelled through seven countries of Europe", cf. also pp. 115–16 and pp. 138–9. Immensely illuminating too is the trilogy of novel-ized memoir by the psychologist and writer, Manès Sperber (*Like a Tear in the Ocean*, comprising *The Burned Bramble*, *The Abyss* and *Journey without End*), (New Jersey: Holmes & Meier, 1988) which first appeared in German at the end of the 1940s and in English in the early 1950s. Sperber was born in 1905 into a Hasidic family in Zablotów, then Austrian Galicia, now Ukraine. Fleeing the war in 1916, his family moved to Vienna. Sperber himself gravi-tated to a secular and political understanding of his times and in 1927, living in Berlin, he joined the communist party. Imprisoned by the Nazis, but released because of his Polish passport, Sperber went to live first in Yugoslavia and then in Paris. He left the communist party in 1938 in protest at the begin-ning of Stalin's purges and in 1939 volunteered for the French army. After its defeat and the German occupation, he escaped to the "free zone". In 1942 Sperber was able to get out of France and to Switzerland, thus narrowly escaping deportation. For Robert Capa himself, also one of these restless refugee boys, see chapter 1 above and (especially) chapter 5 below.

9 This idea is also reflected in chapter 5 below.

10 Funaroff's Apollinaire-influenced poem, *The Bellbuoy*:

> I am that exile
> from a future time
> from shores of freedom
> I may never know,

who hears, sounding in the surf,
tidings from the lips of waves . . . .

Cited in Alan M. Wald's *Exiles from a Future Time. The Forging of the Mid-Twentieth-Century Left* (Chapel Hill & London: University of North Carolina Press, 2002), p. vii. See pp. 204–14 for a portrait of Funaroff as one of Wald's "Three Moderns in Search of an Answer". An assemblage of literary and political commemorations of Funaroff's life and poetry, including by those who knew him personally is at http://www.english.illinois.edu/maps/poets/a_f/funaroff/memoirs.htm (accessed 18 September 2011). The poet Genevieve Taggard (d. 1948) recalled Funaroff as someone who "became a poet *and faced his situation*" (italics mine).

11 Graham, *Spanish Republic at War*, pp. 75, 181–2 and cf. Sandra Souto, "Taking the street: workers' youth organizations and political conflict in the Spanish Second Republic", *European History Quarterly* 34, 2 (2004): 131–56.

12 André Malraux's novel *L'Espoir* (*Man's Hope*), (Paris: Gallimard, 1971), first published in 1938, has an epochal evocation of the battle in Madrid's University City (Malraux had been involved in organizing air support for the Republic). For the siege of Madrid, see also Cox, *Defence of Madrid* and Paul Preston, *We Saw Spain Die: Foreign Correspondents in the Spanish Civil War* (London: Constable, 2008).

13 This artificial beach – the first ever in Spain – was designed for public use and opened in 1932 at Monte de El Pardo in the environs of Madrid. It captures the spirit of the early Republican years – public works (the "sea" was water from the river Manzanares channelled into a dam) plus an aspiration to democratize leisure and grant access to "nature". For more on the "beach", Ana Moreno Garrido, *Historia del turismo español en el siglo XX* (Madrid: Sintesis, 2007), pp. 98–9. The "beach" can be viewed here: http://pasionpormadrid.blogspot.com/2010/02/la-playa-de-madrid.html.

14 Manuel Tagüeña Lacorte, *Testimonio de dos guerras* (Mexico: Ediciones Oasis, 1974); see also Carmen Parga, *Antes que sea tarde* ("Before it is too late"), (Mexico: Porrúa, 2007) which also includes the "playa de Madrid" photograph on p. 41.

15 Paul Preston focuses on the fact that a few of the leading members of the Socialist Youth organization were co-opted by the Spanish Communist Party and thus enjoyed a special political status, see *The Spanish Holocaust*, pp. 347–9, but, socially, and sociologically, speaking, something rather bigger was happening in the wartime Republican Spain, involving young people *en masse*.

16 We know this not least from the records of the *Comandancia de Milicias*, Michael Alpert, *El ejército republicano en la guerra civil* (Madrid: Siglo XXI, 1989), pp. 41 (n. 25), 62; Graham, *Spanish Republic at War*, p. 176. Other work has subsequently borne this out, for example, Ledesma, *Los días de llamas*, pp. 238–40.

17 The latest assessment in Ángel Viñas and Fernando Hernández Sánchez, *El desplome de la República* (Barcelona: Crítica, 2009). For the deadly effects of

Casado, see Eduardo de Guzmán, *La muerte de la esperanza* (Madrid: G. del Toro, 1973) and *Año de la Victoria* (Madrid: G. del Toro, 1974); also Juana Doña, *Querido Eugenio* (Barcelona: Editorial Lumen, 2003) and Aurora Arnáiz, *Retrato hablado de Luisa Julián* (Madrid: Compañía Literaria, 1996), pp. 111 and ff. Aurora Arnáiz was a PCE activist and the wife of José Cazorla, one of the leaders of the JSU, who, as an early thirty something, was in charge of policing the capital for much of the life of the Madrid Defence Council from December 1936 to spring 1937. He was later civil governor of Guadalajara. He was captured in 1939, interrogated under torture, subject to Francoist military trial and executed in April 1940, Preston, *The Spanish Holocaust*, p. 477.

18 For his medical innovation and the political difficulties Crome faced in post, see Paul Preston, "Two doctors and one cause: Len Crome and Reginald Saxton in the International Brigades", *International Journal of Iberian studies* 19, 1 (2006): 5–24. Crome's father would die in a Soviet labour camp; his mother and elder sister were killed by the Germans. Crome himself served as an Allied medical officer with the British forces in Italy and in 1944 was awarded the Military Cross for his achievement in clearing casualties under heavy fire during the battle for Monte Casino. In the postwar most of his publications appertained to his career in the UK as a specialist in the pathology of learning difficulty. He also wrote *Unbroken. Resistance and Survival in the Concentration Camps* (London: Lawrence & Wishart, 1988), based largely on the experience of his brother-in-law, Jonny Hüttner. Obituaries for Crome (b. Dvinsk, Latvia 14 April 1909, d. Stoke-on-Trent, England 5 May 2001) in *The Independent*, 11 May 2001 http://www.independent.co.uk/news/obituaries/dr-len-crome-729104.html; *The Guardian,* 12 May 2001 http://www.guardian.co.uk/news/2001/may/12/guardianobituaries1 and *The Psychiatrist* 26 (2002) http://pb.rcpsych.org/content/26/5/199.1.full (sites last accessed 15 October 2011).

19 Although, as Richard Evans has observed, in some of the current historiography it seems to have become fashionable to write as if the German labour movement of the 1930s were a social minority – which is a statistical absurdity and a notoriously distorting piece of "presentism", Richard J. Evans, "Coercion and Consent in Nazi Germany" (Raleigh Lecture on History, 2006), *Proceedings of the British Academy* 151 (2007), pp. 58–61.

20 Sander began his monumental project of portraiture, *People of the Twentieth Century*, in the early 1920s. A selection from it, published in 1929 as *Face of our Time*, was later seized and destroyed by the Nazis (http://www.tate.org.uk/modern/exhibitions/cruelandtender/sander.htm). (Site accessed, 15 January 2012).

21 The words were written by two "early" concentration camp prisoners in 1933, the political detainees, Johann Esser (a miner) and Wolfgang Langhoff (an actor); the music was composed by Rudi Goguel and was later adapted by Hanns Eisler and Ernst Busch. It was sung by Ernst Busch, and recorded for a later album, *Six Songs for Democracy* (New York: Keynote Recordings 1940).

Much of this recording was made during the shelling of Barcelona in 1938. Busch is accompanied by a chorus from the Thaelmann-Batallion (the 11th International Brigade). Numerous subsequent recordings exist and several websites currently offer access to the original by Busch.

22 Preston, "Theorists of Extermination", *The Spanish Holocaust*, pp. 34–51; Isabelle Rohr, "The use of antisemitism in the Spanish Civil War", *Patterns of Prejudice* 37, 2 (2003) and also *The Spanish Right and the Jews 1898–1945. Antisemitism and Opportunism* (Brighton & Portland: Sussex Academic Press, 2007); Gonzalo Álvarez Chillida, *El antisemitismo en España: la imagen del judío (1812–2002)*, (Madrid: Marcial Pons, 2002).

23 The standard work is Arno Lustiger, *'Shalom Libertad'. Les Juifs dans la guerre d'Espagne* (Paris: Editions du Cerf, 1991), published in German and Spanish in 2001, although the original manuscript was written in German.

24 He was executed by the Polish authorities for killing a police informant.

25 On non-religious Jewish cultural identities, see "The conversion of the Jews", chapter 6 of Alan M. Wald, *Trinity of Passion: The Literary Left and the Antifascist Crusade* (Chapel Hill and London: University of North Carolina Press, 2007), pp. 176–209, esp. 179; cf. also chapter 1 ("Tough Jews in the Spanish Civil War"), pp. 16–45.

26 "Very often there were a lot of Jewish people in the Brigades, a great many, and a lot of them spoke Yiddish *and* something else. And you would always try to get a Jewish person who could speak Yiddish, to another Jewish person – it didn't matter if they were Romanian or Hungarian or what they were, you could get a common language, get a message if you wanted it, that they wanted to send home or say who they were or something like that. But we had on the Ebro, in that cave, three Finns and nobody could speak anything to them. Nobody speaks Finnish. They were all very bad chest wounds. In those days we didn't know that you could operate on chest wounds, we used to strap them up tight and sit them up, but they were miserable. They couldn't breathe; they were strapped up tight as well as being with all these dreadful flesh wounds, very deep ones. And they were all three dying. And we couldn't get anyone who spoke Finnish and they weren't Jewish. Oh! I'll never forget them, they were such beautiful creatures, great blonde things, you know . . . " The words of Patience Darton cited in Jackson, *'For us it was Heaven'*, p. 110. On the cave hospital, Angela Jackson, *Beyond the Battlefield: Testimony, Memory and Remembrance of a Cave Hospital in the Spanish Civil War* (Pontypool: Warren and Pell, 2005).

27 There is to date little published work on antisemitism within the International Brigades, although anecdotal evidence is not hard to find. See also Colin Shindler, "No pasarán. The Jews who fought in Spain", *Jewish Quarterly*, 33, 3 (1986): 34–41; Gerben Zaagsma, "'Red Devils': the Botwin Company in the Spanish Civil War", *East European Jewish Affairs* 33, 1 (2003): 83–99. The identity conflict potentially consequent on the experience of anti-semitism is also broached by Sarah Sackman in "La política de identidad de los judeoame-

ricanos en la guerra civil española", *Congreso Internacional de la Guerra Civil Española 2006*, unpublished conference paper.

28 Javier Cercas, *Soldados de Salamina* (Barcelona: Tusquets Editores, 2001), p. 158 (translation mine).

29 Various of their biographies in Philippe Ganier Raymond, *El cartel rojo* (Tafalla: Editorial Txalaparta, 2008), (French original, *L'Affiche Rouge* [Paris: Arthème Fayard, 1975]). For a study of the three Italian antifascists who were among the Manouchian group members executed, Antonio Bechelloni, "Antifascist resistance in France from the 'Phony War' to the Liberation: identity and destiny in question", in Donna R. Gabaccia and Fraser M. Ottanelli (eds), *Italian Workers of the World: Labor Migration and the Formation of Multiethnic States* (Urbana and Chicago: Illinois University Press, 2001), pp. 222–6. On the difficult relationship between the French communist hierarchy and Manouchian, David Wingeate Pike, *In the Service of Stalin: The Spanish Communists in Exile 1939–1945* (Oxford: Clarendon Press, 1993), pp. 188–91. In 1955 Louis Aragon also wrote a famous poem about Manouchian's executed fighters, "Strophes pour se souvenir", published in *Le roman inachevé* (Paris: Gallimard, 1956). There has been much comment about its final line, "They died for France": see, for example, Bechelloni *above cit.*

30 For all the Western order's retrospective mythologizing of its opposition to Hitler as opposition to the camp universe, in fact that selfsame post-1945 Western order would have almost as its foundational act the massive convulsion of the European continent through which was achieved between 1944 and 1947 none other than an ethnic cleansing "rebranded" as "population transfer". Thus a reordering of "post-Nazi" Europe occurred in accordance with the Hitlerian principle that ethnic homogeneity was the face of the future, and a desirable norm for stabilizing states and societies. Although this was visited upon central and east Europe in the aftermath of both world wars, the origins of the toxic myth clearly lie in *western* Europe – in the very idea of the "coherent" nation state itself.

31 Koestler, *Scum of the Earth*, pp. 89–90. For the French camps, see chapter 1 above. On the multi-ethnic representation of the French resistance, see Robert Guédiguian's widely distributed 2009 French (art house) feature film about the Manouchian group, *The Army of Crime*.

32 Cf. Tal Bruttmann and Laurent Joly, *La France Antijuive. L'agression de Léon Blum à la Chambre des Députés* (Editions des Equateurs, 2006). See also the discussion of Koestler's *Scum of the Earth* in chapter 1 above.

33 McDaniels ran away from home in Mississippi to California where he was adopted by the radical Ohio-born photographer Consuelo Kanaga, a contemporary and associate of a group of artistic practitioners who included Alfred Stieglitz, Edward Weston and Tina Modotti. Video interview with Eluard Luchell McDaniels, 26 August 1985, in the M. Harriman collection, ALBA 48–121, Tamiment Library, New York University; see also Carroll, *Odyssey of the Abraham Lincoln Brigade*, pp. 260–1.

34 Irv Goff interviewed in 1985 by M. Harriman, ALBA collection, Tamiment
    Library, New York University, and again by Jim Carriger c.1991 (privately-
    held audio cassettes, courtesy of Peter N. Carroll); author's interview (October
    2008) with Sylvia Thompson, the widow of the Lincoln brigader and American
    communist party (CPUSA) leader, Bob Thompson.

35 Irv Goff, video interview, Harriman collection; Bill Aalto died in 1958 and
    his telling comes to us only through a third party, in his friend James Foss'
    unpublished memoir of Aalto, "A Hero of the Left", written in the early 1980s,
    one copy of which he donated to the ALBA archive, now held by the Tamiment
    Library, New York University; for Ohio State campus, pp. 16–17.

36 Bill Aalto features as one of the "lives" in *Lives at the Limit*, a book I am
    currently researching which, via a set of signal lives, explores the social and
    existential impact of Republican defeat on a generation of progressives, as well
    as on ideas of political and social progress more broadly.

37 Foss, "A Hero of the Left", p. 52, cf. also p. 33.

38 Including both Marx and Alain Badiou, whose theory of the construction of
    the human subject this is. It is a suggestive hypothesis for historians in that it
    posits how, if not why, social change occurs at the level of the individual (i.e.
    the going beyond habitus or "tradition", or, perhaps even more suggestively
    for the historian, via behaviour which implies "no feel for the game"), Peter
    Hallward, *Badiou: A subject to truth* (Minneapolis: University of Minnesota
    Press, 2003), p. xxiv. For Badiou, one of the routes to such change is through
    "the event". What is of significance in the event thus construed is the part that
    escapes the parameters of the establishment/dominant forces, indeed escapes
    all established notions of *what is occurring*. It is something that cannot be calcu-
    lated, predicted or managed and is based on a radical break with the expected,
    when we are carried beyond the range of predictable response, in a way that
    has existential consequences for everyone. This is the ethical process of radical
    transformation/transfiguration through which the human subject is born. In
    the light of this we can consider James Foss' own comments, made in the mid
    1980s, on how Bill's revelation to Irv Goff went against "obvious" rational
    calculation, "*for some now unknowable reason*" (italics mine), Foss, "A Hero of the
    Left", p. 17. It has something of a void-induced creative blindness to it – which
    takes us back to the idea of thought changing more than it understands; or, in
    Badiou's words "every subject believes something without knowing why"
    (Hallward, *Badiou*, p. xxv). All of which resonates too with some of the histor-
    ical methods adopted in recent years, for example by looking at familiar
    documentation differently, as well as seeking out new kinds of documentation:
    "It has also changed *how* we read – for discrepant tone, tacit knowledge, stray
    emotions, extravagant details, 'minor' events." . . . "New notions of the polit-
    ical – where it is located and how it might be expressed – have revised whose
    stories count, what kind of stories count . . . " Ann Laura Stoler (ed.), *Haunted
    by Empire. Geographies of Intimacy in North American History* (Durham and
    London: Duke University Press, 2006), p. 7. In some ways, the memoir written

by Foss (who was an art historian) stands as an illustration of the technique.

39 For some immensely resonant and historically suggestive material with which to explore the idea of gender as the un-crossable frontier in the 1940s (gender configured as a "necessary constant" when all else seems in flux), see the ideas (and life) of Tatamkhulu Afrika (b. Egypt 1920), especially his remarkable autogiographical novel, *Bitter Eden* (London: Arcadia, 2002), in effect a memoir, whose subterranean story is the one of how gender was inexorably broken in a (Second World War) prisoner-of-war camp, and then remade in a way which both denied the break as well as enshrining it forever. It is a story of private wars won and lost, of the wars Theweleit's Freikorper alluded to without realizing when he opined "we ourselves are the war", and told with the visionary intensity of the poet Afrika was.

40 Vanessa Vieux, "A Short History of Women in the American Medical Bureau 1936–1939", unpublished Senior Thesis, Barnard College, Columbia University, 2002, pp. 26–7. Copy by courtesy of the author.

41 Foss, "A Hero of the Left", pp. 20–1, 71–4; Irv Goff, video interview, Harriman collection, ALBA; Milt Felsen, *The Anti-Warrior: A Memoir* (Iowa City: University of Iowa Press, 1989), pp. 87–9; John Gerassi, *Premature Antifascists: North American Volunteers in the Spanish Civil War* (New York: 1986), pp. 211–12; Carroll, *Odyssey of the Abraham Lincoln Brigade*, pp. 255–6.

42 *La Mise à mort* (Paris: Gallimard, 1965) was Aragon's last novel, or, more accurately, the first volume of the trilogy that constituted his final work. Conceptually and structurally complex, it is an existential disquisition on love, memory and the plurality of human beings.

43 See for example, Amir Weiner, *Landscaping the Human Garden* (Stanford, CA: Stanford University Press, 2003); Amir Weiner (ed.), *Modernity and Population Management* (Stanford, CA: Stanford University Press, 2003); Giorgio Agamben, "The camp as biopolitical paradigm of the modern", in Agamben, *Homo Sacer. Sovereign Power and Bare Life*, pp. 119–88; Peter Holquist, "To count, to extract, to exterminate: population statistics and population politics in late Imperial and Soviet Russia", in Terry Martin and Ronald Grigor Suny (eds), *A State of Nations. Empire and Nation-Making in the Age of Lenin and Stalin* (New York: Oxford University Press, 2001), pp. 111–44; and also, "'Information is the Alpha and Omega of Our Work': Bolshevik Surveillance in its Pan-European Perspective", *Journal of Modern History* 69, 3 (1997): 415–50.

44 Helen Graham, "'Against the State': a genealogy of the Barcelona May Days (1937)", *European History Quarterly* 29, 4 (1999): 485–542 and Ángel Viñas, *El escudo de la República: El oro de España, la apuesta soviética y los hechos de mayo* (Barcelona: Crítica, 2007), pp. 487–548.

45 Josie McLellan, *Antifascism and Memory in East Germany: Remembering the International Brigades 1945–1989* (Oxford: 2004).

46 Ludwig Renn, *Der spanische Krieg* (Berlin: Aufbau-Verlag, 1955), (first

submitted to the publishers in January 1951; finally published in 1955), McLellan, *Antifascism and Memory,* pp. 150–3.

47   On Renn and Uhse – a Prussian aristocrat with a chequered political past – McLellan, *Antifascism and Memory*, pp. 30–2, 119, 150–3.

48   London says this of himself in his memoir, *On Trial (L'Aveu)*, (London: Macdonald and Co., 1970), p. 21.

49   Rudolf Michaelis in a letter in 1973 to his former wife, Margaret, cited in Helen Ennis, *Margaret Michaelis, Love, Loss and Photography* (Port Melbourne, Victoria: National Gallery of Australia, 2005), pp. 76–7.

50   Biography of Rudolf Michaelis in Dieter Nelles, Harald Piotrowski, Ulrich Linse and Carlos García, *Antifascistas alemanes en Barcelona (1933–1939): El grupo DAS, sus actividades contra la red nazi y en el frente de Aragón* (Barcelona, Editorial Sintra, 2010), p. 419 – although the very striking portrait photograph which appears here attributed as Rudolf Michaelis (and also in Ennis, *Margaret Michaelis, above cit.*) we have recently discovered is not in fact Rudolf at all. This confusion and the lack of extant photographs of him, is, of course, an indication of the circumstances of those lives so "swept by travelling" (Durán, *Silences from the Spanish Civil War*, p. 49 and epigraph to ch. 5) where so many things had to be left behind – and repeatedly. For the story of Rudolf and Margaret burying photographs and letters in their Berlin garden before they fled Germany, see Ennis, *Margaret Michaelis*, pp. 84–6. There are two other, rather indistinct, images of Rudolf, one published in Ennis, *ibid.*, p. 35 and the other, also from the Margaret Michaelis archive held at the National Gallery of Australia, which can be viewed online at http://www.123people.de/s/rudolf+michaelis (last accessed 30 September 2011) – along with two misattributed images.

51   Ennis, *Margaret Michaelis*, pp. 170, 225.

52   This is not to say that the impact of the earlier party purges in Hungary (1949) and Czechoslovakia (1952) didn't have an impact in the DDR. Many veterans in East Germany suffered very aggressive questioning about their activities in Spain (McLellan, *Antifascism and Memory*, pp. 58–64). Many suffered work demotions and some unfortunates were handed over to the Soviet authorities and ended in the gulag. There is also evidence that an East German show trial was planned in which German International Brigader leaders (Franz Dahlem and Paul Merker) were earmarked as defendants – Dahlem in particular. It seems probable that an internal power rivalry was a contributory factor here. Dahlem was the most senior brigader veteran and his great popularity with antifascist veterans (both from the Spanish war and from the Nazi camps) meant that he was SED leader Walter Ulbricht's most dangerous rival. But the trial took longer to prepare, and there may have been more ambiguity at the top than in Hungary or Czechoslovakia. (There may also have been an intervention on behalf of Dahlem by DDR president, Wilhelm Pieck.) In any case, the mooted GDR trial ran into the buffers with Stalin's death in 1953. There was, however a later show trial of sorts in the DDR when in 1957

Spanienkämpfer Walter Janka was tried for "counter-revolutionary activities". He served three years in gaol and was subsequently stripped of all official status and even of recognition as an antifascist veteran, McLellan, *Antifascism and Memory*, pp. 1–2. But Janka was not executed or disappeared – which again suggests a different local political culture, as well as a change across time.

53   A resonant philosophical consideration of this question (which applies to more than one of the lives included in this chapter) in Judith Butler's *Antigone's Claim: Kinship Between Life and Death* (New York: Columbia University Press, 2000), esp. pp. 23–5, cf. "Antigone represents not kinship in its ideal form but its deformation and displacement, *one that puts the reigning regimes of representation into crisis and raises the question of what the conditions of intelligibility could have been that would have made her life possible*, indeed, what sustaining web of relations makes our lives possible, those of us who confound kinship in the rearticulation of its terms? What new schemes of intelligibility make our loves legitimate and recognizable, our losses true losses? *This question reopens the relation between kinship and reigning epistemes of cultural intelligibility, and both of these to the possibility of social transformation*" (p. 24, italics mine).

54   On the pattern/intensity of postwar purges, and the greater severity, proportionally, in Hungary and Czechoslovakia see the summary in Robert Bideleux and Ian Jeffries, *A History of Eastern Europe. Crisis and Change*, 2nd edn (Abingdon: Routledge, 2007), pp. 476–7.

55   Field was charged (teleologically) with working to strengthen Western Allied influence and to divide indigenous resistance movements in order to pave the way for a divided Germany in the postwar.

56   Carroll, *Odyssey of the Abraham Lincoln Brigade*, p. 247

57   London, *On Trial,* for example, pp. 83, 92, 113, 135–6.

58   Slánský's Jewish origins unfortunately fitted well with Stalin's newly-discovered anti-Israel paranoia, as Slánský's vague leanings toward Titoism did with the new anti-Tito feeling in Moscow. London, *On Trial*, p. 183; McLellan, *Antifascism and Memory*, p. 59. As both sources indicate, there was from the start in both Czechoslovakia and the DDR a strong element of this distrust and fear of "the enemy within"/contamination driving the obsessive checking and rechecking by officialdom of the "biographies" that those who had been political exiles or who had been veterans of the war in Spain were obliged to compose, McLellan, *ibid.*, pp. 62, 97–8.

59   No simple picture can be drawn here. Some of those functioning as state inquisitors in the trials and policing process had also been International Brigaders themselves – in the Czech case, Zavodsky, head of state security, had been a comrade of London's in Spain (and in Mauthausen). And in the DDR too the leading dissident Brigader, Walter Janka, and his state nemesis, Erich Mielke, head of the Stasi, were both veterans of Spain.

60   McLellan, *Antifascism and Memory*, p. 59.

61   Joel Kovel, *Red Hunting in the Promised Land. Anticommunism and the Making of America* (New York: Basic Books, 1994).

62 Gustavo Durán, *Una enseñanza de la guerra española. Glorias y miserias de la impro-visación de un ejército* (ed. de J. Martín-Artajo), (Madrid: Ediciones Júcar, 1980) for Durán's interesting if exiguous wartime writings. Their practical intona-tion also bespeaks a profound existential change wrought by the war. Durán appears in fictionalized form both in Malraux's *L'Espoir* and Horacio Vázquez-Rial's *El soldado de porcelana* (Barcelona: Ediciones B, 1997), (a novel about Durán's life). There is also a recent biography, Javier Juárez, *Comandante Durán. Leyenda y tragedia de un intelectual en armas* (Barcelona: Debate, 2009), but the best insights into his life come in the exquisite short collection, *Silences from the Spanish Civil War*, by Gustavo's daughter, the poet Jane Durán.

63 Diana Anhalt, *A Gathering of Fugitives: American Political Expatriates in Mexico 1948–1965* (Santa Maria, CA: Archer Books, 2001).

64 Howard Fast, *Departure and Other Stories* (Boston: Little Brown and Co., 1949). In his autobiography, *Being Red* (Boston: Houghton Mifflin, 1990), Fast refers to the inspiration for the story coming from long conversations on Spain with Irv Goff (p. 280).

65 Carroll, *Odyssey of the Abraham Lincoln Brigade*, p. 314.

66 Fast, *Being Red,* pp. 341–2.

67 Miklós Radnóti, "Seventh Eclogue, Lager Heideman, in the mountains above Žagubica, July 1944". English translation by George Gömöri and Clive Wilmer, in Miklós Radnóti, *Forced March* (London: Enitharmon, 2003), pp. 75–6.

68 Toller's related correspondence (May–November 1938) with various American, British and Scandinavian bodies, individuals and governmental/relief agencies is in the SRR (Spanish Refugee Relief) archive, at Columbia University Library (SRR-0 Part 8, Box 34), but the impression it gives is of Toller's vast nervous energy confronting a growing institutional inertia everywhere in matters related to Republican Spain.

69 Alvah Bessie, *Men in Battle* (New York: Scribner's, 1939), pp. 266, and 296; Edwin Rolfe, *The Lincoln Battalion* (New York: Haskell, 1974), pp. 277–80 (first pub. 1939). Toller was the expressionist playwright who had headed the short-lived communist Republic of Bavaria in 1919. His prison poems in *Das Schwalbenbuch* (1923): English edition, *The Swallow Book* (Oxford: Oxford University Press, Humphrey Milford, 1924). On Toller's final months, Robert Payne, *Chungking Diary* (London: William Heinemann, 1945) and extracted in "The man who spared Hitler but didn't spare himself", *The Guardian*, 22 May 1990. Juan Negrín, the Spanish Republican prime minister, gave a funeral oration. It was said that news of Toller's death triggered the final decline of Joseph Roth, whose luminous writing bears witness to the civil wars/cultural wars of Europe's dark twentieth century. Cf. Koestler's epigraph to *Scum of the Earth*.

70 An arresting formulation from Derek Jarman's film *The Garden* (1991).

71 Having caused the betrayal and death of a friend and lover; Michael Ondaatje, *The English Patient* (London: Vintage, 1992).

5 Brutal Nurture

1 Durán, *Silences from the Spanish Civil War*, p. 49.

2 Jennifer Tucker with Tina Campt, "Entwined Practices: Engagements with Photography in Historical Inquiry", full citation in Introduction, endnote 1.

3 The JSU originated as the merged youth association of the Spanish social democratic movement and its smaller communist counterpart, to become during the civil war a mass organization mobilizing young people for the Republican war effort. For the youth unification and wartime JSU, Graham, *Spanish Republic at War*, pp. 75–6, 181–2.

4 This Capa photograph of a lone boy soldier on the Catalan front first appeared in *Regards*, 19 January 1939. See Cynthia Young (ed.), *The Mexican Suitcase: The Rediscovered Spanish Civil War Negatives of Capa, Chim and Taro* (New York: ICP/Göttingen: Steidl, 2010), II, pp. 352–3.

5 For example, Felix Quesada, a member of the Mauthausen Poschacher Kommando, Benito Bermejo (ed.), *Francisco Boix, el fotógrafo de Mauthausen* (Barcelona: RBA, 2002), p. 137.

6 Victor Serge, *The Long Dusk*, p. 87. For a consideration of this, see also chapter 4 above – and note 3 for the reference to this quote.

7 Manuel Moros, *Febrer 1939: L'exili dins la mirada de Manuel Moros* (Perpignan: Mare Nostrum, 2009).

6 Franco's Prisons

1 For a further discussion of Spain's exceptionalism in southern Europe, but also the West's obliviousness to the structural brutality of all the southern European "developmentalist" dictatorships, see Helen Graham and Alejandro Quiroga, "After the fear was over? What came after dictatorships in Spain, Greece and Portugal", in Dan Stone (ed.), *The Oxford Handbook of Postwar European History* (Oxford: Oxford University Press, 2012), pp. 502–25.

2 The photo-essay in chapter 5 also ends with a reflection upon the connections between Spain's civil war, as one form of structural violence, and the later sort inherent in a mass migration that was scarcely a voluntary endeavour for the vast majority of those who undertook it.

3 The core of this prison universe emerged out of an initial process of grouping, investigation and classification – first of prisoners of war (this ongoing from 18 July 1936), then of the soldiers of the Republican army after its surrender at the end of March 1939, and later again of those Republican military refugees who opted and then managed to get back to Spain after the fall of France. This process, plus a parallel one of the Franco regime's defining and refining of various forms of captivity and forced labour, are dealt with in Javier Rodrigo's monograph, *Cautivos. Campos de concentración en la España franquista 1936–1947* (Barcelona: Crítica, 2005). For a definitional overview, pp. xxii–xxx. In summary, "concentration camps" in Francoist Spain were always transitory entities in which prisoners were *en route* elsewhere; some to freedom, many to

be executed, whether or not via a process of summary justice, many to prison (which would constitute the enduring core of the regime's concentrationary universe in the sense of administering punishment) and most to forced labour brigades of different sorts.

4 On the law see Mónica Lanero Táboas, *Una milicia de la justicia. La política judicial del franquismo (1936–1945)*, (Madrid: Centro de Estudios Constitucionales, 1996). The economic workings of autarky in José Luis García Delgado (ed.), *El primer franquismo*. Autarky cut Spain off from world trade and was thus also a form of protectionism that served the interests of the regime's primary backers, the large landowners of central and southern Spain whose antiquated production techniques meant they were uncompetitive in an open market. Autarky's socio-economic and cultural workings (as repression) in Richards, *A Time of Silence*. For punitive social welfare policy see Ángela Cenarro, *La sonrisa de Falange: Auxilio Social en la guerra civil y en la posguerra* (Barcelona: Crítica, 2005) and *Los niños de Auxilio Social*; on the purges of the professions there are many regional studies which indicate the huge scale of the operation. In Catalonia in 1939 of 15,860 public servants, 15,107 lost their jobs. Josep Cruanyes, *Els papers de Salamanca: L'espoliació del patrimoni documental de Catalunya* (Barcelona: Edicions 62, 2003), pp. 16–1, 34–5. Teachers (those who survived) were another major target, in particular primary school teachers, Francisco Morente Valero, *La escuela y el Estado nuevo: La depuración del magisterio nacional* (Barcelona: Ámbito, 1997). But the purge also went deep among secondary and university level teachers too; Carmen Sanchidrián Blanco, Isabel Grana Gil and Francisco Martín Zúñiga, "Análisis y valoración de los expedientes de depuración del profesorado de Instituto de Segunda Enseñanza en el franquismo (1936–1942). Resultados generales", *Revista de Educación* 356 (Sept.–Dec. 2011), consulted via *Red Iris* (accessed 14 August 2011, web address below) suggests that by 1940, the high point of the process, some 30 percent of secondary school teachers had been excluded. The national distribution is still being researched, but it was concentrated especially in the higher echelons of schools in order to discipline the rest of the staff, see Conclusions (no pagination provided online). See also Olegario Negrín Fajardo, "Los expedientes de depuración de los profesores de instituto de segunda enseñanza resueltos por el Ministerio de Educación Nacional (1937–1943)", *Hispania Nova. Revista de Historia Contemporánea* 7 (2007) http://hispanianova.rediris.es (accessed 14 August 2011). On the university, Jaume Claret Miranda, *El atroz desmoche: La destrucción de la universidad española por el franquismo 1936–1945* (Barcelona: Crítica, 2006).

5 It was 1967–8 before the special civilian courts (TOP), established in 1963, pulled ahead of the military tribunals in terms of the number of political opponents tried. Manuel Risques Corbella, "Dictadura y rebelión militar 1936–1968", *Les presons de Franco* (Barcelona: Generalitat de Catalunya/Museu d'Història de Catalunya, 2004), p. 204.

6 Anderson, *The Francoist Military Trials*, pp. 53–6; Preston, *The Spanish*

Holocaust, p. 474 cites the revealing speech by one prosecutor which acknowledged the work of "social cleansing" (*limpieza social*) they were about, and began "I do not care, nor do I even want to know, if you are innocent or not of the charges made against you".

7 Preston, *The Spanish Holocaust*, pp. 492–3, 494, 495.

8 The detailed empirical work – province by province tabulations – on which these figures are based, began back in the 1980s when conditions were very difficult. It then accelerated during the 1990s, spreading much further in terms of geographical coverage, particularly into the centre and north of Spain. The seminal work (on the south, where the greatest volume of extra- and quasi-judicial killing occurred) is by Francisco Moreno Gómez on Córdoba (*La guerra civil en Córdoba 1936–1939*); *Córdoba en la posguerra (La represión y la guerrilla, 1939–1950)*, (Córdoba: Francisco Baena, 1987) and Francisco Espinosa Maestre on Huelva and Seville (latterly publishing *La columna de la muerte: El avance del ejército franquista de Sevilla a Badajoz* (Barcelona: Crítica 2003) and *La justicia de Queipo* (Barcelona: Crítica, 2005). Neither historian was (nor is) a member of a university department, although both are now major authors nationally. The role too of dozens of anonymous local historians across Spain in excavating disparate and often mouldering sources in out-of-the-way places has been crucial in building an accurate national picture of the Francoist repression. That they have largely been private citizens with no formal university affiliation is itself a sociological point worthy of note. Julián Casanova, one of the relatively few university academics involved, has observed that within Spanish academia this work is still seen as maybe "unsafe" and certainly "untoward"/boat-rocking – which is itself of course another after effect of Francoism. Julián Casanova (ed.), *El pasado oculto: Fascismo y violencia en Aragón (1936–1939)*, 1st edn (Madrid: Siglo XXI, 1992). The first synthesis for a general and mainstream readership was produced in 1999, Santos Juliá (coord.), *Víctimas de la guerra civil* (Madrid: Temas de Hoy). All of this work – and its substantial historical implications – still largely passes unnoticed by the community of contemporary Europeanist historians working on countries other than Spain, mainly (one assumes) because they do not read Spanish and the work is rarely translated. Hence the importance of Paul Preston's monumental study, *The Spanish Holocaust*, based on over a decade of primary research. It was published in Spain in spring 2011 and in English (by HarperCollins) in spring 2012. In the course of constructing its own original analysis, Preston's book also serves as an analytical conduit for a mass of local work which is very hard to locate – even inside Spain – because of the circumstances of its publication (in short runs by the authors themselves, or under the auspices of small *ayuntamientos* (town councils)) and which would otherwise have an extremely limited impact.

9 See Preston's Prologue to *The Spanish Holocaust*, pp. xvi–xviii for an explanation of how the continuing terror, and the memory of it, interfered long term with the civil registration of violent deaths and with the investigation by

researchers of such deaths as did manage to be registered by relatives and friends (this more in the north and centre than in the south where many deaths remained undocumented). Preston also provides here (pp. xv–xx) an illuminating *tour d'horizon* of what historians know today, what we might still be able to ascertain, and what historians cannot likely ever know.

10   Richard J. Evans, *The Third Reich in Power 1933–1939* (London: Allen Lane, 2005), p. 70, gives a total of 528 for all the judicial executions carried out between 1933 and 1938 and points out (p. 75) that judicial executions also went up across the board for common crimes of theft, assault, murder etc. But a tally for Nazi state murder obviously extends beyond the 'peacetime' years of 1933–9 to incorporate the subsequent period of foreign war/occupation, which then makes it very hard to make a meaningful overall comparison with Francoism over the longer period – quantitatively or qualitatively. Even more difficult is any comparison with state murder perpetrated by the Stalinist regime. While there are accepted figures for the number of Stalin's political executions, narrowly defined (i.e. executions after some form of "trial"), state murder under Stalin extended far beyond these deaths to include many other forms of mass, extra-judicial killing and "negligent death" (including in the gulag), and of course also to be included here are the victims of famine who died directly as a result of state policy. The current debate between Soviet specialists is both methodologically complex and highly polemical, with disagreements over figures as well as over what should constitute the categories and periodization. For a flavour of this for the wartime period (and in comparative perspective with Nazism), see Timothy Snyder, *Bloodlands. Europe Between Hitler and Stalin* (London: The Bodley Head, 2010), pp. 409–14. Whatever the case, it is clear that the figure for Stalinist state murder runs to millions of victims, and also that these occurred in a historical context whose overwhelming singularity (on this see Ian Kershaw, "War and Political Violence in Twentieth-Century Europe", in *Contemporary European History* 14, 1 (2005): 107–23 (esp. 112–13)) also mitigates against the usefulness of an overall comparison with Francoism (although some aspects of Stalinism and Francoism are certainly comparable, as this chapter and book argue). But regardless of the immense difficulty of the scholarly enterprise, the scale of Francoist state killing and imprisonment, including long after the end of military hostilities on 1 April 1939, inevitably provokes important questions about how to engage in a necessary debate that could produce nuanced and meaningful comparisons – qualitatively as much as quantitatively – of the deaths caused by all the major European totalitarianisms. That Francoism belongs as part of this debate/comparison is clear from the figures already cited: a baseline of 150,000 extra- or quasi- judicial killings over nine years, as compared to "post-war score settling"/extra-judicial killing in Italy 1943–6 (10,000–15,000 deaths) and in France (9,000–10,000 deaths), Mazower, *Dark Continent*, p. 235.

11   Deaths in the camps were not, of course, all executions – for all that they could

be considered culpable deaths – and by 1936 a majority of camp inmates were other than politicals, being those the regime defined as asocial or deviant, including habitual criminals. Evans, *The Third Reich in Power*, pp. 81, 84–5, 87–8.

12 *Anuario Estadístico de España* 1942 (Madrid: Imprenta Nacional, 1942), pp. 722–3; Commission Internationale contre le régime concentrationnaire (CICRC) *Livre Blanc sur le système pénitentiaire espagnol* (Paris: Le Pavois, 1953), p. 206. The CICRC, founded by former deportees of Nazi concentration camps, most notably David Rousset, set out in 1950 to enquire into prison regimes in the Soviet Union, Yugoslavia, Greece and Spain. The history of its investigation in Spain (resisted to the utmost by the Franco regime), is outlined in the *Livre Blanc sur le système pénitentiaire espagnol*, pp. 5–20 and less "diplomatically" in Ricard Vinyes, *Irredentas*, pp. 33–47.

13 *Livre Blanc sur le système pénitentiaire espagnol*, testimony 131, p. 185. Cf., Anderson, *The Francoist Military Trials*, p. 86.

14 Cf. Gutmaro Gómez Bravo and Jorge Marco on impunity as a hallmark of Francoism, *La obra del miedo. Violencia y sociedad en la España franquista (1936–1950)*, (Madrid: Península, 2011), p. 223.

15 This is one of the conclusions to be drawn from the work Conxita Mir on the functioning of the civil courts in the 1940s, *Vivir es sobrevivir*. See a vivid encapsulation of the phenomenon in everyday life in Maruja Torres' "meta-autobiographical" novel *Un calor tan cercano* (Madrid: Alfaguara, 1998) where a destitute Republican parent, desperate for medicines for his child, has to go and abase himself before a local family known to have good connections to the regime, for which reason they are known in the neighbourhood as *los nacionales*.

16 Anderson, *The Francoist Military Trials*, p. 78.

17 *Ibid.*, p. 77.

18 Richards, *A Time of Silence*, p. 79.

19 The evidence in Peter Anderson's study of Cordoba, in *The Francoist Military Trials*, further supports these arguments which also underpin (particularly in regard of Nazi Germany) Ángela Cenarro's seminal article, "Matar, vigilar, delatar: la quiebra de la sociedad civil durante la guerra y la posguerra en España (1936–1948)".

20 *Livre Blanc sur le système pénitentiaire espagnol*, p. 66. But from the ministerial information cited elsewhere in this report (e.g. p. 36 and p. 205) it is clear that the distinction was made in terms of prisoner treatment. The issue, then, was one of recognition, as many prisoner memoirs make clear, in order to confront the situation where politicals were subject to extra punitive treatment and forms of surveillance, but without the regime explicitly recognizing them as such, Ricard Vinyes, *El daño y la memoria: Las prisiones de María Salvo* (Barcelona: Plaza & Janés, 2004), pp. 28–9. Out of a population of 25.9 million the *Anuario Estadístico de España* 1946–47 vol. II, p. 1240, gives the following figures for prisons (i.e. this does NOT include forced labour, encadred in work

brigades of various kinds): 1939 – 270,719; 1940 – 233, 373; 1941 – 159,392; 1942 – 124,423; 1943 – 74,095.

21 On the basis of a population of 70 million. Figures for German penal institutions and SS concentration camps 1934–45 given in Nikolaus Wachsmann, *Hitler's Prisons: Legal Terror in Nazi Germany* (New Haven/London: Yale University Press, 2004), p. 394. Figures for inmates of German penal institutions 1924–44, pp. 392–3. The German rate of incarceration rose considerably, across the board, after the Nazis took control. Evans, *The Third Reich in Power*, p. 79. It should also be noted that, in terms of Spain's total population (c. 23.5m), the incarceration rate in January 1936 was high. (Early 1930s Germany, with three times the population, had an incarceration rate of under 55,000).

22 For a list of state works and private industries which used slave labour, Isaías Lafuente, *Esclavos por la patria: La explotación de los presos bajo el franquismo* (Madrid: Ediciones Temas de Hoy, 2002), pp. 327–34.

23 Gonzalo Acosta Bono *et al.*, *El canal de los presos (1940–1962). Trabajos forzosos: de la represión política a la explotación económica* (Barcelona: Crítica, 2004), based on an interdisciplinary and collective piece of research.

24 Richards, *A Time of Silence*, p. 76.

25 *Livre Blanc sur le système pénitentiaire espagnol*, pp. 59–67. See note 13 above. Of course the Nazis too had many concentration camps which were not death camps *sensu stricto* – i.e. those to which people (or at least some people) were delivered for the purpose of immediate and direct extermination. But in the Nazi camp universe more broadly, as in Franco's, the inmates were entirely disposable, at the mercy of the system/staff and, in both, people were tortured, worked to death, died of culpable neglect, or could be subject to arbitrary execution: Wolfgang Sofsky, *The Order of Terror: The Concentration Camp* (Princeton, Princeton University Press, 1997). Inmates were, in Agamben's terms, beings who could be killed but not sacrificed – since they had been divested of all national, civic or constitutional identity by the imprisoning state. Agamben, *Homo Sacer: Sovereign Power and Bare Life*, for example, pp. 132–3. Nor is the line between mistreatment and disposability ever a clear one. It was already becoming very blurred in the internment camps of Republican France in 1938–39, described by Arthur Koestler in *Scum of the Earth*. See chapter 1 above for a discussion of this.

26 Duilio Susmel, *Vita sbagliata di Galeazzo Ciano* (Milano: Aldo Palazzi Editore, 1962), p. 158.

27 Major examples include the Law/Tribunal for the Repression of Freemasonry and Communism (1940); the law against military rebellion (1943) and the law against banditry and terrorism (1947).

28 A variety of regimes existed here, notably internal exile (*destierro*) and confinement to a specific location (*confinamiento*). It was the prison authorities who took the initial decision whether or not to allow a political prisoner's application to go forward to the national board which could grant parole. The latter's

decisions depended very much on the views of the individual prison authorities and, crucially, on those canvassed from the local authorities in the prisoner's place of origin where local boards were set up to adjudicate the cases referred (these local boards being composed of the mayor [often a Falangist], the local priest and a female representative, chosen from among the "charitable and committed"). Cenarro, "La institucionalización del universo penitenciario", pp. 137–8. For the tendency of these local boards to be harsher and more vindictive than the regime, Anderson, *The Francoist Military Trials*, pp. 127–31.

29 The contagiousness of fear and suspicion in such an atmosphere is conjured acutely in Miguel Durán Pastor, *Sicut Oculi. Vigilantes y vigilados en la Mallorca de la posguerra 1941–1945* (Palma de Mallorca: Miquel Font, 1992), a local history, based on surveillance reports from the Juzgado Militar Especial.

30 There were also civilian warders in most gaols. In men's gaols the increasing demand for warders after the war was supplied by those who had formerly been *alféreces provisionales,* the non-commissioned officer class that had been created in Franco's wartime army. But the exiguous number of female warders (prewar) combined with the sudden growth in the female prison population postwar created a particular need that was filled by female religious personnel – the relevant ministerial order codifying this in women's prisons appears in Franco's BOE (Boletín Oficial del Estado) on 5 September 1938.

31 In both men's and women's prisons, prevailing upon a prisoner on death row to make the act of confession was perceived as a battle won against what the prisoner had previously been/against his or her political and cultural values, Martín Torrent, *¿Qué me dice usted de los presos?* (Alcalá de Henares: Imprenta Talleres Penitenciarios, 1942), pp. 11–12. An indictment of this prevalent attitude from within the Church in the diary of Gumersindo de Estella, a Franciscan friar who was chaplain at the Torrero gaol in Zaragoza, published many years later as *Fusilados en Zaragoza 1936–1939. Tres años de asistencia espiritual a los reos* (Zaragoza: Mira Editores, 2003); Julián Casanova, *La iglesia de Franco*, pp. 306–10. See also chapter 3 above.

32 Vinyes, *Irredentas*, p. 126. Although coercion related to the withholding of sanitary protection was not only a Catholic practice, cf. Anna Funder, *Stasiland. Stories from Behind the Berlin Wall* (London: Granta, 2003), p. 32. On the physical and psychological degradation involved in detention and the prison routine, an especially unflinching account in Consuelo García, *Las cárceles de Soledad Real: Una vida* (Madrid: Ediciones Alfaguara, 1982), pp. 94, 102, 166–69.

33 The main mechanism was the "Board for the redemption (*sic*) of prison sentences through work" (*Patronato central para la redención de penas por el trabajo,* also known as the *Patronato de Nuestra Señora de la Merced*). This was a system whereby, if the prison authorities sanctioned it, an inmate could apply for a scheme which discounted days of sentence against days of prison labour, E. Diéz Echarri, "El sistema de la Redención de Penas por el Trabajo. Sus funda-

mentos, su aplicación y sus consecuencias", *Revista de la Escuela de Estudios Penitenciarios* 36 (March 1948): 43–7. In the same source, Clemente Rodríguez, "Ventajas de los penados trabajadores en los Destacamentos", 37 (April 1948): 71–6.

34 Fidalgo, *A Young Mother in Franco's Prisons.* See chapter 3 for more on Pilar Fidalgo.

35 Letter from Aida Landa (Matilde's sister) to Miquel Ferrà, 19 October 1942, cited in David Ginard i Ferón, *L'esquerra mallorquina i el franquisme* (Palma: Edicions Documenta Balear, 1994), p. 162. See also by the same author *Matilde Landa, De la Institución Libre de Enseñanza a las prisiones franquistas* (Barcelona: Flor del Viento, 2005). From Aida's letter we also learn that Matilde's body was not returned to her family but buried by the authorities, evidently with full Catholic ceremonial, without their knowledge, intervention or consent – thus in Matilde Landa's death the regime sought to achieve what it had failed to during her life.

36 Ángeles García Madrid, *Réquiem por la libertad* (Madrid: Editorial Alianza Hispánica, 2003), p. 61; Ricard Vinyes, "El universo penitenciario durante el franquismo", in Carme Molinero *et al.*, *Una inmensa prisión*, pp. 164–9; Vinyes, Armengou and Belis, *Los niños perdidos del franquismo*, pp. 68–9, 131; Fuensanta Escudero Andújar, *Lo cuentan como lo han vivido (república, guerra y represión en Murcia)*, (Murcia: Universidad de Murcia, 2000), pp. 133, 139–40, 154.

37 By 1943 12,042 children were recorded as being under state tutelage. But there were many more thousands in state institutions: Patronato de la Merced, *Memoria* (1944); cf. also Vinyes, *Irredentas*, p. 98.

38 A preliminary discussion of where this aspect of the afterlife of violence led in Preston, *The Spanish Holocaust*, p. 525. In regard of the civil guard lieutenant in provincial Córdoba who had taken part in many executions and who then shot himself in the head at a local dance held to celebrate the outbreak of the civil war, see the discussion here above in chapter 2 of "terror and fiesta" where the local rebel authorities organized fêtes and dances to follow the executions of those deemed social and political enemies, requiring the local population to attend both.

39 Michel de Castillo, *Tanguy, Histoire d'un enfant d'aujourd'hui* (Paris: Gallimard, 1957): English translation: *A Child of Our Time* (New York: Alfred A. Knopf, 1957).

40 The documentary, *Els nens perduts del franquisme* (Televisió de Catalunya, 2002) is discussed above in chapter 3. The broader social ramifications of this state-driven abuse of children is taken up in chapter 7, in the discussion of similar, long-term abuses in the private sector in Spain, also involving Church personnel, which have continued right up until the present day.

41 This supposition has informed the perspective of sociologist Juan Linz, just as it underpins the work of historian Stanley G. Payne. A counter-argument runs throughout Paul Preston's *The Politics of Revenge: Fascism and the Military in 20th Century Spain* (London: Routledge, 1995 [first pub. 1990]).

42 Hannah Arendt, *The Origins of Totalitarianism* (San Diego/New York/London: Harcourt Brace & Company, 1973), p. 186.

43 Here see also Thomas Kühne, *Belonging and Genocide: Hitler's Community 1918–1945* (New Haven, CT: Yale University Press, 2010), which argues that *Volksgemeinschaft* and genocide not only went hand in hand but actually presupposed one another.

44 Concerned as it is with the social and cultural continuities of Francoism and the ways in which earlier forms of repression lived on in late Francoism as an "afterlife of violence", this essay does not rehearse the familiar political and economic explanation of how and why the regime was able to survive the defeat of the Nazi new order in Europe whose victory it had desired. The three poles of this explanation – Cold War, Concordat and consumer society – can be followed up easily in the standard texts and here in chapter 7.

45 See here the depiction of the adult children of those who had formed the socially feudal retaining classes of the agrarian deep south in Miguel Delibes' novel, *Los santos inocentes* (The Holy Innocents), (Barcelona: Planeta, 1981). Set on a *cortijo* (aristocratic estate) in Extremadura during the 1960s, it shows a younger generation that has no ostensible politics or sense of the past, but which is no longer prepared to accept the hierarchical social relations of the *cortijo* whose lengthy prolongation was one of the main social consequences of Francoist victory in 1939. The solutions found by the children are individual ones – migration of one form or another.

46 See the searing, if oblique, depiction of this in Carlos Saura's 1981 film *Deprisa Deprisa*. One of the few historians to think through the intimate, intrahistorical links between the social history of Francoist developmentalism and Spain's experience of brutal nation-building is Michael Richards, *After the Civil War: Memory and the Shaping of Spanish Society since 1936* (Cambridge: Cambridge University Press, forthcoming 2012) and also "Between memory and history: Social relationships and ways of remembering the Spanish civil war", *International Journal of Iberian Studies* 19, 1 (2006): 85–94 and "Grand narratives, collective memory, and social history: public uses of the past in post-war Spain", in Carlos Jerez-Farrán and Samuel Amago (eds), *Unearthing Franco's Legacy: Mass graves and the recovery of historical memory in Spain* (Notre Dame, Ind.: University of Notre Dame Press, 2010), pp. 121–45. Some of the same ideas/theories can be deduced from the material in Antonio Cazorla's social history of Francoism, *Fear and Progress: Ordinary Lives in Franco's Spain 1939–1975* (Oxford: Wiley-Blackwell, 2009) but the author never explicitly makes the argument.

47 Cazorla, *Fear and Progress*, p. 96.

48 The voluminous – and highly bureaucratic – archive of the Sección Femenina is available for consultation at the Archivo General de la Administración, Alcalá de Henares (Madrid) where one can read a lengthy narrative of late totalitarian decay in the SF cadres' obsessive references to these baby baskets (*canastillas*) and the minutiae of their contents. By the late 1960s the baskets

had come to stand for an "abuse" of the whole system whereby many young
women bought their way out of "active service" in the SF.

49 Correspondence with Mercedes Esteban-Maes Kemp, May–August 2003;
January–March 2005 and interview, 21 July 2011.

50 Paul Preston, *The Triumph of Democracy in Spain* (London: Routledge, 1990), p.
57.

51 "Eurocommunism" denotes the movement (in the 1970s and 80s) of western
European communist parties towards a position of greater critical distance
from the Soviet Union, in search of a theory and practice of social transformation more in keeping with local conditions.

7 The Afterlife of Violence

1 Etkind, "Post-Soviet Hauntology", 194–5.

2 William Faulkner, *Requiem for a Nun* (London: Chatto & Windus, 1953, [first
pub. 1951]).

3 Etkind, "Post-Soviet Hauntology", 182–3 gives details of one civic memory
project to identify and commemorate a series of mass graves at Sandarmokh, a
pine forest near the Belomor Canal in northwest Russia, where some nine thousand men and women of sixty ethnicities were shot in 1937 and 1938. Over
time, the memorial project brought together the efforts of people who
included: a political prisoner; a retired NKVD officer who had been a perpetrator; the child of someone whose father was also an NKVD perpetrator and
then himself a victim of the Terror; the son of a Soviet military family with no
particular direct or personal involvement; a local artist; and several other local
enthusiasts including a present-day police officer who had been a deputy in
the Russian parliament during the 1990s. Theirs too was a story of confronting
a deaf or obstructive "authority". In the end the grave was uncovered in 1997
and commemorated entirely by private effort – as was the case with other sites.
At Sandarmokh the monument is a stone angel with hands tied, waiting to be
shot. Above the angel (of history?) an inscription reads: "People, do not kill
each other." None of those involved in the project was a professional historian.
Viewed comparatively, the Russian state is further away from addressing the
legacy of Stalinism than the Spanish state is from recognizing the effects of
Francoism – not least because the state in Russia can still make great play of
the Second World War as "the Great Patriotic War" in a way that the Spanish
state cannot with the civil war.

4 Sociological Francoism is conventionally defined as those sectors whose
commitment to the dictatorship (during its lifetime) was driven less by
ideology and more by a pragmatic self-interest – so its bedrock was the new
white collar lower middle class and managerial sectors generated by the
economic liberalization of the later 1950s and 60s. Francoism also came to be
perceived by such constituencies as providing a general sense of security and
even existential well-being – a view obviously also shared by ideologically
committed Francoists of all conditions and which, since the end of the regime,

seems to have become autonomously powerful, and increasingly so, among socially conservative constituencies, as a reaction both to economic uncertainty and the speed of social change.

5 There are some other contenders here, of course – the debates around the legacy of communism in Romania, for example, or those over "double genocide" in the Baltic States or Hungary. But as discussed a little later in this chapter, in Spain it is the lack of any alibi or "screen" of foreign occupation or control which raises the stakes of the debate, that is to say, raises the stakes in recognizing what the history of extreme violence "between nationals" was about.

6 Spain's Communist Party (PCE) while an important player during the transition, ceased to be one thereafter.

7 Notwithstanding the differences of political context, see Etkind, "Post-Soviet Hauntology", 182.

8 This frequently means outright corruption, which is an explosive phenomenon, in every sense, today in Spain. It has, for example, been an integral part of the Judge Garzón affair in that the political assault on him, while focussing on his bid to facilitate the excavation of the mass graves/extrajudicially murdered, is very probably fuelled as much, if not more, by the desire of sectors of the political class to paralyse his investigations into widespread corruption (see the discussion of the Garzón affair at the start of chapter 1). Corruption as a mode of state activity in Spain goes back much further than the Franco regime, of course. Indeed it was effectively institutionalized by the Restoration monarchy which governed Spain from 1875. For this reason, my analysis does not dwell upon corruption as a specific Franco effect. Nevertheless, corruption was the fuel upon which the dictatorship ran. Moreover, Franco inflected its practices as a means of implicating the regime's servants, to enforce loyalty and keep them "in the game" – rather in the same way as the "memory of murder" too was deployed with other sectors. For corruption, like the "fellowship of blood", (Raymond Carr, *Spain: A History* [Oxford: Oxford University Press, 2000], p. 265), was both a threat and a promise – in that it was *tacitly* understood within the culture of the regime to be a material reward; but the threat of exposure always loomed.

9 For more on the subject of these abductions and on the documentary itself, see chapters 3 and 6.

10 *Death in El Valle* is available as a dvd. For the story and the story of the film: http://www.deathinelvalle.com/ (accessed 21 November 2011).

11 José María Marín Arce, "Diez años de Gobierno del PSOE (1982–1992)", *Espacio, tiempo y forma*. Serie V, *Historia contemporánea* 13 (2000): 189–209.

12 See chapter 2 above.

13 Carlos Giménez's *Paracuellos* (first series 1977–82) see http://www.carlosgimenez.com/obra/paracuellos.htm (accessed 24 Dec. 2010).

14 Francisco Espinosa Maestre, *Callar al mensajero. La represión franquista. Entre la libertad de información y el derecho al honor* (Barcelona: Península, 2009), p. 47 where the author recounts his own experience of politically-inspired bureau-

cratic (including university/academic) obstruction of his attempts to research the repression that followed the 18 July 1936 coup in Seville. He observes somewhat ironically that the very professor who had adopted a "nothing can be done" attitude to his thesis proposal in 1978, refusing outright to supervise it, was the same person who in 1990 would end up publishing the result of the research in a volume edited by himself.

15 The case of Salvaleón (Badajoz) in 1980 in Espinosa Maestre, *La columna de la muerte*, pp. 249–50; also the three photographs opposite page 261 showing the exhumation of remains, the ceremony-procession of transfer to, and their reburial in, the local cemetery. The very first was in Granada in 1976. Francisco Espinosa Maestre, "La memoria de la represión y la lucha por su reconocimiento: en torno a la creación de la comisión interministerial", in dossier: "Generaciones y memoria de la represión franquista: un balance de los movimientos por la memoria, *Hispania Nova. Revista de Historia Contemporánea* 6 (2006). Consulted on Red Iris http://hispanianova.rediris.es/6/dossier/6d007.pdf, 24.

16 Among the works published, Tomasa Cuevas, *Cárcel de mujeres (1939–1945)*, (Barcelona: Sirocco, 1986, and subsequent editions). Cuevas, herself a political prisoner, traversed Spain in difficult circumstances and impecunious condition in order to record the testimonies of other women like herself, the results of which eventually became her book; Ángeles García-Madrid, *Requiém por la libertad* (Madrid: Editorial Alianza Hispánica, 2003); García, *Las cárceles de Soledad Real*; Neus Catalá, *De la resistencia a la deportación: 50 testimonios de mujeres españolas* (Barcelona: Adgena, n.d., c.1984); and also by the journalist Montserrat Roig, *Noche y niebla: Los catalanes en los campos nazis* (Barcelona: Península, 1978), [original in Catalan, 1977].

17 Cf. Francisco Espinosa Maestre, *Contra el olvido. Historia y memoria de la guerra civil* (Barcelona: Crítica, 2006), pp. 177–84.

18 Macías and Silva, *Las fosas de Franco*. The appearance in 1999 of a multi-author volume, *Víctimas de la guerra civil*, edited by the eminent historian Santos Juliá, signified the dissemination to the general public in Spain of twenty years of specialist empirical work on the repression. See chapters 3 and 6 for a more detailed discussion of this specialist historiography.

19 For the movement's early approach to request UN support in November 2002, Espinosa, *Contra el olvido*, p. 192.

20 In this regard, see the ineffable essay by the best-selling publicist of Francoist revisionism, Pío Moa, "La sociedad homosexual: El feminismo como ideología", in *La sociedad homosexual y otros ensayos* (Madrid: Criterio Libros, 2001), in which, as the title suggests, everything (more or less) is blamed on feminism. On Moa and his work, see Helen Graham, "New Myths for Old", *Times Literary Supplement*, 11 July 2003.

21 An extreme source of the racking up of political tension (*crispación*) was for some considerable time the radio presenter and media commentator, Federico Jiménez Losantos, who used to host a morning programme on the COPE

during which time he became infamous for his sound-bite bigotry, a Spanish minting of the rightwing American "shock jock" format: on Jiménez Losantos' content and style, José María Izquierdo, "El ángel animador", *El País*, 1 August 2010.   http://www.elpais.com/articulo/reportajes/angel/animador/elpepusocdmg/20100801elpdmgrep_2/Tes (accessed 16 January 2012).

22 See the Introduction above.

23 In numerous cases, including in Poland, Hungary and Romania, the rehabilitation of nationalism has involved a notorious squaring of the circle which derives from endemic antisemitism: the Jews are first blamed for "bringing communism" and then for "deciding" subsequently to dismantle it and profit from the process – a piece of fantasy which recapitulates the Nazi ideology of Jews as simultaneously communists and capitalists.

24 Sergio Alonso, "La JMJ sitúa en España la 'persecución más sangrienta' a la Iglesia", *Público*, 25 August 2011. http://www.publico.es/espana/393041/la-jmj-situa-en-espana-la-persecucion-mas-sangrienta-a-la-iglesia (accessed 16 January 2012).

25 There are references to pension payments made in the 1960s to Spaniards (or in some cases to their immediate families) among the records of one Paris-based former prisoners' association whose papers are now held in the Archivo General de la Guerra Civil Española, Salamanca. I am grateful to Peter Anderson for this information. José Luis Rodríguez Jiménez, *Los esclavos españoles de Hitler* (Barcelona: Planeta, 2002); Rafael García Pérez, "El envío de trabajadores españoles a Alemania durante la segunda guerra mundial", *Hispania* 170 (1998): 1031–65; Christian Leitz, "Nazi Germany and Francoist Spain, 1936–1945", in Sebastian Balfour and Paul Preston (eds), *Spain and the Great Powers in the Twentieth Century* (New York: Routledge, 1999), pp. 140–1.

26 Account of the meeting in letter from Magdalena Maes to Ramón Sender (senior), 15 June 1977; author's interview and correspondence with Magdalena Maes in July 2003 and July 2011.

27 The end of Spain's formal transition, with the promulgation of its new constitution in December 1978, also coincided with the end of the papacy of Paul VI, who had been responsible for enacting the policy of the Second Vatican Council (Vatican II). Magdalena Maes would comment some years later, with typically mordant wit, that, however it had come about, she had received her apology at around the same time as Galileo ("no sé si fue a Galileo o a mí a quien se lo pidieron primero, pero por ahí anda la cosa").

28 Espinosa Maestre, *Callar al mensajero*, pp. 45–56; Diego Barcala, "El cine español aún se exilia para burlar la censura", *Público*, 27 May 2011. http://www.publico.es/espana/315761/el-cine-espanol-aun-se-exilia-para-burlar-la-censura (accessed 16 January 2012).

29 *Ibid.*, p. 53 for the remarks of the Supreme Court judges. Remarkable too is the frequency with which, right up to the present time, public authorities in Spain respond to mention of the extrajudicially murdered with terms such as "inopportune". See chapter 3 for a further discussion of how the dominant

unspoken social assumption in Spain is to see the victims as somehow to blame for the "embarrassment" they "provoke", rather than as an opportunity to engage in restorative justice or other social initiatives.

30 Including, for Almonte specifically, Espinosa, *La guerra civil en Huelva* (fourth edn, 2005), pp. 553–5. Although, as Espinosa points out in paying tribute to Ruiz Vergara's pioneering work, *Rocío* the documentary carried information on extrajudical murders that had never been recorded in the Almonte civil register (only an approximate quarter of the subsequently substantiated killings were thus recorded – a not uncommon phenomenon, as was discussed in chapter 3 above): F. Espinosa Maestre, *Callar al mensajero*, p. 48. So in fact *Rocío* itself had provided invaluable clues for empirical historical work. Espinosa's own work on the repression in Huelva indicates the clear links between the killings of July 1936 and events in 1932 when the Republican mayor of Almonte had sought to bring a legal claim to establish the rights of the municipality over land acquired by powerful local landowning interests during the disentail-ments of the mid-nineteenth century. In 1932 this provoked a violent response (the disruption of a local council meeting) by sectors who later, in July 1936, would lead the "cleansing" vigilantism, F. Espinosa, "La religión al servicio de la política: algunas claves de la represión en Almonte (Huelva)", unpublished essay courtesy of the author. Significant too was the deliberate obfuscation/mythologization of the events of 1932 subsequently during the Franco dictatorship, whereby a conflict over landownership and economic power was represented solely as a response to the Republic's secularizing initia-tives (which had included the removal from the council chamber of a plaque to the Virgin of El Rocío).

31 For an overview summary, Graham, *The Spanish Civil War: A Very Short Introduction*, pp. 141–4.

32 Interview, 21 July 2011. On the power of exhumation, see the opening essay by the artist, Francesc Torres, *Dark is the room where we sleep*, esp. pp. 21–2. The physical remains of victims, subject to forensic analysis, can also of course in many cases provide irrefutable proof of the fact that they were murdered.

33 The reference is to Agamben's idea, discussed in chapter 6. One can contrast the comments of Federico García Lorca's niece Laura, who runs the García Lorca Foundation, that one should not look for bones but rather look for a name – in an interview with Fergal Keane on BBC Radio 4's "Taking a Stand: Federico García Lorca and the Bones of the Past", broadcast on 3 February 2009 and which in some ways implies an artificial binary, for physical recovery is integrally bound up with naming too. In this regard, compare the resonant, but also deeply practical, civic memory initiatives, *Todos los Nombres* (All the Names), a cumulative, work-in-progress online database of those executed in the Francoist repression, at http://www.todoslosnombres.org/ and also *Todos los Rostros* (All the Faces), an interactive website containing much photographic material on the Francoist prison universe, and presented in comparative

perspective at http://todoslosrostros.blogspot.com/ (accessed 16 January 2012).

34 Cf. Peter Anderson, "In the name of the Martyrs. Memory and Retribution in Francoist Southern Spain 1936–45", *Cultural and Social History* 8, 3 (2011): 355–70.

35 Michael Taussig, *The Magic of the State* (London/New York: Routledge, 1997), pp. 3, 111, 113–14, 159–60.

36 The Partido Popular sought for as long as possible to oppose any condemnation of the July 1936 coup, something which eventually passed through the Spanish parliament in November 2002, along with a formal recognition of the victims of the civil war and the Franco regime – albeit with this expressed in a discreet and ultimately conservative formulation. The PP also resisted any recognition of the anti-Franco guerrilla as such, and in 2006 opposed the Council of Europe statement condemning the crimes of Franco, and, as the incumbent government in Spain at that time, set out to block any follow-on symbolic initiatives inside the country. The PP also opposed a memory law root and branch, including the limited symbolic achievement of the 2007 law (discussed below).

37 *El País* report of 11 July 1999, cited in Espinosa *Contra el olvido*, p. 306 (n. 16).

38 For example, the Belgian Nazi collaborator and member of the Waffen SS, Léon Degrelle, a war criminal in his country of origin but a resident in Spain since 1945, praised Hitler and denied the existence of the gas chambers in Spain's national media (including television) on more than one occasion during the 1980s. Espinosa, *Callar al mensajero*, pp. 57–63.

39 *La Razón* 13 December 2009, at http://observatorioantisemitismo.fcje.org/?m =200912 (accessed 26 December 2010). "Tu muerte fue injusta e innecesaria y te debemos el recuerdo. Espero verte algún día ahí arriba, con tu dulce sonrisa. ¡Hasta siempre!".

40 The late Tony Judt referred to the way in which "accepting the Holocaust" has become a kind of formal European "entry ticket": *Postwar: A History of Europe since 1945*, pp. 803–4. It would take until 1991 for a Spanish constitutional court ruling to lay the groundwork for it to become illegal in Spain to justify the Holocaust (1995): Espinosa, *Callar al mensajero*, pp. 59–60. There was a landmark prosecution in Valencia in 1998. Spain's relatively late recognition of Israel (under the PSOE in 1986) was in part due to longstanding Francoist alliances with the Arab bloc in the international arena. This was tactical, but of course it is also true that Francoism, like all its European homologues, was deeply antisemitic, as we have seen from the rebels' own civil war discourse, as discussed in chapter 2 above.

41 For the killings in Jedwabne, see the reference in chapter 1. The memorial was daubed with swastikas, antisemitic slogans and the comment that there was no need to apologize for Jedwabne. http://www.bbc.co.uk/news/world-europe-14749852 (accessed 1 September 2011). Maciej Giertych, MEP and chairman of the League of Polish Families, in an address to the European Parliament in

July 2006, had called for statues to be erected to Franco across Europe, to recognize his status as a defender of European civilization, Nora Langenbacher and Britta Schellenberg (eds), *Is Europe on the "right" path? Right-wing extremism and right-wing populism in Europe* (Berlin: Friedrich-Ebert-Stiftung, 2011), p. 29.

42 Jorge Ruiz Lardizábel, "Polonia repudia las Brigadas Internacionales", *El País*, 9 March 2007 at http://www.elpais.com/articulo/internacional/Polonia/repudia/Brigadas/Internacionales/elpepuint/20070309elpepiint_7/Tes; Pablo X. De Sandoval, "El Senado defiende a los brigadistas comunistas polacos repudiados en su país", *El País,* 23 March 2007 at http://www.elpais.com/articulo/espana/Senado/defiende/brigadistas/comunistas/polacos/repudiados/pais/elpepuesp/20070323elpepinac_12/Tes. For more on the IBs and the Polish brigaders, see chapter 4; http://www.lamoncloa.gob.es/ IDIOMAS/9/Gobierno/News/2011/18072011PolishInternationalBrigadeVolunteers.htm (all sites accessed 7 September 2011).

43 Walter Benjamin, "Theses on the Philosophy of History", VI, published in Walter Benjamin, *Illuminations. Essays and Reflections* (edited and with an introduction by Hannah Arendt) (New York: Schocken Books, 2007), p. 255 [first published in English in 1968].

44 Giles Tremlett and John Hooper, "Spain's Catholics to fight Socialist reform", *The Guardian*, 25 October 2004; Giles Tremlett, "Spanish church prepares for battle on gay marriage", *The Guardian*, 2 October 2004; Juan G. Bedoya, "La Iglesia cree que la crisis sumará manifestantes contra el aborto", *El País*, 11 October 2009.

45 Interview with Ana Isabel (Anabel) Almendral (Oppermann), *La Opinión de Zamora*, 13 July 2004.

46 For syphilis as a stock-in-trade metaphor of moral panic and, earlier, of degenerationist/social darwinist discourse, see for example Daniel Pick, *Faces of Degeneration* (Cambridge: Cambridge University Press, 1989). For its use by Francoist soldiers and medics, Preston, "Theorists of Extermination", in *The Spanish Holocaust*, pp. 34–51. The theme of Francoism's reduction of its political enemies to the status of "moral degenerates" is also explored at various points in chapters 2, 3 and 6 of this book.

47 For this memoir and for Amparo's story see chapter 3.

48 From February to April 2005, Miguel Ángel Mateos published a total of eight articles in *La Opinión-El Correo de Zamora*, the dates of these as follows: 17 February, 3 April, 4 April, 5 April, 6 April, 7 April, 8 April, 24 April 2005.

49 The uncensored version was screened in May 2010 in Portugal: Diego Barcala, "El cine español aún se exilia para burlar la censura", *Público*, 27 May 2010. http://www.publico.es/espana/315761/el-cine-espanol-aun-se-exilia-para-burlar-la-censura. (accessed 12 September 2011).

50 This is the unifying theme of Francisco Espinosa's previously cited book of essays, *Callar al mensajero*.

51 Nizkor (from the Hebrew, "we will remember") is an NGO whose main focus

is human rights violations in Latin America, although Europe also falls within its ambit.

52 *El Pais*, 2 June 2008, cited in Anderson, *The Francoist Military Trials*, p. 78.

53 Raphael Minder, "Spain Confronts Decades of Pain over Lost Babies", *New York Times*, 6 July 2011 at http://www.nytimes.com/2011/07/07/world/europe/07iht-spain07.html?_r=1; Giles Tremlett, "Victims of Spanish 'stolen babies network' call for investigation", *The Guardian*, 27 January 2011 at http://www.guardian.co.uk/world/2011/jan/27/spain-alleged-stolen-babies-network; Vicenç Navarro, "Los niños perdidos del franquismo", *El País*, 24 December 2008 at http://www.elpais.com/articulo/opinion/ninos/perdidos/franquismo/elpepiopi/20081224elpepiopi_10/Tes; Rafael Quílez, "Mi padre me confesó que nos habían comprado a un cura por 150.000 pesetas", El Mundo (Niños Robados Microsite) at http://www.elmundo.es/especiales/2010/09/espana/ninos_robados/juanluis_antonio.html (all sites accessed 18 October 2011). The information here in chapter 7 is mainly based on the author's interview with the television journalist Montserrat Armengou, who, with Ricard Belis, produced *Els nens perduts del franquisme* and who has recently (summer 2011) completed a new documentary on the subject of the subsequent children trafficking, *¡Devolvedme a mi hijo!* (Televisió 3 de Catalunya).

54 See Antonio Altarriba/Kim, *El arte de volar* (Alicante: Edicions de Ponent, 2009), (The Art of Flying) for a (literally) graphic depiction of structural violence and its long-term effects. This is a cartoon book (drawings by Kim), in the spirit, though not the style, of Spiegelman's *Maus*, which explains why Altarriba's father, having lived Spain and Europe's dark twentieth century, not only in its physical camps and prisons but also those of the repeated failures and frustrations of the defeated, chose in old age to take his life. For an austere, unflinching study of the irreparable damage wrought by the camps – the French concentration camps for Spanish Republicans – see Alberto Morais' film, *Las Olas* (The Waves), (Spain, 2011).

55 My thanks to Paul Preston for relating this comment made to him by a member of the audience at a public lecture he gave in Spain in 2003.

56 The links between *desmemoria* and this disengagement, as well as the dangers this is storing up in Spain, are major themes in Isaac Rosa's extraordinary novel, *El vano ayer* (Barcelona: Seix Barral, 2004). (The title might be translated as "Yesterday in Eclipse".)

57 Indications of the ongoing "memory" problem in Spain continue to appear: the slippage that in 2009 allowed the appearance in the national press of a commemorative celebration of a Nazi guard is now visible too in Spain's academy – with the current polemic over certain entries in the new, publicly-funded *Diccionario Biográfico español* (National Dictionary of Biography) published in 2011 by the Real Academia de la Historia, and in which the Franco regime is described in terms that notoriously fail to mention that it was a dictatorship.

Bibliography

Primary Sources

Archives

Abraham Lincoln Brigade Archives (ALBA), Tamiment Library, New York University.

Archivo General de la Administración, Alcalá de Henares, Madrid (AGA).

Archivo General de la Guerra Civil Española, Salamanca.

Archivo Histórico Nacional, Madrid (AHN).

Archivo Histórico Provincial de Zamora (AHPZ).

Archivo del Partido Comunista de España (Madrid).

Barayón Family Private Archive.

Berg Collection, New York Public Library.

British National Archives, London (NA).

Bronx County Historical Society (New York).

Department of the Army, USA (documentation released under the Freedom of Information Act [FOIA]).

Federal Bureau of Investigation, USA (documentation released under FOIA).

Finnish National Archive, Helsinki.

Imperial War Museum Archive, London.

Library of Congress, Washington.

New York Historical Society.

Port of New York Passenger Records.

Quaker Archive, Friends House, London.

Quaker Archive (American Friends Service Committee), Philadelphia.

Registro Civil of Toro, Juzgado de Toro (Zamora).

Spanish Refugee Relief (SRR) Archive, Columbia University Library.

Newspapers, periodicals and official publications

El Socialista, 1937.

Anuario Estadístico de España 1940–51.

Boletín del Movimiento de Falange Española Tradicionalista y de las J.O.N.S. Año VII, n° 193, 10 September 1943.

Dirección General de Prisiones, *Memorias 1956–1978*.

La Opinión-El Correo de Zamora, 2004; 2005.

El País (Madrid) 2000–.

Patronato central para la redención de penas por el trabajo, *Memorias 1939–1955*.

Redención (1939–40).
Revista de Estudios Penitenciarios (1945–48).

Interviews

Alan Ansen †
Magdalena Maes Barayón
Thekla Clark
Bernard Perlin
Elliot Stein
Sylvia Thompson
Piero Tosi
Donald Windham †

Unpublished sources

Bannan, Tom, "The Long Memory of Evil: Genocide, Memory, and Identity in Bosnia-Herzegovina", MA Dissertation, Royal Holloway University of London, 2009.
Foss, James, "A Hero of the Left" (unpublished memoir of Bill Aalto).
Thomas, Maria, "The Faith and the Fury: The Construction of Anticlerical Collective Identities in Early Twentieth-Century Spain", unpublished article, forthcoming, *European History Quarterly*.
Vieux, Vanessa, "A Short History of Women in the American Medical Bureau 1936–1939" (unpublished Senior Thesis, Barnard College, Columbia University, 2002).

Published Sources

Diaries, memoirs, speeches, reports, collections of documents and other contemporary or eyewitness accounts

Anhalt, Diana, *A Gathering of Fugitives. American Political Expatriates in Mexico 1948–1965* (Santa Maria, CA: Archer Books, 2001).
Altarriba, Antonio/Kim, *El arte de volar* (Alicante: Edicions de Ponent, 2009).
Antelme, Robert, *The Human Race* (Northwestern Evanston, Illinois: The Marlboro Press, 1998).
Arnáiz, Aurora, *Retrato hablado de Luisa Julián* (Madrid: Compañía Literaria, 1996).
Ayerra Redín, Marino, *No me avergoncé del evangelio (desde mi parroquia)*, 2nd edn (Buenos Aires: Editorial Periplo, 1959).
Bahamonde, Antonio, *Un año con Queipo: Memorias de un nacionalista* (Barcelona: Ediciones Españolas, 1938).
Barral, Carlos, *Años de Penitencia* (Barcelona: Tusquets, [1975] 1990).

Belaustegui Mas, Calixto, *Fundamentos del trabajo penitenciario* (Madrid: Talleres Penitenciarios de Alcalá de Henares, 1952).

Bermejo, Benito (ed.), *Francisco Boix, el fotógrafo de Mauthausen* (Barcelona: RBA, 2002).

Bertrán Güell, Felipe, *Preparación y desarrollo del alzamiento nacional* (Valladolid: Librería Santarén, 1939).

Bessie, Alvah, *Men in Battle* (New York: Scribner's, 1939).

Brenan, Gerald, *Personal Record 1920–1972* (London: Jonathan Cape, 1974).

Catalá, Neus, *De la resistencia a la deportación. 50 testimonios de mujeres españolas* (Barcelona: Adgena, n.d., c.1984).

Commission Internationale contre le régime concentrationnaire (CICRC), *Livre Blanc sur le système pénitentiaire espagnol* (Paris: Le Pavois, 1953).

Copado, P. Bernabé (S.J.), *Con la columna Redondo: Combates y conquistas. Crónica de guerra* (Sevilla: Imprenta de la Gavidia, 1937).

Cox, Geoffrey, *Defence of Madrid* (London: Victor Gollancz, 1937).

Crome, Len, *Unbroken. Resistance and Survival in the Concentration Camps* (New York: Schocken Books, 1988).

Delaprée, Louis, *Morir en Madrid* (edición de Martin Minchom), (Madrid: Raices, 2009), [first pub. in French 1937].

Djilas, Milovan, *Wartime* (London: Secker and Warburg, 1980).

Doña, Juana, *Querido Eugenio* (Barcelona: Editorial Lumen, 2003).

Doña, Juana, *Desde la noche y la niebla. Mujeres en las cárceles franquistas* (Madrid: Ediciones de la Torre, 1978).

Downes, Donald, *The Scarlet Thread. Adventures in Wartime Espionage* (New York: The British Book Centre, 1953).

Durán, Gustavo, *Una enseñanza de la guerra española. Glorias y miserias de la improvisación de un ejército* (ed. de Martín-Artajo, José), (Madrid: Ediciones Júcar, 1980).

Durán, Jane, *Silences from the Spanish Civil War* (London: Enitharmon Press, 2002).

Estella, Gumersindo de, *Fusilados en Zaragoza 1936–1939: Tres años de asistencia espiritual a los reos* (Zaragoza: Mira Editores, 2003).

Fast, Howard, *Being Red* (Boston: Houghton Mifflin, 1990).

Felsen, Milt, *The Anti-Warrior. A Memoir* (Iowa City: University of Iowa Press, 1989).

Fidalgo, Pilar, *A Young Mother in Franco's Prisons* (London: United Editorial Ltd, 1939).

Fisher, Harry, *Comrades. Tales of a Brigadista in the Spanish Civil War* (Lincoln and London: University of Nebraska Press, 1998).

Fontserè, Carles, *Un exiliado de tercera. En París durante la Segunda Guerra Mundial* (Barcelona: Acantilado, 2004).

García, Consuelo, *Las cárceles de Soledad Real: Una vida* (Madrid: Ediciones Alfuaguara, 1982).

García Madrid, Ángeles, *Réquiem por la libertad* (Madrid: Editorial Alianza Hispánica, 2003).

Guzmán, Eduardo de, *La muerte de la esperanza* (Madrid: G. del Toro, 1973).

Guzmán, Eduardo de, *Año de la Victoria* (Madrid: G. del Toro, 1974).

Healey, Dorothy and Isserman, Maurice, *Dorothy Healey Remembers. A Life in the American Communist Party* (New York/Oxford: Oxford University Press, 1990).

Hughes, Langston, *The Collected Works*, Vol. 9. *Essays on Art, Race, Politics, and World Affairs* (edition by Christopher C. De Santis), (Columbia and London: University of Missouri Press, 2002).

Jiménez, Mona, "My dear mama: don't worry", a photographic installation, reproduced in *Contact Sheet* no. 73 (Syracuse, NY: Light Work [gallery], n.d. [1991]). (The installation was based on photographs and letters sent [c.1939–40] from Gurs internment camp [southern France] by her father, Mike Jiménez, born in Spain but a US citizen, who volunteered for the International Brigades and fought in the Spanish Republican guerrilla.)

Jiménez Margalejo, Carlos, *Memorias de un refugiado español en el Norte de África, 1939–1956* (Madrid: Fundación Largo Caballero/Ediciones Cinca, 2008).

Kluger, Ruth, *Landscapes of Memory: A Holocaust Girlhood Remembered* (London: Bloomsbury, 2004).

Knickerbocker, Hubert Renfro, *The Siege of the Alcazar: A war-log of the Spanish revolution* (London: Hutchinson, 1937).

Koestler, Arthur, *Scum of the Earth* (London: Eland, [1941] 2006).

Koltsov, Mijail, *Diario de la guerra de España* (Madrid: Akal, 1978).

Langdon-Davies, John, *Behind the Spanish Barricades. Reports from the Spanish Civil War* (London: Reportage Press, [1936] 2007).

Lasala Navarro, Gregorio, *La mujer delincuente en España y su tratamiento correccional* (Buenos Aires: DG de Institutos Penales de la Nación Argentina, 1948).

London, Artur, *On Trial* (London: Macdonald and Co., 1970).

Lord, James, *My Queer War* (New York: Farrar, Straus and Giroux, 2010).

Loyd, Anthony, *My war gone by, I miss it so* (London: Penguin, 1999).

Malonda, Ángeles, *Aquello sucedió así* (Madrid: Dept. de Publicaciones de la Asociación de Cooperativas Farmacéuticas, 1983).

Martín Blázquez, José, *I Helped to Build an Army* (London: Secker and Warburg, 1939).

Marzani, Carl, *The Education of a Reluctant Radical* (New York: Topical Books, 1992–5) 4 vols: 1. *Roman Childhood* (1992); 2. *Growing Up American* (1993); 3. *Spain, Munich and Dying Empires*; 4. *From Pentagon to Penitentiary* (1995)).

Mera, Cipriano, *Guerra, exilio y cárcel de un anarcosindicalista* (Paris: Ruedo Ibérico, 1976).

Ministerio de la Justicia, *Crónica del Patronato Nacional de San Pablo (1943–1951)* (Madrid: Gráficas Reunidas, 1951).

Miró, Joan, *Epistolari català* (Barcelona: Fundació Joan Miró, 2009).

Mola Vidal, Emilio, *Obras completas* (Valladolid: Librería Santarén, 1940).

Moros, Manuel, *Febrer 1939: L'exili dins la mirada de Manuel Moros* (Perpignan: Mare Nostrum, 2009).

Núñez, Mercedes, *Cárcel de Ventas* (Paris: Éditions de la Librarie du Globe, 1967).

O' Donnell, Peadar, *Salud!: An Irishman in Spain* (London: Methuen and Co., 1937).

Pérez del Pulgar, José Agustín, *La solución que da España al problema de sus presos politicos* (Valladolid: Publicaciones Redención, 1939).

Parga, Carmen, *Antes que sea tarde* (Madrid: Compañía Literaria, 1996).

Parshina, Elizaveta, *La brigadista* (Barcelona: RBA, 2005).

Payne, Robert, *Chungking Diary* (London: William Heinemann, 1945).

Pemán, José María, *Arengas y crónicas de guerra* (Cádiz: Establecimientos Cerón, 1937).

Rolfe, Edwin, *The Lincoln Battalion* (New York: Haskell, 1974).

Roth, Joseph, *The White Cities. Reports from France 1925–39* (London: Granta, 2004).

Rousset, David, *L'univers concentrationnaire* (Paris: Les Éditions de Minuit, [1946] 1965).

Rousset, David, *Les jours de notre mort* (Paris: Hachette, 1993).

Ruiz Vilaplana, Antonio, *Doy fe . . . un año de actuación en la España nacionalista* (Paris: Editions Imprimerie Coopérative Etoile S.A., 1938).

Salut, Emil, *Vivers de revolucionaris: apunts històrics del districte cinquè* (Barcelona: Libreria Catalònia, 1938).

Sánchez del Arco, Manuel, *El sur de España en la reconquista de Madrid* (Seville: Editorial Sevillana, 1937).

Schlayer, Felix, *Diplomat im roten Madrid* (Berlin, 1938).

Semprún, Jorge, *Le Grand Voyage* (Paris: Gallimard, 1963), (autobiographical novel).

Semprún, Jorge, *Quel Beau Dimanche!* (Paris: Bernard Grasset, 1980).

Semprún, Jorge, *Literature or Life* (New York: Viking, 1997).

Semprún, Jorge, *Viviré con su nombre, morirá con el mío* (Barcelona: Tusquets, 2003).

Sender Barayón, Ramón, *A Death in Zamora* (Albuquerque: University of New Mexico Press, 1989; 2nd edn (Calm Unity Press, 2003). Spanish edition: *Muerte en Zamora* (Barcelona: Plaza & Janés, 1990).

Sperber, Manès, *Like a Tear in the Ocean* (trilogy comprising *The Burned Bramble*, *The Abyss* and *Journey without End*), (New Jersey: Holmes & Meier, 1988).

Starinov, Ilya Grigoryevich, *Over the Abyss: My Life in Soviet Special Operations* (New York: Ivy Books, 1995).

Tagüeña Lacorte, Manuel, *Testimonio de dos guerras* (Mexico: Ediciones Oasis, 1974).

Tisa, John, *Recalling the Good Fight. An Autobiography of the Spanish Civil War* (South Hadley, MA: Bergin and Garvey, 1985).

Toller, Ernst, *I was a German* (New York: Paragon, 1991).

Torrent, Martín, *¿Qué me dice usted de los presos?* (Alcalá de Henares: Imprenta Talleres Penitenciarios, 1942).

Whitaker, John T., "Prelude to World War: A Witness from Spain", *Foreign Affairs* 21, 1 (October 1942).

Whitaker, John T., *We Cannot Escape History* (New York: Macmillan, 1943).

Wolff, Milton, *Another Hill* (Urbana and Chicago: University of Illinois Press, 1994), (autobiographical novel).

Wolff, Milton, *Member of the Working Class* (Lincoln, NE: iUniverse, 2005).

Woolsey, Gamel, *Death's Other Kingdom* (London: Longmans, Green & Co., 1939).

Yates, James, *Mississippi to Madrid. Memoir of a Black American in the Abraham Lincoln Brigade* (Greensboro, NC: Open Hand Publishing, 1989).

Zugazagoitia, Julián, *Guerra y vicisitudes de los españoles* (Paris: Librería Española, 1968).

Secondary Sources

Abad, Francisco *et al.*, 'Dossier. Camp de la Bota. La memòria dels vençuts', *L'Avenç*, no. 291, May 2004.

Acosta Bono, Gonzalo *et al.*, *El canal de los presos (1940–1962). Trabajos forzosos: de la represión política a la explotación económica* (Barcelona: Crítica, 2004).

Agamben, Giorgio, *Homo Sacer. Sovereign Power and Bare Life* (Stanford, CA: Stanford University Press, 1998).

Águila, Juan José del, *El TOP. La represión de la libertad (1963–1977)* (Barcelona: Planeta, 2001).

Aguilar Fernández, Paloma, *Memoria y olvido de la guerra civil española* (Madrid: Alianza,1996).

Alfaya, José Luis, *Como un río de fuego: Madrid 1936* (Barcelona: Ediciones Internacionales Universitarias, 1998).

Allcock, John B., "Rural–urban differences and the break-up of Yugoslavia", *Balkanologie. Revue d'études pluridisciplinaires* IV, 1–2 (December 2002).

Altaffaylla Kultur Taldea, *Navarra 1936. De la esperanza al terror* (Tafalla: author-editor, 1992) 2 vols.

Alpert, Michael, *El ejército republicano en la guerra civil* (Madrid: Siglo XXI, 1989).

Álvarez Fernández, José Ignacio, *Memoria y trauma en los testimonios de la represión franquista* (Barcelona: Anthropos, 2007).

Álvarez Bolado, Alfonso, *Para ganar la guerra, para ganar la paz. Iglesia y guerra civil 1936–1939* (Madrid: Universidad Pontificia de Comillas, 1995).

Álvarez Chillida, Gonzalo, *El antisemitismo en España: la imagen del judío (1812–2002)*, (Madrid: Marcial Pons, 2002).

Álvaro Dueñas, Manuel, *'Por ministerio de la ley y voluntad del Caudillo': La Jurisdicción Especial de Responsabilidades Políticas (1939–1945)*, (Madrid: Centro de Estudios Políticos y Constitucionales, 2006).

Anderson, Peter, "Singling Out Victims: Denunciation and Collusion in the Post-Civil War Francoist Repression in Spain, 1939–1945", *European History Quarterly,* vol. 39, 1 (2009).

Anderson, Peter, "In the Interests of Justice? Grassroots Prosecution and Collaboration in the Francoist Military Trials, 1939–1945", *Contemporary European History*, 18, 1, 2009.

Anderson, Peter, *The Francoist Military Trials. Terror and Complicity, 1939–1945* (London and New York: Routledge, 2010).

Anderson, Peter, "In the Name of the Martyrs. Memory and Retribution in Francoist Southern Spain 1936–45", *Cultural and Social History* 8, 3 (2011).

Appadurai, Arjun, "Disjuncture and Difference in the Global Cultural Economy", in Simon During (ed.), *The Cultural Studies Reader*, 3rd edn (London: Routledge, 2007).

Applebaum, Anne, *Gulag. A History* (London: Penguin, 2003).

Arco Blanco, Miguel Ángel, *Hambre de Siglos. Mundo rural y apoyos sociales del franquismo en Andalucía oriental (1936–51)*, (Granada: Comares, 2007).

Arendt, Hannah, *The Origins of Totalitarianism* (San Diego/New York/London: Harcourt Brace & Company, 1973).

Aróstegui, Julio and Marco, Jorge (eds), *El último frente: La resistencia armada antifranquista en España, 1939–1952* (Madrid: Catarata, 2008).

Badiou, Alain, *Ethics. An essay on the understanding of evil* (London: Verso, 2001).

Badiou, Alain, *Polemics* (London: Verso, 2006).

Badiou, Alain, *The Century* (Cambridge: Polity Press, 2007).

Balfour, Sebastian, *Dictatorship, Workers and the City: Labour in Greater Barcelona since 1939* (Oxford: Clarendon Press, 1989).

Balfour, Sebastian, *Deadly Embrace: Morocco and the Road to the Spanish Civil War* (Oxford: Oxford University Press, 2002).

Ballbé, Manuel, *Orden público y militarismo en la España constitucional (1812–1983)* (Madrid: Alianza Editorial, 1983).

Bartov, Omer, *Mirrors of Destruction: War, Genocide and Modern Identity* (New York/Oxford: Oxford University Press, 2000).

Bartov, Omer, "Eastern Europe as the Site of Genocide", *Journal of Modern History* 80, 3 (2008).

Baxell, Richard, *British Volunteers in the Spanish Civil War: The British Battalion in the International Brigades 1936–1939* (London: Routledge/Cañada Blanch Studies on Contemporary Spain, 2004).

Bechelloni, Antonio, "Antifascist resistance in France from the 'Phony War' to the Liberation: identity and destiny in question", in Gabaccia, Donna R., and Ottanelli, Fraser M. (eds), *Italian Workers of the World. Labor Migration and the Formation of Multiethnic States* (Urbana and Chicago: Illinois University Press, 2001).

Bedmar González, Arcángel, *Lucena: de la segunda república a la guerra civil* (Córdoba: n.p., 1998).

Bedmar González, Arcángel, *República, guerra y represión: Lucena 1931–1939* (Lucena: Ayuntamiento de Lucena, 2000).

Benjamin, Walter, *Illuminations. Essays and Reflections* (edited and with an introduction by Hannah Arendt), (New York: Schocken Books, [1968] 2007).

Bideleux, Robert and Jeffries, Ian, *A History of Eastern Europe. Crisis and Change*, 2nd edn (Abingdon: Routledge, 2007).

Blinkhorn, Martin, *Carlism and Crisis in Spain 1931–1939* (Cambridge: Cambridge University Press, 1975).

Bloxham, Donald and Moses, A. Dirk (eds), *The Oxford Handbook of Genocide Studies* (Oxford: Oxford University Press, 2010).

Bonet Baqué, Núria, Cardona Alcaide, Amanda and Corbella López, Gerard, *Tàrrega 1936–61. Aproximació a la repressió, l'exili i la vida quotidiana* (Tàrrega: Ajuntament de Tàrrega, 2008).

Bosch, Aurora, *Ugetistas y libertarios: guerra civil y revolución en el País Valenciano, 1936–1939* (Valencia: Institución Alfonso El Magnánimo, 1983).

Botti, Alfonso, *Cielo y dinero: el nacionalcatolicismo en España 1881–1975* (Madrid: Alianza, 1992).

Bougarel, Xavier, "Yugoslav Wars: The 'revenge of the countryside' between sociological reality and nationalist myth", *East European Quarterly* XXXIII, 2 (1999).

Boyd, Carolyn P., "'Responsibilities' and the Second Spanish Republic 1931–1936", *European History Quarterly* 14 (1984).

Boyd, Carolyn P., *Historia Patria: Politics, History and National Identity in Spain 1875–1975* (Princeton: Princeton University Press, 1997).

Bruttmann, Tal and Joly, Laurent, *La France Antijuive. L'agression de Léon Blum à la Chambre des Députés* (Editions des Equateurs, 2006).

Buchanan, Tom, "Edge of Darkness: British 'Front-line' Diplomacy in the Spanish Civil War, 1936–1937", *Contemporary European History* 12, 3 (2003).

Buchanan, Tom and Conway, Martin (eds), *Political Catholicism in Europe, 1918–1965* (Oxford: Clarendon Press, 1996).

Butler, Judith, *The Psychic Life of Power: Theories in Subjection* (Stanford, CA: Stanford University Press, 1997).

Butler, Judith, *Antigone's Claim: Kinship Between Life and Death* (New York: Columbia University Press, 2000).

Butler, Judith, *Precarious Life: The Powers of Mourning and Violence* (London/New York: Verso, 2006).

Butler, Judith, *Frames of War: When is life grievable?* (London: Verso, 2009).

Carmichael, Cathie, "Violence and Ethnic Boundary Maintenance in Bosnia in the 1990s", *Journal of Genocide Research* 8, 3 (2006).

Carmichael, Cathie, "Brothers, Strangers and Enemies: Ethno-Nationalism and the Demise of Communist Yugoslavia", in Dan Stone (ed.), *The Oxford Handbook of Postwar European History* (Oxford: Oxford University Press, 2012).

Caron, Vicki, *Uneasy Asylum: France and the Jewish Refugee Crisis 1933–1942* (Stanford, CA: Stanford University Press, 1999).

Carr, Raymond, *Spain: A History* (Oxford: Oxford University Press, 2000).

Carroll, Peter N., *The Odyssey of the Abraham Lincoln Brigade. Americans in the Spanish Civil War* (Stanford, CA: Stanford University Press, 1994).

Carroll, Peter N., Small, Melvin, and Nash, Michael H., *The Good Fight Continues: World War II Letters from the Abraham Lincoln Brigade* (New York: New York University Press, 2006).

Carroll, Peter N. and Fernández, James D. (eds), *Facing Fascism: New York and the Spanish Civil War* (New York: Museum of the City of New York/New York Press, 2007).

Casanova, Julián *et al.* (eds), *El pasado oculto. Fascismo y violencia en Aragón (1936–1939)*, 1st edn (Madrid: Siglo XXI, 1992).

Casanova, Julián, *Anarchism, the Republic and the Civil War in Spain 1931–1936* (London and New York: Routledge, 2005).

Casanova, Julián, *La iglesia de Franco* (Barcelona: Crítica, 2009).

Casanova, Julián *The Spanish Republic and the Civil War* (Cambridge: Cambridge University Press, 2010).

Casanova, Julián, Espinosa, Francisco, Mir, Conxita and Moreno Gómez, Francisco, *Morir, matar, sobrevivir: la violencia en la dictadura de Franco* (Barcelona: Crítica, 2001).

Casas de la Vega, Rafael, *El terror: Madrid 1936* (Madrid: Fénix, 1994).

Casquete, Jesús and Cruz, Rafael (eds), *Políticas de la muerte: Usos y abusos del ritual fúnebre en la Europa del siglo XX* (Madrid: Catarata, 2009).

Castillo, Juan José, *Propietarios muy pobres: sobre la subordinación política del pequeño campesino en España (la Confederación Nacional Católico-Agraria, 1917–1942)* (Madrid: Servicio de Publicaciones Agrarias,1979).

Cate-Arries, Francie, *Spanish Culture behind Barbed Wire: Memory and Representation of the French Concentration Camps 1939–1945* (Lewisburg, PA: Bucknell University Press, 2004).

Cazorla Sánchez, Antonio, *Las políticas de la victoria: La consolidación del Nuevo Estado franquista (1938–1953)*, (Madrid: Marcial Pons, 2000).

Cazorla, Antonio, *Fear and Progress: Ordinary Lives in Franco's Spain 1939–1975* (Oxford: Wiley-Blackwell, 2009).

Cenarro, Ángela, *El fin de la esperanza: fascismo y guerra civil en la provincia de Teruel (1936–1939)*, (Teruel: Diputación Provincial de Teruel, 1996).

Cenarro, Ángela, "Matar, vigilar y delatar: la quiebra de la sociedad civil durante la guerra y la posguerra en España (1936–1948)", *Historia Social* 44 (2002).

Cenarro, Ángela, "La lógica de la guerra, la lógica de la venganza: violencia y fractura social en una comunidad bajoaragonesa, 1939–1940", in Mir, Conxita, Catalán, Jordi and Ginard, David (coords.), *Enfrontaments civils: Postguerres i reconstruccions: II Guerra civil de 1936 i franquisme* (Lleida: Associació Recerques i Pagès Editors, 2002).

Cenarro, Ángela, "La institucionalización del universo penitenciario", in Carme Molinero *et al.* (eds), *Una inmensa prisión: Los campos de concentración y las prisiones durante la guerra civil y el franquismo* (Barcelona: Crítica, 2003).

Cenarro, Ángela, *La sonrisa de Falange: Auxilio Social en la guerra civil y en la posguerra* (Barcelona: Crítica, 2005).

Cenarro, Ángela, "Memories of Repression and Resistance. Narratives of Children Institutionalized by Auxilio Social in Postwar Spain", *History & Memory* 20, 2 (2008).

Cenarro, Ángela, *Los niños de Auxilio Social* (Madrid: Espasa Calpe, 2009).

Cervera, Javier, *Madrid en guerra. La ciudad clandestina 1936–1939* (Madrid: Alianza, 1998).

Christian Jr., William A., *Moving Crucifixes in Modern Spain* (Princeton, NJ: Princeton University Press, 1992).

Christian Jr., William A., *Visionaries: The Spanish Republic and the Reign of Christ* (Berkeley/Los Angeles, CA: University of California Press, 1996).

Cifuentes Checa, Julia & Maluenda Pons, Pilar, *El asalto a la República: Los orígenes del franquismo en Zaragoza (1936–1939)*, (Zaragoza: Institución 'Fernando el Católico', 1995).

Claret Miranda, Jaume, *El atroz desmoche: La destrucción de la universidad española por el franquismo 1936–1945* (Barcelona: Crítica, 2006).

Claudín, Fernando, *The Communist Movement: From Comintern to Cominform* (Harmondsworth: Penguin, 1975).

Cobo Romero, Francisco, *La guerra civil y la represión franquista en la provincia de Jaén (1936–1950)*, (Jaén: Diputación de Jaén, 1993)

Cobo Romero, Francisco, *Conflicto rural y violencia política: El largo camino hacia la dictadura. Jaen 1917–1950* (Jaén: Universidad de Jaén/Universidad de Granada, 1998).

Cobo Romero, Francisco, "El voto campesino contra la II República: La derechización de los pequeños propietarios y arrendatarios agrícolas jiennenses 1931–1936", *Historia Social*, 37 (2000).

Cobo Romero, Francisco, *Revolución campesina y contrarrevolución franquista en Andalucía: conflictividad social, violencia política y represión franquista en el mundo rural andaluz, 1931–1950* (Granada: University of Granada, 2004).

Cohen, Stanley, *States of Denial: Knowing about Atrocities and Suffering* (Cambridge: Polity Press, 2001).

Collier, George Allen, *Socialists of Rural Andalusia* (Stanford, CA: Stanford University Press, 1987).

Collum, Danny D. and Berch, Victor A. (eds), *African-Americans in the Spanish Civil War: This Ain't Ethiopia But It'll Do* (Boston, MA: G.K. Hall, 1991).

Connolly, John, "The Uses of *Volksgemeinschaft*: Letters to the NSDAP Kreisleitung Eisenach, 1939–1940", *Journal of Modern History* 68, 4 (1996).

Conway, Martin and Romijn, Peter (eds), *The War for Legitimacy in Politics and Culture 1936–1946* (Oxford: Berg, 2008).

Crome, Ilana, "Obituary: Leonard Crome", *The Psychiatrist* 26 (2002).

Cruanyes, Josep, *Els papers de Salamanca. L'espoliació del patrimoni documental de Catalunya* (Barcelona: Edicions 62, 2003).

Cruz, Rafael, "¡Luzbel vuelve al mundo! Las imágenes de la Rusia Soviética y la acción colectiva en España", in Cruz, Rafael and Pérez Ledesma, Manuel (eds), *Cultura y movilización en la España contemporánea* (Madrid: Alianza, 1997).

Cruz, Rafael, *En el nombre del pueblo: República, rebelión y guerra en la España de 1936* (Madrid: Siglo XXI, 2006).

Cruz, Rafael, "El sabor fúnebre de la política española entre 1876 y 1940", Casquete, Jesús and Cruz, Rafael (eds), *Políticas de la muerte: usos y abusos del ritual fúnebre en la Europa del siglo XX* (Madrid: Catarata, 2009).

Cueva, Julio de la, "The Stick and the Candle: Clericals and Anticlericals in Northern Spain, 1898–1913", *European History Quarterly* 26, 2 (1996).

Cueva, Julio de la, "Clericalismo y movilización católica durante la restauración", in Cueva, Julio de la and López Villaverde, Ángel Luis (eds), *Clericalismo y asociacionismo católico en España: de la restauración a la transición* (Cuenca: Universidad Castilla-La Mancha, 2005).

Cuevas, Tomasa, *Cárcel de mujeres (1939–1945)*, (Barcelona: Sirocco, 1986).

Deák, István, Gross, Jan T. and Judt, Tony (eds), *The Politics of Retribution in Europe. World War II and Its Aftermath* (Princeton: Princeton University Press, 2000).

Delgado, Manuel, *Luces iconoclastas. Anticlericalismo, espacio y ritual el la España contemporánea* (Barcelona: Ariel, 2001).

Diéz Echarri, E., "El sistema de la Redención de Penas por el Trabajo. Sus fundamentos, su aplicación y sus consecuencias", *Revista de la Escuela de Estudios Penitenciarios* 36 (March 1948).

Dios Vicente, Laura de, "Control y represión en Zamora (1936–1939). La violencia vengadora ejecutada sobre el terreno", *Historia y Comunicación Social* 7 (2002).

Douglas, Mary, *Purity and Danger* (Abingdon, Oxon: Routledge Classics, 2002).

Dulić, Tomislav, *Utopias of Nation: Local Mass Killings in Bosnia and Herzegovina, 1941–42* (Uppsala: Acta Universitatis Upsaliensis, 2005).

Durán Pastor, Miguel, *Sicut Oculi. Vigilantes y vigilados en la Mallorca de la posguerra 1941–1945* (Palma de Mallorca, Miquel Font, 1992).

Ealham, Chris, *Class, Culture and Conflict in Barcelona, 1898–1937* (Routledge/Cañada Blanch: London, 2005).

Ealham, Chris, "Anarchism and Illegality in Barcelona, 1931–37", *Contemporary European History* 4, 2 (1995).

Ealham, Chris, "La lluita pel carrer, els vendedors ambulants durant la II República', *L'Avenç* 230 (1998).

Ennis, Helen, *Margaret Michaelis, Love, Loss and Photography* (Port Melbourne, Victoria: National Gallery of Australia, 2005).

Ennis, Helen and Mendelson, Jordana *et al.*, *Margaret Michaelis: Fotografía, vanguardia y política en la Barcelona de la República* (Valencia: IVAM, 1998).

Escudero Andújar, Fuensanta, *Lo cuentan como lo han vivido (república, guerra y represión en Murcia)*, (Murcia: Universidad de Murcia, 2000).

Espías Bermúdez, Ángel, "Memorias, Año 1936. Hechos acaecidos en Zamora y provincia", *Ebre 38. Revista Internacional de la guerra civil* 2 (2003).

Espinosa Maestre, Francisco, *La justicia de Queipo (violencia selectiva y terror fascista en la II División en 1936): Sevilla, Huelva, Cádiz, Córdoba, Málaga y Badajoz* (Córdoba: Bibliofilia Montillana, Cofradía de la Viña y el Vino, 2000).

Espinosa Maestre, Francisco, *La columna de la muerte. El avance del ejército franquista de Sevilla a Badajoz* (Barcelona: Crítica, 2003).

Espinosa Maestre, Francisco, *La justicia de Queipo* (Barcelona: Crítica, 2005).

Espinosa Maestre, Francisco, *La guerra civil en Huelva*, 1st edn (Huelva: Diputación Provincial de Huelva, 1996) and 4th edn (Huelva: Diputación Provincial de Huelva, 2005).

Espinosa Maestre, Francisco, *Contra el olvido. Historia y memoria de la guerra civil* (Barcelona: Crítica, 2006).

Espinosa Maestre, Francisco, "La memoria de la represión y la lucha por su reconocimiento: en torno a la creación de la comisión interministerial", in dossier: "Generaciones y memoria de la represión franquista: un balance de los movimientos por la memoria", *Hispania Nova. Revista de Historia Contemporánea* 6 (2006).

Espinosa Maestre, Francisco, *Callar al mensajero. La represión franquista. Entre la libertad de información y el derecho al honor* (Barcelona: Península, 2009).

Espinosa Maestre, Francisco, *Violencia roja y azul. España 1936–1950* (Barcelona: Crítica, 2010).

Etkind, Alexander, "Post-Soviet Hauntology. Cultural Memory of the Soviet Terror", *Constellations* 16, 1 (2009).

Evans, Richard J., *The Third Reich in Power 1933–1939* (London: Allen Lane, 2005).

Evans, Richard J., *Rituals of Retribution: Capital Punishment in Germany 1600–1987* (Oxford: Oxford University Press, 1996).

Fitzpatrick, Sheila and Gellately, Robert (eds), *Accusatory Practices: Denunciation in Modern European History, 1789–1989* (Chicago: University of Chicago Press, 1997).

Funder, Anna, *Stasiland. Stories from Behind the Berlin Wall* (London: Granta, 2003).

Ganier Raymond, Philippe, *El cartel rojo* (Tafalla: Editorial Txalaparta, 2008).

García de Consuegra Muñoz, Gabriel, López López, Ángel and López López, Fernando, *La represión en Pozoblanco* (Córdoba: Francisco Baena, 1989).

García Delgado, José Luis (ed.), *El primer franquismo: España durante la Segunda Guerra Mundial* (Madrid: Siglo XXI Editores, 1989).

García Pérez, Rafael, "El envío de trabajadores españoles a Alemania durante la segunda guerra mundial", *Hispania* 170 (1998).

Gellately, Robert and Kiernan, Ben (eds), *The Specter of Genocide: Mass Murder in Historical Perspective* (Cambridge: Cambridge University Press, 2003).

Gemie, Sharif, "The Ballad of Bourg-Madame: Memory, Exile and the Spanish Republican Refugees of the *Retirada* of 1939", *International Review of Social History* 51 (2006).

Gerassi, John, *The Premature Antifascists: North American Volunteers in the Spanish Civil War, 1936–39: An Oral History* (New York: Praeger, 1986).

Gerlach, Christian, *Extremely Violent Societies: Mass Violence in the Twentieth-Century World* (Cambridge: Cambridge University Press, 2010).

Gerwarth, Robert, "The Central European Counter-Revolution: Paramilitary Violence in Germany, Austria and Hungary after the Great War", *Past and Present* 200 (2008).

Gibson, Ian, *La represión nacionalista de Granada en 1936 y la muerte de Federico García Lorca* (Paris: Ruedo Ibérico, 1971).

Gibson, Ian, *Paracuellos cómo fue* (Barcelona: Argos Vergara, 1983).

Gibson, Ian, *Federico García Lorca. A Life* (London: Faber & Faber, 1989).

Ginard i Ferón, David, *L'esquerra mallorquina i el franquisme* (Palma: Edicions Documenta Balear, 1994).

Ginard i Ferón, David, *Matilde Landa, De la Institución Libre de Enseñanza a las prisiones franquistas* (Barcelona: Flor del Viento, 2005).

Gómez Bravo, Gutmaro, *La redención de penas: La formación del sistema penitenciario franquista, 1936–1950* (Madrid: Catarata, 2007).

Gómez Bravo, Gutmaro, *El exilio interior: Cárcel y represión en la España franquista, 1939–1950* (Madrid: Taurus, 2009).

Gómez Bravo, Gutmaro and Marco, Jorge, *La obra del miedo: Violencia y sociedad en la España franquista (1936–1950)*, (Madrid: Península, 2011).

González Calleja, Eduardo, "La defensa armada del 'orden social' durante la Dictadura de Primo de Rivera (1923–1930)", in García Delgado, José Luis (ed.), *España entre dos siglos (1875–1931). Continuidad y cambio* (Madrid: Siglo XXI, 1991).

González Calleja, Eduardo and Rey Reguillo, Fernando, *La defensa armada contra la revolución. Una historia de las "guardias cívicas'" en la España del siglo XX* (Madrid: CSIC, 1995).

González Calleja, Eduardo, *El Máuser y el sufragio. Orden público, subversión y violencia política en la crisis de la Restauración (1917–1931)*, (Madrid: CSIC, 1999).

Graham, Helen, *Socialism and War: The Spanish Socialist Party in Power and Crisis 1936–1939* (Cambridge: Cambridge University Press, 1991).

Graham, Helen, "'Against the State': a genealogy of the Barcelona May Days (1937)", *European History Quarterly* 29, 4 (1999).

Graham, Helen, *The Spanish Republic at War* (Cambridge: Cambridge University Press, 2002).

Graham, Helen, "New Myths for Old", *Times Literary Supplement*, 11 July 2003.

Graham, Helen, *The Spanish Civil War: A Very Short Introduction* (Oxford: Oxford University Press, 2005).

Graham, Helen, and Labanyi, Jo (eds), *Spanish Cultural Studies: an Introduction: the Struggle for Modernity* (Oxford and New York: Oxford University Press, 1995).

Graham, Helen and Quiroga, Alejandro, "After the fear was over? What came after dictatorships in Spain, Greece and Portugal", in Stone, Dan (ed.), *The Oxford Handbook of Postwar European History* (Oxford: Oxford University Press, 2012).

Granja Fernández, Pilar de la, *Represión durante la guerra civil y la posguerra en la provincia de Zamora* (Zamora: Instituto de Estudios Zamoranos Florián de Ocampo, 2002).

Gross, Jan Tomasz, *Neighbours: the Destruction of the Jewish Community of Jedwabne* (Princeton: Princeton University Press, 2000).

Gross, Jan Tomasz, *Fear. Anti-Semitism in Poland After Auschwitz: An Essay in Historical Interpretation* (New York: Random House, 2007).

Hallward, Peter, *Badiou: A subject to truth* (Minneapolis: University of Minnesota Press, 2003).

Harouni, Rahma, "Le débat autour du statut des étrangers dans les années 1930", *Mouvement Social* 188 (1999).

Hayden, Robert M., "Recounting the Dead: The Rediscovery and Redefinition of Wartime Massacres in Late- and Post-Communist Yugoslavia", in Watson, Rubie S. (ed.), *Memory, History and Opposition under State Socialism* (Santa Fe, NM: School of American Research Press, 1994).

Haynes, Michael and Husan, Rumy, *A Century of State Murder? Death and Policy in Twentieth-Century Russia* (London/Sterling, VA: Pluto Press, 2003).

Hernández Holgado, Fernando, *Mujeres encarceladas. La prisión de Ventas: de la República al franquismo, 1931–1941* (Madrid: Marcial Pons, 2003).

Holquist, Peter, "'Information is the Alpha and Omega of Our Work': Bolshevik Surveillance in its Pan-European Perspective", *Journal of Modern History* 69, 3 (1997).

Holquist, Peter, "To count, to extract, to exterminate: population statistics and population politics in late Imperial and Soviet Russia", in Martin, Terry and Suny, Ronald Grigor (eds), *A State of Nations: Empire and Nation-Making in the Age of Lenin and Stalin* (New York: Oxford University Press, 2001).

Horkheimer, Max and Adorno, Theodor, *Dialectics of Enlightenment* (London: Verso Editions, 1979).

Iturralde, Juan de, *La guerra de Franco, los vascos y la Iglesia*, 2 vols (San Sebastián: Publicaciones del Clero Vasco, 1978).

Izquierdo Martín, Jesús and Sánchez León, Pablo, *La guerra que nos han contado. 1936 y nosotros* (Madrid: Alianza, 2006).

Jackson, Angela, *Beyond the Battlefield: Testimony, Memory and Remembrance of a Cave Hospital in the Spanish Civil War* (Pontypool: Warren and Pell, 2005).

Jackson, Angela, *'For us it was Heaven': The Passion, Grief and Fortitude of Patience Darton – From the Spanish Civil War to Mao's China* (Brighton, Portland, Toronto: Sussex Academic Press, 2012).

Jackson, Julian, *France. The Dark Years, 1940–1944* (Oxford: Oxford University Press, 2001).

Jones, Adam, "Gender and Genocide", in Stone, Dan (ed.), *The Historiography of Genocide* (Basingstoke: Palgrave Macmillan [2008] 2010).

Juárez, Javier, *Comandante Durán: Leyenda y tragedia de un intelectual en armas* (Barcelona: Debate, 2009).

Judt, Tony, *Postwar. A History of Europe since 1945* (London: Heinemann, 2005).

Juliá, Santos (coord.), *Víctimas de la guerra civil* (Madrid: Temas de Hoy, 1999).

Kovel, Joel, *Red Hunting in the Promised Land: Anticommunism and the Making of America* (New York: Basic Books, 1994).

Kühne, Thomas, *Belonging and Genocide: Hitler's Community 1918–1945* (New Haven, CT: Yale University Press, 2010).

Kalyvas, Stathis N., *The Logic of Violence in Civil War* (Cambridge: Cambridge University Press, 2006).

Labanyi, Jo, "Women, Asian Hordes and the Threat to the Self in Giménez Caballero's *Genio de España*", *Bulletin of Hispanic Studies* LXXIII (1996).

Lafuente, Isaías, *Esclavos por la patria: La explotación de los presos bajo el franquismo* (Madrid: Ediciones Temas de Hoy, 2002).

Lama, José María, *Una biografía frente al olvido: José González Barrero, Alcalde de Zafra en la segunda República* (Badajoz: Diputación de Badajoz, 2000).

Lanero Táboas, Mónica, *Una milicia de la justicia: La política judicial del franquismo (1936–1945)*, (Madrid: Centro de Estudios Constitucionales, 1996).

Lannon, Frances, *Privilege, Persecution and Prophecy: The Catholic Church in Spain 1875–1975* (Oxford: Clarendon Press, 1987).

Ledesma, José Luis, *Los días de llamas de la revolución. Violencia y política en la retaguardia republicana de Zaragoza durante la guerra civil* (Institución Fernando el Católico, Zaragoza, 2003).

Leitz, Christian, "Nazi Germany and Francoist Spain, 1936–1945", in Balfour, Sebastian and Preston, Paul (eds), *Spain and the Great Powers in the Twentieth Century* (New York: Routledge, 1999).

Lincoln, Bruce, "Revolutionary Exhumations in Spain, July 1936", *Comparative Studies in Society and History* 27, 2 (1985).

Lindqvist, Sven, *Exterminate All the Brutes* (London: Granta, 2002).

Lindqvist, Sven, *Desert Divers* (London: Granta, 2002).

Lindsey, Rose, "From atrocity to data: historiographies of rape in Former Yugoslavia and the gendering of genocide", *Patterns of Prejudice* 36, 4 (2002).

López Villaverde, Ángel Luis and Sánchez Sánchez, Isidro, *Honra, agua y pan. Un sueño comunista de Cipriano López Crespo (1934–1938)*, (Cuenca: Universidad Castilla-La Mancha, 2004).

Lowe, Sid, *Catholicism, War and the Foundation of Francoism: The Juventud de Acción Popular in Spain* (Brighton & Portland: Sussex Academic Press, 2010).

Lowenthal Felstiner, Mary, *To Paint Her Life: Charlotte Salomon in the Nazi Era* (Berkeley and Los Angeles, CA/London: University of California Press, 1997).

Lustiger, Arno, *'Shalom Libertad'. Les Juifs dans la guerre d'Espagne* (Paris: Editions du Cerf, 1991).

Macías, Santiago and Silva, Emilio, *Las fosas de Franco: los republicanos que el dictador dejó en la cuneta* (Madrid: Temas de Hoy, 2006).

Marco, Jorge, *Hijos de una guerra. Los hermanos Quero y la resistencia antifranquista* (Granada: Comares, 2010).

Mariani, Laura, *Quelle dell'Idea. Storie di detenute politiche 1927–1948* (Bari: De Donato, 1982).

Marín Arce, José María, "Diez años de Gobierno del PSOE (1982–1992)", *Espacio, tiempo y forma. Serie V, Historia contemporánea* 13 (2000).

Martín Barrio, Adoración, Sampedro Talabán, María de los Ángeles and Velasco Marcos, María Jesús, "Dos formas de violencia durante la guerra civil. La represión en Salamanca y la resistencia armada en Zamora", in Aróstegui, Julio (coord.), *Historia y memoria de la guerra civil*, 3 vols, II (Valladolid: Junta de Castilla y León, 1988).

Mateos, Miguel Ángel, *La República en Zamora (1931–1936): Comportamiento político electoral en una sociedad tradicional* (Zamora: IEZ Florián de Ocampo, 1995).

Mazower, Mark, *Dark Continent: Europe's Twentieth Century* (London: Penguin, 1998).

Mazower, Mark (ed.), *After the War was Over: Reconstructing the family, nation, and state in Greece, 1943–1960* (Princeton, NJ: Princeton University Press, 2000).

Mazower, Mark, *Inside Hitler's Greece: The Experience of Occupation 1941–1944* (New Haven and London: Yale University Press, 2001).

McLellan, Josie, *Antifascism and Memory in East Germany: Remembering the International Brigades 1945–1989* (Oxford: Clarendon, 2004).

Merridale, Catherine, *Death and Memory in Russia* (London: Granta, 2000).

Mir, Conxita, *Vivir es sobrevivir: Justicia, orden y marginación en la Cataluña rural de posguerra* (Lleida: Editorial Milenio, 2000).

Moa, Pío, "La sociedad homosexual: El feminismo como ideología", in *La sociedad homosexual y otros ensayos* (Madrid: Criterio Libros, 2001).

Molinero, Carme and Ysàs, Pere, *El règim franquista. Feixisme, modernització i consens* (Vic: Eumo, 1992).

Molinero, Carme *et al.* (eds), *Una inmensa prisión: Los campos de concentración y las prisiones durante la guerra civil y el franquismo* (Barcelona: Crítica, 2003).

Molins i Fábrega, N., and Bartolí, Josep, *Campos de concentración, 1939–194 . . .* (Mexico City: Iberia, 1944).

Montellà, Assumpta, *La Maternitat d'Elne: Bressols dels exiliats* (Barcelona: 2005).

Montero Moreno, Antonio, *Historia de la persecución religiosa en España 1936–1939* (Madrid: Biblioteca de los Autores Cristianos, 1961).

Moreno Gómez, Francisco, *La guerra civil en Córdoba* (Madrid: Alpuerto, 1985).

Moreno Gómez, Francisco, *Córdoba en la posguerra (La represión y la guerrilla, 1939–1950)*, (Córdoba: Francisco Baena, 1987).

Moreno Gómez, Francisco, "La represión en la España campesina", in García Delgado, José Luis (ed.), *El primer franquismo: España durante la segunda guerra mundial* (Madrid, 1989).

Morente Valero, Francisco, *La escuela y el Estado nuevo: La depuración del magisterio nacional* (Barcelona: Ámbito, 1997).

Mulaj, Klejda, *Politics of Ethnic Cleansing: Nation-State Building and Provision of In/Security in Twentieth-Century Balkans* (New York: Lexington Books, 2008).

Negrín Fajardo, Olegario, "Los expedientes de depuración de los profesores de instituto de segunda enseñanza resueltos por el Ministerio de Educación Nacional (1937–1943)", *Hispania Nova. Revista de Historia Contemporánea* 7 (2007).

Nelles, Dieter, Piotrowski, Harald, Linse, Ulrich and García, Carlos, *Antifascistas alemanes en Barcelona (1933–1939): El grupo DAS, sus actividades contra la red nazi y en el frente de Aragón* (Barcelona, Editorial Sintra, 2010).

Nelson, Cary, *The Aura of the Cause* (Urbana and Chicago: University of Illinois Press, 1997).

Nelson, Cary and Hendricks, Jefferson (eds), *Madrid 1937: Letters of the Abraham Lincoln Brigade from the Spanish Civil War* (New York and London: Routledge, 1996).

Nerín, Gustau, *La guerra que vino de África* (Barcelona: Crítica, 2005).

Nuñez Diaz-Balart, Mirta and Rojas Friend, Antonio, *Consejo de guerra: Los fusila-*

mientos en el Madrid de la posguerra (1939–1945) (Madrid: Compañía Literaria, 1997).

Olmedo Alonso, Ángel, *Llerena 1936: Fuentes orales para la recuperación de la memoria histórica* (Badajoz: Diputación de Badajoz, 2010).

Ortiz Heras, Manuel, *Violencia política en la II República y el primer franquismo* (Madrid: Siglo XXI, 2006).

Passerini, Luisa, *Memory and Totalitarianism* (Oxford: Oxford University Press, 1992).

Passerini, Luisa, *Europe in Love: Love in Europe. Imagination and Politics in Britain between the Wars* (London: I.B. Tauris, 1999).

Paxton, Robert, *Vichy France. Old Guard and New Order, 1940–1944* (New York: Knopf, 1972).

Paz, Abel, *Durruti en la revolución española* (Madrid: Fundación Anselmo Lorenzo, 1996).

Pérez Díaz, Victor, *The Return of Civil Society* (Cambridge, MA: Harvard University Press, 1993).

Petrou, Michael, *Renegades. Canadians in the Spanish Civil War* (Vancouver: UBC Press, 2008).

Pick, Daniel, *Faces of Degeneration* (Cambridge: Cambridge University Press, 1989).

Pike, David Wingeate, *¡Vae Victis! Los republicanos españoles refugiados en Francia 1939–1944* (Paris: Ruedo Ibérico, 1969).

Pike, David Wingeate, *In the Service of Stalin: The Spanish Communists in Exile 1939–1945* (Oxford: Clarendon Press, 1993).

Pike, David Wingeate, *Spaniards in the Holocaust: Mauthausen, the horror on the Danube* (Routledge/Cañada Blanch Studies on Contemporary Spain, 2000), and updated edition in Spanish, *Españoles en el holocausto: Vida y muerte de los republicanos en Mauthausen* (Barcelona: Mondadori, 2003).

Pike, David Wingeate, *France Divided: The French and the Civil War in Spain* (Brighton, Portland, Toronto: Sussex Academic Press, 2011).

Pons Prades, Eduardo, *Republicanos españoles en la Segunda Guerra Mundial* (Madrid: La Esfera de los Libros, 2003).

Popov, Nebojša (ed.), *The Road to War in Serbia: Trauma and Catharsis* (Budapest: Central European University Press, 2000).

Prada Rodrígues, Julio, *La España masacrada: La represión franquista de guerra y posguerra* (Madrid: Alianza, 2010).

Preston, Paul, *The Triumph of Democracy in Spain* (London: Routledge, 1990).

Preston, Paul, *Franco. A Biography* (London: HarperCollins, 1993).

Preston, Paul, *The Politics of Revenge: Fascism and the Military in 20th Century Spain* (London: Routledge, [1990] 1995).

Preston, Paul, *Comrades* (London: HarperCollins, 1999).

Preston, Paul, *Doves of War: Four Women of Spain* (London: HarperCollins, 2002).

Preston, Paul, *We Saw Spain Die. Foreign Correspondents in the Spanish Civil War* (London: Constable, 2008).

Preston, Paul, *The Spanish Holocaust: Inquisition and Extermination in Twentieth-Century Spain* (London: HarperCollins, 2012).

Preston, Paul, "Two doctors and one cause: Len Crome and Reginald Saxton in the International Brigades", *International Journal of Iberian Studies* 19, 1 (August 2006).

Quiroga, Alejandro, *Making Spaniards. Primo de Rivera and the Nationalization of the Masses, 1923–30* (Basingstoke: Palgrave Macmillan, 2007).

Quiroga, Alejandro and Arco Blanco, Miguel Ángel del, *Soldados de Díos y Apóstoles de la Patria: Las derechas españoles en la Europa de entreguerras* (Granada: Comares, 2010).

Raguer, Hilari, *Gunpowder and Incense: The Catholic Church and the Spanish Civil War* (Routledge/Cañada Blanch Studies on Contemporary Spain, 2007).

Reig Tapia, Alberto, *Ideología e Historia (sobre la represión franquista y la guerra civil)*, (Torrejón de Ardoz, Madrid: Akal, 1986).

Reig Tapia, Alberto, *Memoria de la guerra civil. Los mitos de la tribu* (Madrid: Alianza, 1999).

Richards, Michael, *A Time of Silence: Civil War and the Culture of Repression in Franco's Spain, 1936–1945* (Cambridge: Cambridge University Press, 1998).

Richards, Michael, *After the Civil War: Memory and the Shaping of Spanish Society since 1936* (Cambridge: Cambridge University Press, forthcoming 2012).

Richards, Michael, "Biology and Morality in the Spanish Civil War: Psychiatrists, Revolution and Women Prisoners in Málaga", *Contemporary European History* 10 (2001).

Richards, Michael, "Between memory and history: Social relationships and ways of remembering the Spanish civil war", *International Journal of Iberian Studies* 19, 1 (2006).

Richards, Michael, "Grand narratives, collective memory, and social history: public uses of the past in post-war Spain", in Jerez-Farrán, Carlos and Amago, Samuel (eds), *Unearthing Franco's Legacy: Mass graves and the recovery of historical memory in Spain* (Notre Dame, Ind.: University of Notre Dame Press, 2010).

Ripa, Yannick, "La tonte purificatrice des republicaines pendant la guerre civile espagnole", *Identités fémenines et violences politiques (1936–1946). Les cahiers de l'Institut d'Histoire du temps présent* 31 (1995).

Risques, Manuel Corbella, "Dictadura y rebelión militar 1936–1968", *Les presons de Franco* (Barcelona: Generalitat de Catalunya/Museu d'Història de Catalunya, 2004).

Rodrigo, Javier, *Cautivos. Campos de concentración en la España franquista 1936–1947* (Barcelona: Crítica, 2005).

Rodrigo, Javier, *Hasta la raíz: Violencia durante la guerra civil y la dictadura franquista* (Madrid: Alianza, 2008).

Rodríguez, Clemente, "Ventajas de los penados trabajadores en los Destacamentos", *Revista de la Escuela de Estudios Penitenciarios* 37 (April 1948).

Rodríguez Jiménez, José Luis, *Los esclavos españoles de Hitler* (Barcelona: Planeta, 2002).

Rodríguez Sánchez, Gregorio, *El habito y la cruz: religiosas asesinadas en la guerra civil española* (Madrid: Edibesa, 2006).

Rohr, Isabelle, "The use of antisemitism in the Spanish Civil War", *Patterns of Prejudice* 37, 2 (2003).

Rohr, Isabelle, *The Spanish Right and the Jews, 1898–1945: Antisemitism and Opportunism* (Brighton & Portland: Sussex Academic Press, 2007).

Roig, Montserrat, *Noche y niebla: Los catalanes en los campos nazis* (Barcelona: Península, 1978).

Romero Salvadó, Francisco, *Spain 1914–1918: Between War and Revolution* (London: Routledge, 1999).

Romero Salvadó, Francisco and Smith, Ángel (eds), *The Agony of Spanish Liberalism: From Revolution to Dictatorship, 1913–1923* (Basingstoke: Palgrave Macmillan, 2010).

Rosenstone, Robert A., *Crusade of the Left: The Lincoln Battalion in the Spanish Civil War* (New York: Pegasus, 1969).

Rousso, Henri, *Le syndrome de Vichy de 1944 à nos jours* (Paris: Éditions de Seuil, 1990).

Ruiz, David, Sánchez, Isidro and Ortiz, Manuel (eds), *España franquista: causa general y actitudes sociales ante la dictadura* (Castilla-la Mancha: Servicio de Publicaciones de la Universidad de Castilla-La Mancha, 1993).

Ruiz, Julius, *Franco's Justice: Repression in Madrid after the Spanish Civil War* (Oxford: Clarendon Press [Oxford Historical Monographs], 2005).

Ruiz González, Cándido and Blanco Rodríguez, Juan Andrés, "La represión en la provincia de Zamora durante la guerra civil y el franquismo", in Berzal de la Rosa, Enrique (coord.), *Testimonio de voces olvidadas*, II (Valderas, León: Fundación 27 de Marzo, 2007).

Ruiz González, Cándido, Granja Fernández, Pilar de la and Martín González, Eduardo, "Un largo período de represión", in Blanco Rodríguez, Juan Andrés (ed.), *A los 70 años de la Guerra Civil española: actas del Encuentro celebrado en Zamora, 21 y 22 de diciembre de 2006* (Zamora: Centro de la UNED de Zamora, 2010).

Sabín, J.M., *Prisión y muerte en la España de la postguerra* (Madrid: Muchnik, 1996).

Salomón Chéliz, María Pilar, *Anticlericalismo en Aragón: Protesta popular y movilización política (1900–1939)*, (Zaragoza: Prensas Universitarias de Zaragoza, 2002).

Sánchez Recio, Glicerio, *La República contra los rebeldes y los desafectos: La represión económica durante la guerra civil* (Alicante: Universidad de Alicante, 1991).

Sánchez Ruano, Francisco, *Islam y guerra civil española: Moros con Franco y con la República* (Madrid: La Esfera de los Libros, 2004).

Sánchez Sánchez, Isidro, "El pan de los Fuertes. La 'buena prensa' en España", in Cueva, Julio de la and López Villaverde, Ángel Luis (eds), *Clericalismo y asociacionismo católico en España: de la restauración a la transición* (Cuenca: Universidad Castilla-La Mancha, 2005).

Sánchez Tostado, Luis Miguel, *Víctimas: Jaén en guerra (1936–1950)*, (Jaén: Ayuntamiento de Jaén, 2005).

Sanchidrián Blanco, Carmen, Grana Gil, Isabel and Martín Zúñiga, Francisco, "Análisis y valoración de los expedientes de depuración del profesorado de Instituto de Segunda Enseñanza en el franquismo (1936–1942). Resultados generales", *Revista de Educación* 356 (2011).

Schinkel, Willem, *Aspects of Violence: A Critical Theory* (Basingstoke: Palgrave Macmillan, 2010).

Scott, James C., *Domination and the Arts of Resistance: Hidden Transcripts* (New Haven, CT: Yale University Press, 1990).

Shindler, Colin, "No pasarán. The Jews who fought in Spain", *Jewish Quarterly* 33, 3 (1986).

Shore, Marci, *Caviar and Ashes: A Warsaw Generation's Life and Death in Marxism 1918–1968* (New Haven and London: Yale University Press, 2006).

Simeón Riera, José Daniel, *Entre la rebelió y la tradició (Llíria durante La República y la Guerra Civil, 1931–1939)*, (Valencia: Diputació de València, 1993).

Skoutelsky, Rémi, *Novedad en el frente. Las brigadas internacionales en la guerra civil* (Madrid: Temas de Hoy, 2006).

Skoutelsky, Rémi, *L'espoir guidait leurs pas: Les volontaires français dans les Brigades Internationales 1936–1939* (Paris: Grasset, 1998).

Skoutelsky, Rémi (and Lefebvre, Michel), *Les Brigades Internationales: Images Rétrouvées* (Paris: Éditions du Seuil, 2003).

Snyder, Timothy, Bloodlands. *Europe Between Hitler and Stalin* (London: The Bodley Head, 2010).

Sofsky, Wolfgang, *The Order of Terror: The Concentration Camp* (Princeton: Princeton University Press, 1997).

Solé i Sabaté, Josep, *La repressió franquista a Catalunya 1938–1953* (Barcelona: Edicions 62, 1985).

Solé i Sabaté, Josep and Villarroya i Font, Joan, *L'ocupació militar de Catalunya, març 1938–febrer 1939* (Barcelona: L'Avenç, 1987).

Solé i Sabaté, Josep and Villarroya i Font, Joan, *La repressió a la reraguarda de Catalunya (1936–1939)*, (Barcelona, PAM, 1989).

Soo, Scott, "Putting memory to work: A comparative study of three associations dedicated to the memory of the Spanish republican exile in France", in Altink, Henrice and Gemie, Sharif (eds), *At the Border: Margins and Peripheries in Modern France* (Cardiff: University of Wales Press, 2007).

Soo, Scott, *The Routes to Exile: Spanish Civil War Refugees and their Hosts in South-Western France* (University of Wales Press, 2011).

Southworth, Herbert R., *El mito de la cruzada de Franco* (Paris: Ruedo Ibérico, 1963).

Southworth, Herbert R., *Conspiracy and the Spanish Civil War: The Brainwashing of Francisco Franco* (London and New York: Routledge, 2002).

Souto, Sandra, "Taking the street: workers' youth organisations and political conflict in the Spanish Second Republic", *European History Quarterly* 34, 2 (2004).

Stein, Louis, *Beyond Death and Exile: The Spanish Republicans in France 1939–1955* (Cambridge, MA: Harvard University Press, 1979).

Stoler, Ann Laura (ed.), *Haunted by Empire: Geographies of Intimacy in North American History* (Durham and London: Duke University Press, 2006).

Stone, Dan, "The 'Final Solution': a German or European Project?" in Stone, Dan, *Histories of the Holocaust* (Oxford: Oxford University Press, 2010).

Stone, Dan (ed.), *The Oxford Handbook of Postwar European History* (Oxford: Oxford University Press, 2012).

Suárez, A and Colectivo '36, *El libro blanco sobre las cárceles franquistas 1939–1976* (Paris: Ruedo Ibérico, 1976).

Susmel, Duilio, *Vita sbagliata di Galeazzo Ciano* (Milano: Aldo Palazzi Editore, 1962).

Sweets, John F., *Choices in Vichy France: The French under Nazi Occupation* (Oxford: Oxford University Press, 1994).

Taussig, Michael, *The Magic of the State* (London/New York: Routledge, 1997).

Taussig, Michael, *Law in a Lawless Land: Diary of a Limpieza in Columbia* (University of Chicago Press, 2003).

Theweleit, Klaus, *Male Fantasies* (vol. 1, *Women, Floods, Bodies, History*) (Minneapolis: University of Minnesota Press, 1987).

Thomas, Hugh, *The Spanish Civil War*, 3rd edn (London: Hamish Hamilton, 1977).

Thomas, Maria, "The front line of Albion's perfidy. Inputs into the making of British policy towards Spain. The racism and snobbery of Norman King", *International Journal of Iberian Studies* 20, 2 (2007).

Thomas, Maria, "Disputing the Public Sphere: Anticlerical Violence, Conflict and the Sacred Heart of Jesus. April 1931–July 1936", *Cuadernos de Historia Contemporánea* 33 (2011).

Thomas, Maria, "'We have come to place you at liberty and to burn the convent': Masculinity, Sexuality and Anticlerical Violence during the Spanish Civil War", Abraham Lincoln Brigade Archive, George Watt Memorial Essay Prize 2011, http://www.albavolunteer.org/2011/12/masculinity-sexuality-and-anticlerical-violence-during-the-scw/.

Timmons, Stuart, *The Trouble with Harry Hay: A Biography* (Boston: Alyson Publications, 1990).

Torres, Francesc, *Dark is the room where we sleep* (New York and Barcelona: Actar, 2007).

Tortella, Gabriel, *Spain: An Economic History* (Cambridge, MA: Harvard University Press, 2000).

Tucker, Jennifer with Campt, Tina, "Entwined Practices: Engagements with Photography in Historical Inquiry", *History and Theory* Theme Issue 48 (December 2009).

Ugarte Tellería, Javier, *La nueva Covadonga insurgente. Orígenes sociales y culturales de la sublevación de 1936 en Navarra y el País Vasco* (Madrid: Biblioteca Nueva, 1998).

Vázquez Montalbán, Manuel, *Crónica sentimental de España* (Barcelona: DeBolsillo, 2003), (articles from *Triunfo*, first published as a book in 1969).

Vázquez Montalbán, Manuel, *Barcelonas* (London: Verso, 1992).

Vilanova i Vila-Abadal, Francesc, *Repressió política i coacció econòmica: Les responsabi-*

litats polítiques de republicans i conservadors catalans a la postguerra (1939–1942) (Barcelona: Publicacions de l'Abadia de Montserrat, 1999).

Villegas, Jean-Claude, *Plages d'Exil: Les camps de refugiés espagnols en France – 1939* (n.p.: BDIC, 1989).

Vincent, Mary, *Catholicism in the Second Spanish Republic: Religion and Politics in Salamanca1930–1936* (Oxford: Clarendon Press, 1996).

Vincent, Mary, "The Martyrs and the Saints: Masculinity and the Construction of the Francoist Crusade", *History Workshop Journal* 47 (1999).

Vincent, Mary, "The Keys to the Kingdom: Religious Violence in the Spànish Civil War", in Ealham, Chris and Richards, Michael (eds), *The Splintering of Spain: Cultural History and the Spanish Civil War* (Cambridge: Cambridge University Press, 2005).

Vincent, Mary, *Spain 1833–2002: People and State* (Oxford: Oxford University Press, 2007).

Vinyes, Ricard, *Irredentas: Las presas políticas y sus hijos en las cárceles franquistas* (Madrid: Temas de Hoy, 2002).

Vinyes, Ricard, "El universo penitenciario durante el franquismo", in Molinero, Carme *et al.* (eds), *Una inmensa prisión: Los campos de concentración y las prisiones durante la guerra civil y el franquismo* (Barcelona: Crítica, 2003).

Vinyes, Ricard, *El daño y la memoria: Las prisiones de María Salvo* (Barcelona: Plaza & Janés, 2004).

Vinyes, Ricard, Armengou, Montserrat and Belis, Ricard, *Los niños perdidos del franquismo* (Barcelona: Plaza & Janés, 2002).

Viñas, Ángel, *La soledad de la República: el abandono de las democracias y el viraje hacia la Unión Soviética* (Barcelona: Crítica, 2006).

Viñas, Ángel, *El escudo de la República: el oro de España, la apuesta soviética y los hechos de mayo* (Barcelona: Crítica, 2007).

Viñas, Ángel, *El honor de la República: entre el acoso fascista, la hostilidad británica y la política de Stalin* (Barcelona: Crítica, 2009).

Viñas, Ángel and Hernández Sánchez, Fernando, *El desplome de la República* (Barcelona: Crítica, 2009).

Virgili, Fabrice, *Shorn Women: Gender and Punishment in Liberation France* (Oxford/New York: Berg, 2002).

Wachsmann, Nikolaus, *Hitler's Prisons: Legal Terror in Nazi Germany* (New Haven/London: Yale University Press, 2004).

Wagner, Sarah E., *To Know Where He Lies: DNA Technology and the Search for Srebrenica's Missing* (Berkeley: University of California Press, 2008).

Wald, Alan, *Exiles from a Future Time: The Forging of the Mid-Twentieth- Century Left* (University of North Carolina: Chapel Hill & London, 2002).

Wald, Alan M., *The Literary Left and the Antifascist Crusade* (Chapel Hill: University of North Carolina Press, 2007).

Webster, Justin, 'El valle de Díos', in *Granta* en español 1 (special issue: *El silencio en boca de todos*), pp. 134–59.

Weiner, Amir, *Landscaping the Human Garden* (Stanford, CA: Stanford University Press, 2003).

Weiner, Amir (ed.), *Modernity and Population Management* (Stanford, CA: Stanford University Press, 2003).

Weiss, Gordon, *The Cage: The Fight for Sri Lanka and the Last Days of the Tamil Tigers* (London: The Bodley Head, 2011).

Werth, Nicolas, "The Crimes of the Stalin Regime: Outline for an Inventory and Classification", in Stone, Dan (ed.), *The Historiography of Genocide* (Basingstoke: Palgrave Macmillan [2008] 2010).

Whelan, Richard, *Robert Capa: A biography* (London: Faber, 1985).

Young, Cynthia (ed.), *The Mexican Suitcase: The Rediscovered Spanish Civil War Negatives of Capa, Chim and Taro* (New York: ICP/Göttingen: Steidl, 2010), II.

Zaagsma, Gerben, "'Red Devils': the Botwin Company in the Spanish Civil War", *East European Jewish Affairs* 33, 1 (2003).

Zemon Davis, Natalie, "The Rites of Violence: Religious Riot in Sixteenth-Century France", *Past and Present* 59, 1 (1973).

Novels, short stories, poetry

Afrika, Tatamkhulu, *Bitter Eden* (London: Arcadia, 2002).

Aragon, Louis, *Le roman inachevé* (Paris: Gallimard, 1956).

Aragon, Louis, *La Mise à mort* (Paris: Gallimard, 1965).

Aub, Max, *El laberinto mágico*, 6 vols (*Campo cerrado*; *Campo abierto*; *Campo de sangre*; *Campo francés*; *Campo del moro*; *Campo de los almendros*), (Madrid: 2003), (first pub. 1943–1968). *Campo cerrado* published in English, *Field of Honour* (London: Verso, 2009).

Auden, Wystan H., *The Age of Anxiety: A Baroque Eclogue* (Princeton and Oxford: Princeton University Press, 2011).

Barea, Arturo, *The Forging of a Rebel,* 3 vols *(The Forge*; *The Track*; *The Clash),* (London: Granta, 2001), (first pub. 1941–46).

Cercas, Javier, *Soldados de Salamis* (Barcelona: Tusquets Editores, 2001).

Delibes, Miguel, *Los santos inocentes* (Barcelona: Planeta, 1981).

Durán, Jane, *Silences from the Spanish Civil War* (London: Enitharmon Press, 2002).

Castillo, Michel de, *Tanguy, Histoire d'un enfant d'aujourd'hui* (Paris: Gallimard, 1957). English edition: *A Child of Our Time* (New York: Alfred A. Knopf, 1957).

Fast, Howard, *Departure and Other Stories* (Boston: Little Brown and Co., 1949).

Jergović, Miljenko, *Sarajevo Marlboro* (London: Penguin, 1997).

Malraux, André, *L'Espoir* (Paris: Gallimard, 1971).

Mariani, Diego, *New Finnish Grammar* (Sawtry, Cambs.: Dedalus, 2011).

Marsé, Juan, *Si te dicen que caí* (Mexico: Novaro, 1973; Spain: Seix Barral, 1976). English translation: *The Fallen* (London: Quartet Books, 1994).

Marsé, Juan, *Un día volveré* (Barcelona: Plaza y Janés, 1982).

Mehmedinović, Semezdin, *Sarajevo Blues* (San Francisco: City Lights Books, 1998).

Modiano, Patrick, *La place de l'étoile* (Paris: Gallimard, 1968).

Modiano, Patrick, *Dora Bruder* (Berkeley and Los Angeles, CA/London: University of California Press, 1999).

Müller, Herta, *The Land of Green Plums* (London: Granta, 1996). German, *Herztier* (Hamburg: Rowohlt Verlag, 1993).

Ondaatje, Michael, *Anil's Ghost* (London: Bloomsbury, 2000).

Radnóti, Miklós, *Forced March* (London: Enitharmon, 2003).

Rolfe, Edwin, *Collected Poems* (edition by Nelson, Cary and Hendricks, Jefferson), (Urbana and Chicago: University of Illinois Press, 1993).

Rosa, Isaac, *El vano ayer* (Barcelona: Seix Barral, 2004).

Roth, Joseph, *Hotel Savoy* (London: Granta, 2000).

Saura, Carlos, *¡Esa luz!* (Huesca: Instituto de Estudios Altoaragoneses, 1995).

Scott Fox, Lorna, "Double duty", *London Review of Books* 25, 10 (2003).

Sebald, Winfried Georg, *The Emigrants* (London: The Harvill Press, 1996).

Sebald, Winfried Georg, *Austerlitz* (London: Penguin, 2002).

Semprún, Jorge, *Veinte años y un día* (Barcelona: Tusquets, 2003).

Serge, Victor, *The Long Dusk* (New York: The Dial Press, 1946).

Toller, Ernst, *The Swallow-Book-Das Schwalbenbuch* (London: Humphrey Milford, 1924).

Torres, Maruja, *Un calor tan cercano* (Madrid: Alfaguara, 1998).

Vázquez-Rial, Horacio, *El soldado de porcelana* (Barcelona: Ediciones B, 1997).

Yourcenar, Margaret, *Coup de Grace* (Henley-on-Thames: Aidan Ellis, 1983).

Films, documentaries and radio programmes

Armengou, Montserrat and Belis, Ricard, *Els nens perduts del franquisme* (Spain, 2002).

Armengou, Montserrat, *¡Devolvedme a mi hijo!* (Spain, forthcoming).

Camino, Jaime, *Las Largas Vacaciones del 36* (Spain, 1976).

Channel 4, *Sri Lanka's Killing Fields* (2011).

García-Lorca de los Ríos, Laura, on BBC Radio 4, "Taking a Stand: Federico García Lorca and the Bones of the Past" (presented by Fergal Keane), 3 February 2009.

Guédiguian, Robert, *The Army of Crime* (France, 2009).

Haneke, Michael, *The White Ribbon* (Austria/Germany/France/Italy, 2009).

Makepeace, Anne, *Robert Capa: In Love and War* (USA, 2003).

Michie, Helena, *Le dernier jour au camp du Rivesaltes* (France, 2009).

Renais, Alain, *Nuit et Brouillard* (*Night and Fog*), (France, 1955).

Schlöndorff, Volker, *Der Fangschuss* (France/West Germany, 1976).

Taberna, Helena, *La Buena Nueva* (Spain, 2008).

Woodhead, Leslie, *A Cry from the Grave* (UK/USA/Netherlands, 1999).

Websites

Asociación para la Recuperación de la Memoria Histórica (ARMH):
http://www.memoriahistorica.org
International Center of Photography, New York, Mexican Suitcase Exhibition:
http://museum.icp.org/mexican_suitcase/
International Criminal Tribunal for the former Yugoslavia (ICTY):
http://www.icty.org/x/file/Outreach/view_from_hague/jit_srebrenica_en.pdf
International State Crime Initiative website (Kings College London, Universities
of Harvard, Hull and Ulster):
http://statecrime.org/state-studies/gg-sri-lanka/237
Margaret Michaelis Archive, National Gallery of Australia:
http://www.123people.de/s/rudolf+michaelis
La Moncloa: Gobierno de España:
http://www.lamoncloa.gob.es/IDIOMAS/9/Gobierno/News/2011/
18072011PolishInternationalBrigadeVolunteers.htm
El Mundo, Niños Robados Microsite:
http://www.elmundo.es/especiales/2010/09/espana/ninos_robados/
juanluis_antonio.html
Observatorio de Antisemitismo en España:
http://observatorioantisemitismo.fcje.org/?m=200912
"Paracuellos" by Carlos Giménez (first series 1977–82):
http://www.carlosgimenez.com/obra/paracuellos.htm
Srebrenica museum site, Potočari:
http://www.potocarimc.ba
Todos los Nombres:
http://www.todoslosnombres.org/
Todos los Rostros:
http://todoslosrostros.blogspot.com/

Index